The Meaning of the
Nuclear Revolution

CORNELL STUDIES IN SECURITY AFFAIRS

edited by Robert J. Art *and* Robert Jervis

The Meaning of the Nuclear Revolution

STATECRAFT AND THE PROSPECT OF ARMAGEDDON

ROBERT JERVIS

Cornell University Press

ITHACA AND LONDON

THIS BOOK WAS WRITTEN UNDER THE AUSPICES OF THE
INSTITUTE OF WAR AND PEACE STUDIES AND THE RESEARCH
INSTITUTE ON INTERNATIONAL CHANGE, COLUMBIA UNIVERSITY.

First published 1989 by Cornell University Press.
First published, Cornell Paperbacks, 1990.
International Standard Book Number 0-8014-2304-X (cloth)
International Standard Book Number 0-8014-9565-2 (paper)
Library of Congress Catalog Card Number 88-43443

Printed in the United States of America

*Librarians: Library of Congress cataloging information
appears on the last page of the book.*

⊗ The paper in this book meets the minimum requirements of the American National
Standard for Information Sciences–Permanence of Paper for Printed Library
Materials, ANSI Z39.48-1984.

To Alexa and Lisa

Contents

Preface

Nuclear weapons have existed for only half a century, a very brief period by historical standards. In a sense, the human race is just becoming accustomed to their presence. Yet most of us have lived with nuclear weapons all our lives. The idea that not only could we die at any moment—this has been true for any given individual throughout history—but that everyone and everything we care about could be destroyed in a twinkling, must remain always frightening, however familiar it is.

Our merely living with nuclear weapons has not been sufficient to give us an understanding of their influence on world politics. It is of course a fallacy to believe that "big" causes must have "big" effects, but I believe that the fact that nuclear weapons could destroy the world has changed the way people think and the way nations behave. I also believe that a better understanding of their role can make the world safer. None of us can, nor should we, put the nightmare of nuclear holocaust out of our minds. Indeed, it is important that it be there if we are to understand that large-scale violence is no longer a viable tool of statecraft.

This book explores some of the effects of nuclear weapons on world politics, particularly on relations between the superpowers. Several of the chapters were written in response to invitations to address selected topics and have been extensively rewritten for publication here. Chapters 3 and 7 are new.

I have not discussed the consequences of the recent changes in Soviet domestic and foreign policy, even though they may be the most important developments in world politics since 1945. Even if they fell within my area of expertise, they are simply too new and too rapidly changing to be analyzed here. Furthermore, I doubt that they will lead to the abolition of nuclear weapons. And, as long as they do not, they will leave intact much of the framework this book presents. I also have said little about arms control because I think the underlying principles are those which operate in the more general arena of nuclear strategy and international politics. But the general perspective stressed by arms control infuses this book: what is important is not each side's unilateral decision on what arms to build, but rather the ways in which such decisions interact to produce an overall configuration.

I am grateful to my friends who have commented on drafts of these essays: Robert Art, Richard Betts, McGeorge Bundy, Joseph Grieco, Ole Holsti, Deborah Larson, Joshua Lederberg, Joseph Nye, George Quester, Edward Rhodes, John Ruggie, Glenn Snyder, Jack Snyder, and Marc Trachtenberg. Kay Scheuer and Holly Bailey of Cornell University Press and Joanne Ainsworth of the Guilford Group worked their usual magic on the manuscript. William Daugherty provided the index.
The Institute of War and Peace Studies at Columbia University provided a stimulating home, and its staff typed endless versions of the manuscript with hardly a complaint. The research was supported by a grant from the Ford Foundation to the Research Institute on International Change.
In ways they might not recognize—or approve—my students have contributed greatly to this book by their questions, arguments, and friendly skepticism. Although at times I thought classes might run more smoothly if they would only sit there and take notes, this book—not to mention the classes—has been greatly improved by their insights.

Chapter 1 is very loosely based on "The Nuclear Revolution and the Common Defense," published in *Political Science Quarterly*, 101, no. 5 (1986). A version of Chapter 2 appeared (under the same title) in *Journal of Strategic Studies*, 9 (December 1986). Chapter 4 is a revision of "Morality and Nuclear Strategy," published in *International Ethics in the Nuclear Age*, ed. Robert Myers (Lanham, Md.: University Press of America, 1987), sponsored by the Carnegie Council on Ethics and International Affairs. An abridgment of Chapter 5 appears in *Lurching toward the Brink*, ed. George Simpson (Washington, D.C.: Center for Strategic and International Studies, 1989). An earlier version of Chapter 6 was published by the Political Science Department of the University of Illinois at Urbana. I thank the editors and publishers concerned for permission to use this material.

ROBERT JERVIS

New York, New York

The Meaning of the
Nuclear Revolution

[1]

The Theory of the
Nuclear Revolution

[After nuclear war, the] two sides would have neither powers,
nor laws, nor cities, nor cultures, nor cradles, nor tombs.
—*Charles de Gaulle, May 31, 1960*

A nuclear war cannot be won and must never be fought.
—*Joint statement of President Ronald Reagan and First
Secretary Mikhail Gorbachev, November 21, 1985*

CONTRADICTIONS AND PUZZLES

The most important points often are the simplest ones. No one can
win an all-out nuclear war. While this statement is open to dispute, I
maintain that it is correct and that its implications have not been fully
appreciated. The odder implications are discussed in later chapters;
here I want to present the underpinnings of the argument.

We need to explain a series of remarkable if familiar contradictions:
the United States and the Soviet Union possess unprecedented military
might, yet they cannot protect themselves; the absence of war between
the great powers since 1945 coexists with unprecedented fear of total
destruction; what the United States and the USSR threaten to do to one
another during war would be suicidal, yet attempts to moderate these
threats are often greeted as dangerous if not aggressive; the superpowers threaten each other with enormous devastation yet avoid serious provocations; levels of arms have varied greatly since 1945, and
yet the basic outlines of the status quo have remained unchanged. We

I am grateful to McGeorge Bundy for the reference to and translation of de Gaulle's
statement.

[1]

need to understand what nuclear weapons have done to world politics, yet the attempts to maintain familiar intellectual frameworks compound rather than alleviate the dilemmas. The key to solving these puzzles is an understanding of the transformation of the nature and sources of security in the nuclear era.

First let me explain some basic concepts, sketch the difference between military victory—which is no longer possible in a war between the superpowers—and political victory, which depends on the threat of war, and explain why the superpowers' nuclear arsenals provide greater protection for allies than is often believed. Parts of this discussion will be familiar to experts in the field. I will then treat the central claim of this book—that nuclear weapons have drastically altered statecraft—as a theory. That is, I will ask what consequences should follow if it is true and see whether international behavior since 1945 has been consistent with these theoretically generated expectations.

The difficulties in coming to grips with the implications of nuclear weapons are perhaps best epitomized by our inability to answer the straightforward question of whether these weapons have made the United States—and the world—more or less secure. The common reply—that nuclear weapons have both decreased the chance of world war and increased the destruction that would result were such a war to occur—is not a direct answer, although it may well be correct. Thus it is not a contradiction for public opinion to affirm simultaneously that nuclear war would mean annihilation and that nuclear weapons have served the cause of peace.[1]

But evaluating this trade-off is so difficult that decision makers have made ambivalent if not inconsistent responses. In early 1949, five days after President Truman told a trusted adviser that "the atomic bomb was the mainstay and all he had; that the Russians would probably have taken over Europe a long time ago if it were not for that," he asked, "Wouldn't it be wonderful . . . if we could take [our atomic stockpile] and dump it into the sea?"[2] President Eisenhower displayed the same contradictory attitudes. Early in his administration, he argued

---

1. This position is presented as a contradiction by Daniel Yankelovich in *Voter Options on Nuclear Arms Policy* (New York: Public Agenda Foundation, and Providence, R.I.: Center for Foreign Policy Development, Brown University, 1984), p. 3.

2. Quoted in David Lilienthal, *The Journals of David E. Lilienthal* (New York: Harper & Row, 1964), 2:466-73. In NSC-68, which Truman endorsed, it was also said that "it appears that it would be to the long-term advantage of the United States if atomic weapons were to be effectively eliminated from national peacetime armaments" (John Gaddis and Thomas Etzold, eds., *Containment: Documents on American Policy and Strategy, 1945-1950* [New York: Columbia University Press, 1978], p. 417).

that nuclear weapons were not different in kind from conventional ones. When discussing disarmament proposals in 1955 he also told his press secretary that "of course, the Reds were proposing to eliminate all atomic weapons, . . . which would leave them with the preponderance of military power in Europe."[3] But when Secretary of State John Foster Dulles said that of course everyone knew that because of the vast Soviet superiority in manpower, the United States could not agree to abolish nuclear weapons, Eisenhower vigorously dissented: According to the records of the National Security Council (NSC) meeting, "the President said that if he knew any way to abolish atomic weapons which would ensure the certainty that they would be abolished, he would be the very first to endorse it, regardless of any general disarmament. He explained that he was certain that with its great resources the United States would surely be able to whip the Soviet Union in any kind of war that had been fought in the past or any other kind of war than an atomic war."[4] This was not an isolated outburst: the next day he said that "he would gladly accept nuclear disarmament [even without conventional disarmament] if he was sure he could get the genuine article. . . . He would gladly go back to the kind of warfare which was waged in 1941."[5] The 1986 Reykjavik summit meeting called up the same ambivalence.

The difficulties stem in part from the fact that the trade-off between the chance of war and the consequence of war is an extremely painful one, the kind that people try to avoid facing.[6] The ambivalence also may represent an instinctive recognition of the fact that nuclear weapons are very powerful in one sense but not in another. John Thibaut and Harold Kelley draw the general distinction between fate-control and behavior-control.[7] As the terms indicate, the former is the ability to determine what happens to others, the latter is the ability to control their behavior. Both we and the Soviets have fate-control over the other, but it is far from clear how much this can translate into behavior-control. Indeed, the possession of nuclear weapons can decrease the state's freedom of action by increasing the suspicion with which it is viewed.

3. Quoted in Stephen Ambrose, *Eisenhower the President* (New York: Simon & Schuster, 1984), p. 246; for similar statements see pp. 153, 491.

4. *Foreign Relations of the United States, 1952–1954*, vol. 2, *National Security Affairs* (Washington, D.C.: Government Printing Office, 1984), pt. 2, p. 1469 (hereafter cited as *FRUS*).

5. Ibid., pt. 1, p. 688.

6. Robert Jervis, *Perception and Misperception in International Politics* (Princeton: Princeton University Press, 1976), pp. 128–42.

7. John Thibaut and Harold Kelley, *The Social Psychology of Groups* (New York: Wiley, 1959), pp. 101–11.

India, China, and Israel may have decreased the chance of direct attack by developing nuclear weapons, but they have not increased their general political prestige or influence.

The Impossibility of Military Victory

President Reagan and First Secretary Gorbachev formally ratified what has long been understood: both sides (not to mention bystanders) would suffer so much in a total war that they both would lose. President Eisenhower recognized this reality, often giving vent to his exasperation with those who thought that military victory was possible. Even before the Soviet Union was capable of doing overwhelming damage to the United States, he noted the problems of postwar reconstruction. As he put it to the Joint Chiefs of Staff when they talked of a world war: "I want you to carry this question home with you: Gain such a victory [as would follow from a nuclear attack], and what do you do with it? Here would be a great area from the Elbe to Vladivostok . . . torn up and destroyed, without government, without its communications, just an area of starvation and disaster. I ask you what would the civilized world do about it? I repeat that there is no victory except through our imaginations."[8] Later, when he considered Soviet retaliation, his concern was not with who would come out ahead. He told the critic of his disarmament policy that "even assuming that we could emerge from a global war today as the acknowledged victor, there would be a destruction in the country [such] that there would be no possibility of our exercising a representative free government for, I would say, two decades at the minimum."[9] At an NSC meeting he asked, "What would we do with Russia, if we should win in a global war?" Indeed, "the only thing worse than losing a global war was winning one; . . . there would be no individual freedom after the next global war."[10]

As he continued to contemplate the growing Soviet arsenal, Eisenhower wrote to a friend: "We are rapidly getting to the point that no

8. Ambrose, *Eisenhower the President*, p. 206. Similarly, at an NSC meeting Eisenhower mused about the difficulties of occupying Russia, which "would be far beyond the resources of the United States. . . . A totalitarian system was the only imaginable instrument by which Russia could be ruled for a considerable interval after the war" (*FRUS, 1952–1954*, vol. 2, pt. 1, p. 636; also see ibid., pp. 639–41, 804).

9. Quoted in Fred Greenstein, *The Hidden-Hand Presidency* (New York: Basic Books, 1982), p. 47.

10. This is the paraphrase of Robert Cutler, Eisenhower's Special Assistant for National Security Affairs, in *FRUS, 1952–1954*, vol. 2, pt. 1, p. 397. In public, however, Eisenhower reversed this formulation: he told a press conference on September 30, 1953, that "the only possible tragedy greater than winning a war would be losing it."

[4]

war can be *won*. War implies a contest; when you get to the point that contest is no longer involved and the outlook comes close to destruction of the enemy and suicide for ourselves—an outlook that neither side can ignore—then arguments as to the exact amount of available strength as compared to somebody else's are no longer the vital issues."[11] Eisenhower's views were not unusual: others asked similar questions about what American war aims might be and the policy statements that tried to answer these questions are both few and inadequate.[12] Eisenhower was not completely consistent. Indeed, in the course of one NSC meeting he said: "After the first exchange of thermonuclear blows . . . the United States would have to pick itself up from the floor and try to win through to a successful end." But later in the same meeting he declared that, "one thing he was dead sure: No one was going to be the winner in such a nuclear war. The destruction might be such that we might have ultimately to go back to bows and arrows."[13]

What is new about this world with nuclear weapons (or, to be more precise, mutual second-strike capability, where neither side can launch a first strike that is successful enough to prevent retaliation from the other) is not overkill, but mutual kill—the side that is "losing" the war as judged by various measures of military capability can inflict as much destruction on the side that is "winning" as the "winner" can on the "loser."[14] Furthermore, the level of destruction would far surpass that accompanying previous wars. Even a decision maker who was willing to risk a crushing defeat for his own country might be restrained by the unimaginable loss of worldwide life and civilization.[15]

11. Dwight D. Eisenhower to Richard Simon, April 4, 1956, Ann Whitman File, DDE Diary, box 8, "Apr. 56 Misc (5)," Dwight D. Eisenhower Library, Abilene, Kans.

12. See the papers associated with NSC-20/4, "U.S. Objectives with Respect to the USSR to Counter Soviet Threats to U.S. Security," in *FRUS, 1948*, vol. 1, *General: The United Nations* (Washington, D.C.: Government Printing Office, 1976), pt. 2, pp. 589–669; NSC-79, "United States and Allied War Objectives in the Event of Global War," *FRUS, 1950*, vol. 1, *National Security Affairs; Foreign Economic Policy* (Washington, D.C.: Government Printing Office, 1977), pp. 390–99. (also see the discussion on pp. 94–100, 197–200, 390–93). For the Eisenhower administration's attempt to deal with this problem, see *FRUS, 1952–1954*, vol. 2, pt. 1, pp. 379–434, 635–46. Also see David Rosenberg, "The Origins of Overkill: Nuclear Weapons and American Strategy, 1945–1960," *International Security*, 7, (Spring 1983), 13–14.

13. Minutes of the 272d Meeting of the National Security Council, January 12, 1956, Ann Whitman File, NSC series, box 7, pp. 6, 13 (also see p. 3), Eisenhower Library.

14. Thomas Schelling, *Arms and Influence* (New Haven: Yale University Press, 1960), chapter 1.

15. The most recent and careful studies indicate that the environmental effects of nuclear war would be enormous, although not as cataclysmic as had been portrayed a

Nuclear weapons are different not only in the scale of destruction they can bring, but also in their speed. This is not to say that destruction would *have* to be carried out quickly. As I will discuss in later chapters, protracted or slow-motion wars of punishment are logical possibilities. But in the past, punishment *had* to be slow. Conventional bombing, blockades, and even poison gas simply could not extinguish all cities overnight. Both sides then knew that there would be time for bargaining during the war: momentary impulse or inadvertent escalation could not lead to mutual suicide. The possibility that all cities could be destroyed within a period of hours, without any room for negotiations or second thoughts, can deter where the danger of total destruction would not if it had to be carried out a little bit at a time. In the latter case a state might be confident that its greater willingness to bear pain, its advantageous bargaining position, or its greater skill would permit it to prevail. But these assets could not prevent an all-out nuclear attack arising out of the adversary's planned strategy, the overwhelming emotion of its leaders, or its strategic forces escaping central control.[16]

In the past, mutual vulnerability did not dominate and so conflict could be total. There could be wars without bargaining in which each side simply tried to reduce the other's military capabilities because the stronger side could win by destroying its adversary if need be. The former would pay some price for doing so, but it would not be prohibitive. Of course, few situations reached this extreme. As Paul Kecskemeti has shown, even World War II did not end in "unconditional surrender."[17] The losers had some bargaining power, in part because it was understood that the defeated countries could not be ruled without at least a modicum of cooperation on their part. But the main stages of the conflict involved military battles in which each side tried to gain the upper hand. The side that surrendered or accepted unfavorable peace terms did so because it realized that if the conflict continued, it would fall further and further behind, eventually facing complete defeat.

Wars, even large-scale wars, often paid off for the winner. Sometimes

---

few years earlier. See Starley Thompson and Stephen Schneider, "Nuclear Winter Reappraised," *Foreign Affairs*, 64 (Summer 1986), 981–1005.

16. As Schelling notes, "if cities could be destroyed indefinitely, but at a rate not exceeding one per week or one per day, or even one per hour, nobody could responsibly ignore the possibility that the war might be stopped before both sides ran out of ammunition or cities" (*Arms and Influence*, p. 163). For a comparison of nuclear bargaining with wars of attrition in which pain is inflicted only slowly, see George Quester, "Crises and the Unexpected," *Journal of Interdisciplinary History*, 18 (Spring 1988), 701–19.

17. Paul Kescskemeti, *Strategic Surrender* (New York: Atheneum, 1964).

the winner was simply better off militarily and politically after the war than before it. But even when this was not the case, as it was not for the European states in 1918 and 1945, the winners still were better off in having fought the war than they would have been had they made the concessions necessary to avoid it. (This was not true for czarist Russia because World War I destroyed the regime, although not the country.)

Mutual vulnerability has made a crucial difference in how we view war, but not everything has changed. In earlier eras waging war could be very costly even to the side that was winning; that victory was possible did not mean it was possible at an acceptable price. In addition, states did not have to believe that they could win in order rationally to decide to fight. If the gains of victory were high and the difference between losing a war and making the concessions necessary to avoid it were slight, even a small chance of victory could justify the decision to go to war. Futhermore, in many cases states fought even though they lacked any clear idea of how a conflict might be brought to a favorable conclusion. This situation was perhaps true for Germany and certainly for Great Britain in September 1939 and even more so for Great Britain in the period between the fall of France and the German invasion of Russia and for the Japanese when they attacked Pearl Harbor.[18]

What is new, however, is that the other side must cooperate if the state is not to be destroyed. Neither the United States nor the Soviet Union can impose its will on the other by superior military power. Thus Bernard Brodie's famous sentences: "The writer... is not for the moment concerned about who will *win* the next war in which atomic bombs are used. Thus far the chief purpose of our military establishment has been to win wars. From now on its chief purpose must be to avert them. It can have almost no other useful purpose."[19] It might

18. See, for example, David Reynolds, "Churchill and the British 'Decision' to Fight On in 1940: Right Policy, Wrong Reasons," in Richard Langhorne, ed., *Diplomacy and Intelligence during the Second World War* (Cambridge: Cambridge University Press, 1985), pp. 147–67.

19. Bernard Brodie et al., *The Absolute Weapon* (New York: Harcourt, Brace, 1946), p. 76. As Brodie and others later noted, it was really the development of much larger bombs, especially thermonuclear ones, that brought about the situation he foresaw in 1945. Winston Churchill put it eloquently in 1955: "There is an immense gulf between the atomic and the hydrogen bomb. The atomic bomb, with all its terrors, did not carry us outside the scope of human control or manageable events in thought or action, in peace or war. But [with the development of the H-bomb], the entire foundation of human affairs was revolutionized, and mankind placed in a situation both measureless and laden with doom." Interestingly enough, it was in this speech that Churchill voiced the

seem that this assessment would not apply to limited wars. After all, the Warsaw Pact forces might defeat NATO in a conventional war in Europe (or vice versa), and the situation could look like the prenuclear era. But that view would be misleading. The victory would not only be one of arms but also of bargaining, because it would require the maintenance of limits on the weapons that would be used and the targets that would be attacked.

To conclude that military victory is impossible may seem to be a commonplace, but that should not lead us to overlook what a revolutionary change it represents. Throughout recorded history, all-out war has been a useful tool of statecraft; the ability of states to resort to the highest level of violence has been a major engine of international change. Because military victory is impossible, the many patterns that rested on the utility of superior force have also been altered. Even great military success cannot limit the damage that the other superpower can inflict. As a result, force and the threat of it cannot support foreign policy in the same way that it did in the past. But while most of the history of American doctrine and war planning has been the attempt to design substitutes for damage limitation, these attempts have not come to grips with the fundamental characteristics of nuclear politics. U.S. policy has been incoherent, it has conjured up unrealistic dangers, and it has ignored real problems.

Deterrence by Denial and Deterrence by Punishment

Mutual second-strike capability has drastically altered the ways in which states can use force to reach their goals. In the past, successful armies could simultaneously seize desired territory, punish the other side, limit or diminish the effectiveness of the other side's arms, and, most important in this context, keep the adversary from doing these things to the state. Strategic nuclear weapons can inflict punishment; they can also decrease the other side's military capability; they can even facilitate the taking of territory. But as long as the other side has a sufficient number of well-protected nuclear weapons, they cannot prevent the adversary from destroying what the state values. As we will see, this does not mean that weapons are less important than they

hope that safety might be "the sturdy child of terror" (*Hansard*, March 1, 1955, vol. 537, 5th ser., cols. 1894–95. I am grateful to McGeorge Bundy for calling my attention to the less-well-known portion of this speech).

were in the past or even that states cannot benefit by increasing their nuclear arsenals. But the weapons produce their influence by processes that are very different from those operating in the past.

Previously, strong states were able to discourage others from attacking them by being able to repel such an attack—what Glenn Snyder calls "deterrence by denial."[20] Military superiority was meaningful in a direct and straightforward sense. Defense now being impossible, the superpowers deter their adversaries not by threatening to defeat them, but by raising the cost of the conflict to unacceptably high levels— what is called "deterrence by punishment." It is the prospect of fighting the war rather than the possibility of losing it that induces restraint.

The exact ways a nuclear war might be fought have been much discussed and debated. But whatever the method, the destruction would be enormous. Thus deterrence by punishment is not a matter of subtleties; the influence of the fear of war on political leaders is not sensitive to the details of doctrine and war planning that preoccupy the specialists.[21] Thus it is not surprising that variations in American nuclear strategy have not produced variations in Soviet or American international behavior.

Although neither side can deny the other the ability to destroy it, perhaps denial can work at lower levels of violence. That is, the United States might be able to beat back conventional attacks in Europe or deny the Soviets the ability to gain other war aims. But even such capabilities would not permit escape from the powerful shadow of punishment. Soviet war aims must include absorbing no more punishment than the objectives merit, an aim that nuclear weapons make easy to thwart. Of course, the American threat to use such weapons is undercut by the Soviet ability to respond similarly. But this problem does not disappear even if the United States can deny other Soviet war aims without resorting to a pure policy of punishment. In the absence of the ability to protect itself, the United States risks destruction in any war with the USSR, even if the United States is successful in immediate military terms.

Because it is mutual second-strike capability and not nuclear weapons per se that has generated the new situation, it is possible to imagine a world in which such weapons existed, and yet deterrence by denial resumed its previous role. If defense were possible through any one

---

20. Glenn Snyder, *Deterrence and Defense* (Princeton: Princeton University Press, 1961).
21. This point has been stressed by McGeorge Bundy: see "To Cap the Volcano," *Foreign Affairs*, 48 (October 1969), 13; "The Bishops and the Bomb," *New York Review of Books*, June 16, 1983, pp. 3–8.

of three mechanisms, the analysis presented here would be negated. First and most obvious would be the development of a defensive shield that could protect society against nuclear attack. But such protection is impossible in this century if not forever. Defenses of lesser potency that could be deployed within the next ten or twenty years will not be considered here because they would not alter mutual vulnerability, although they might enhance some forms of coercion and make others more difficult. A second theoretical possibility would be for a state to gain the ability to destroy all the adversary's strategic forces in a first strike. As with a defensive shield—and perhaps in conjunction with it—this ability could produce protection no matter what the adversary tried to do to the state. But this prospect is not technologically feasibile either. Third, the United States and the Soviet Union could agree to reductions in strategic forces so drastic that, perhaps in conjunction with the deployment of defenses, one or both sides could protect themselves. The barriers to such a world are more political than technical, but both sides' rhetoric notwithstanding, this development also seems so unlikely that it can be put aside.

Although the contrast between deterrence by denial and deterrence by punishment is central to understanding the nuclear era, the transformation from one to the other is not unqualified. Nuclear weapons have greatly enhanced the role of punishment, not created it.[22] Naval blockades, raids on the other side's towns and farmlands, as well as what we now call "conventional" bombing, all inflicted punishment before 1945.[23] Much of the theory of air power in the 1920s and 1930s was based on the expected efficacy of bombing civilians and the belief that the outcome of the war would be determined by which nation could stand the most punishment.[24] Indeed, even before the development of airplanes, Ivan Bloch foresaw that battlefield defense was so strong and weapons of firepower so dreadful that "the future of war [would be] not fighting, but famine, not the slaying of men but the bankruptcy of nations and the break-up of the whole social orga-

22. See George Quester, *Deterrence before Hiroshima* (New York: Wiley, 1966).

23. See John Herz, *International Politics in the Atomic Age* (New York: Columbia University Press, 1959), pp. 96–108. Examples of punitive raids are presented in Schelling, *Arms and Influence*, pp. 178–79.

24. The picture, of course, is a complicated and controversial one. For a variety of reasons, the power of bombing was often overestimated, as I have discussed in "Deterrence and Perception," *International Security*, 7 (Winter 1982–83), 14–18. Also see Malcolm Smith, *British Air Strategy between the Wars* (Oxford: Clarendon Press, 1986), for a discussion of air doctrines that were not aimed at punishment and the argument that the fact that the British stance in the 1930s was meant to deter rather than to fight explains in part the RAF's lack of preparation actually to carry out bombing campaigns.

nization." The decisive factors then would be "the quality of toughness and capacity for endurance, of patience under privation, of stubbornness under reverse or disappointment."[25] Opposing sides could and did simultaneously attack each other's values. England could bomb Germany while Germany was bombing England; Britain could blockade Germany as Germany was cutting deeply into Britain's seaborne supply lines. In earlier eras, countries could simultaneously destroy each other's croplands; states without modern technology could assassinate each other's leaders.

Neither now nor in the past do the costs have to be overwhelming in order to deter nations from war. They just have to be high enough to make going to war less attractive than the alternative. In the past, states have been deterred from fighting wars they believed they could win because the costs have been expected to be too high.[26] Today, the United States refrains from invading Libya not because it could not do so successfully or because Libya or the USSR would retaliate (although terrorists might), but because the unfavorable allied and neutral reaction would outweigh the gains. But when nuclear weapons are not involved, the level of pain is not likely to rise to unacceptable levels or to be totally uncorrelated with the fortunes on the battlefield. For example, in World War II the Allied war effort—including bombing—slowly reduced the German ability to bomb England. And if the terms of peace were very demanding, the pain was worth bearing as long as there was a chance to stave off a defeat.

Two conceptual points need to be stressed. First, the relevant distinction is between deterrence by denial and deterrence by punishment, not between counterforce and countervalue, although the distinctions often are parallel. The use or threat of force exerts pressure either by making it impossible for the other side to reach its objectives or by exacting an unacceptable price for doing so. Usually the threat to destroy civilian targets fits into the latter category and the threat to destroy military targets into the former, but this connection is not rigid and invariant. Thus, in a long conventional conflict, destroying civilian targets such as factories could prevent the other side from carrying on the war. On the other hand, destroying military forces not directly involved in the war does more to punish the other side than to affect

25. Quoted in Michael Howard, "Men against Fire: Expectations of War in 1914," *International Security*, 9 (Summer 1984), 43.

26. This is especially likely if a war of attrition is foreseen. See John Mearsheimer, *Conventional Deterrence* (Ithaca: Cornell University Press, 1983); for a good discussion of the domestic impact of prolonged wars, see Arthur Stein, *The Nation at War* (Baltimore: Johns Hopkins University Press, 1980).

the course of battle. For example, in a war limited to Europe, the American threat to destroy Soviet forces in the Far East would be much more punishment than denial.

Second, the distinction between denial and punishment is blurred to the extent that force works through both channels simultaneously. Carl von Clausewitz noted that one method of warfare is "to influence the enemy's expenditure of effort; in other words, . . . to make the war more costly to him,"—deterrence by punishment. The most important way of doing this "is to wear down the enemy . . . using the duration of the war to bring about a gradual exhaustion of his physical and moral resistance."[27] Killing or disabling the enemy's soldiers not only makes it harder for him to reach his objectives, it also inflicts pain on the society. Bombing North Vietnam was supposed both to reduce its capability to wage war and to inflict sufficient pain so that it would come to the peace table. The United States accepted an unsatisfactory end to that war because the costs of continued fighting were too high, costs that would have been lower had the military balance in Indochina been more favorable. In the future as well, successful fighting would punish as it denies. American destruction of Soviet armies would not only endanger the success of the military mission, it would also destroy a valued instrument of their Soviet state. Indeed, as long as technology does not permit a quick victory, any war between large, industrialized, and resilient states will inflict enormous costs on each side even if neither consciously pursues a strategy of punishment. In contrast, the threat of nuclear war is a form of deterrence by denial in that no reasonable objective could be reached through an all-out conflict.

Policies can also combine punishment and denial, either by holding at risk targets that serve both functions or by planning to employ one or the other depending on the circumstances. Indeed, most American strategies have been based on seeking denial if the violence can be contained and seeking punishment if it cannot. Over the past decade the latter aspect of the policy has changed as American decision makers have changed their analysis of what the Soviets value—shifting attention from their cities to economic recovery and then to the leadership's control of the USSR. But, at least since the 1960s, the United States has sought to make denial the first line of deterrence, keeping the possibility of extreme punishment as the ultimate threat.

Nevertheless, the distinction between the two kinds of deterrence is still a valid one. One does not have to be a Marxist to believe that at

27. Carl von Clausewitz, *On War*, ed. and trans. Michael Howard and Peter Paret (Princeton: Princeton University Press, 1976), p. 93, emphasis omitted.

a certain point, a quantitative change becomes a qualitative change. The denial of the adversary's aims that was possible in the past entailed the protection of the state. The fact that the two effects are now severed, the ease with which each superpower can punish the other, the fact that such punishment does not depend on gaining military advantage, and the overwhelming nature of the destruction that is possible, all conspire drastically to alter the role of force between the superpowers.

Hostages

Because of mutual vulnerability, each superpower has involuntarily given the other hostages.[28] Three characteristics of hostages are particularly important. First, they can perform their functions only as long as they survive. The adversary is restrained because the state can hurt it; once the state has destroyed what the adversary values, this motive for holding back disappears. Thus Schelling points out that "no cities" was a misleading name for the McNamara strategy which held out the possibility of limited and counterforce wars. Rather, it should have been called the "cities" strategy because it stressed the value of cities and the influence that is provided only as long as at least some of them remained intact.[29] Inflicting pain on the other side by destroying some hostages provides bargaining leverage not directly—because there is nothing the state could do to reverse the destruction—but by making more credible the threat to continue and to increase the punishment.[30]

Second, the holding of hostages predates the advent of nuclear weapons, just as deterrence by punishment does. We should expect hostages to be taken whenever states are unable physically to protect their values, although the phenomenon may not be limited to this condition. Thus when armies were not large enough to defend all of the state's territory, attacks on civilians and property were common. Furthermore, in these circumstances states recognized the value of keeping hostages alive. The king of Sparta opposed immediately attacking Athenian territory, noting that the Athenians "will be more inclined to give way,

28. Some have argued that the United States has welcomed this situation and has foregone opportunities to alter it. The former claim is questionable at best. The latter is almost certainly false; at minimum, it could be made plausible only by careful historical research, coupled with the difficult analysis of the hypothetical situations that would have arisen had the United States acted differently. For a good discussion, see Warner Schilling, "U.S. Strategic Nuclear Concepts in the 1970s: The Search for Sufficiently Equivalent Countervailing Parity," *International Security*, 6 (Fall 1981), 49–79.

29. Schelling, *Arms and Influence*, pp. 192–98. Of course more recently there has been a vigorous debate about whether the Soviets value their cities.

30. Ibid., pp. 170–74; Snyder, *Deterrence and Defense*, p. 71.

[13]

since their land will still be untouched and, in making up their minds, they will be thinking of advantages which they still possess and which have not yet been destroyed. For you must think of their land as though it was a hostage in your possession, and all the more valuable the better it is looked after."[31] The nuclear era is unique, however, in that the value of the hostages is greater than what is at stake in the conflict, and defeating the other side's army cannot effectively protect the hostages.

Third, the exchange of hostages can facilitate cooperation. Thus in premodern times some agreements were possible only because one or both sides could send valued members of the community to the other side, where they could be killed if the sender reneged on its commitments. Modern corporations use analogous devices to see that their subsidiaries and others they deal with do not take advantage of them.[32] Much of the recent discussion of the ability of states to cooperate in the anarchic international environment stresses that hostages (in the form of values that would be sacrificed if conflict increased) discipline states against breaking agreements.[33] At any point in a continuing relationship, one state is likely to have gained more than the other and, through a tacit or an explicit understanding, will be expected to even the balance. Facing a short-run loss, the state will be tempted to renege on its promises. Understanding this dynamic at the start, in the absence of hostages states will hesitate to enter into arrangements that could prove highly advantageous over the long-run because they fear the other side will terminate them whenever it sees an immediate benefit in doing so. Of course hostages do not solve all problems of cooperation, but the effect helps explain why mutual vulnerability yields benefits as well as potential doom.

NUCLEAR REVOLUTION

The result of mutual vulnerability is what has been called the nuclear revolution.[34] The term "revolution" often is used quite freely. Thus

31. Thucydides, *The Peloponnesian War*, trans. Rex Warner (Harmondsworth, Engl.: Penguin Books, 1956), pp. 58–59.
32. Oliver Williamson, "Credible Commitments: Using Hostages to Support Exchange," *American Economic Review*, 73 (September 1983), 519–40.
33. See, for example, the articles in *World Politics*, 37 (October 1985), also published as *Cooperation under Anarchy*, ed. Kenneth Oye (Princeton: Princeton University Press, 1985).
34. The first analysis—which is still among the best—is Brodie et al., *The Absolute*

Albert Wohlstetter talks of "revolutionary changes in precision" guidance in missiles and a "revolution in microelectronics."[35] But I mean the term quite literally—a change that turns established truths about the relationships between force and statecraft on their heads. In the past, it was possible for conflict of interest to be total in that whatever one side won, its adversary lost. Although the nuclear era is often referred to as one of total conflict, the situation is very different today. The very fact that war could be total in the sense of destroying both sides means that the conflict of interest cannot be total.[36]

The claim that mutual second-strike capability has drastically altered the relationships between force and foreign policy underpins many of the detailed arguments being made here. So it stands to reason that those who disagree on the specific issues see nuclear weapons as less revolutionary. It is not that they think such weapons are only large conventional explosives, but that they believe they can be understood within the intellectual framework that was developed in the era when deterrence by denial prevailed. That is, they engage in what Hans Morgenthau called "conventionalization."[37] Thus it is not surprising that Paul Nitze not only stresses the importance of military advantage and multiple nuclear options but, long before these specific issues arose, argued that the nuclear revolution was a myth. As a member of the Strategic Bombing Survey, Nitze was one of the first Americans to visit Hiroshima. Although he did not minimize "the extent of the destruction" according to one historian, "he was also impressed at the number of people who had nonetheless managed to survive. Nitze

---

Weapon. For an excellent recent treatment, see Michael Mandelbaum, *The Nuclear Revolution* (Cambridge: Cambridge University Press, 1981). My own arguments on this point are in Jervis, *The Illogic of American Nuclear Strategy* (Ithaca: Cornell University Press, 1984), chap. 1.

35. Albert Wohlstetter, "Between an Unfree World and None," *Foreign Affairs*, 63 (Summer 1985), 990; also see Wohlstetter, "Swords without Shields," *The National Interest*, no. 8 (Summer 1987), 40.

36. For a discussion of the way in which the nuclear revolution has heightened both common and conflicting interests, see Jervis, *Illogic of American Nuclear Strategy*, pp. 29–34. To argue for the revolutionary nature of nuclear weapons does not mean that all earlier ideas no longer apply. The most important of these is Clausewitz's argument that war is not separate from politics but, rather, is subordinate to it. Military advantage is not an end in itself; it must serve political objectives. For further discussion, see Bernard Brodie, *War and Politics* (New York: Macmillan, 1973), chap. 1, and the concluding Chapter 7 below.

37. See Hans Morgenthau, "The Fallacy of Thinking Conventionally About Nuclear Weapons," in David Carlton and Carlo Schaerf, eds., *Arms Control and Technological Innovation* (New York: Wiley, 1976), pp. 256–64. My discussion is in *Illogic of American Nuclear Strategy*, pp. 56–63.

immediately began to question, he said, the 'common, popular view' that the atomic bomb 'was an absolute weapon and that this changed everything.' "[38] It followed that while the details of prenuclear strategies and tactics would have to be changed to accommodate the new technology, the basic intellectual guidelines remained:

> It is a copybook principle in strategy that, in actual war, advantage tends to go to the side in a better position to raise the stakes by expanding the scope, duration or destructive intensity of the conflict. By the same token, at junctures of high conflict short of war, the side better able to cope with the potential consequences of raising the stakes has the advantage. The other side is the one under greater pressure to scramble for a peaceful way out. To have the advantage at the utmost level of violence helps at every lesser level.[39]

There is no doubt that Nitze is correct that this is a copybook principle of strategy. But the question is whether the copybook still applies.

Claims for Military Victory

The disagreement about whether a major war could produce a military victory brings the issue of whether old guidelines are still usable most sharply into focus. As noted earlier, the central implication of the nuclear revolution is that it cannot. Paul Nitze and others disagree. What is intriguing is the standard they employ. Thirty years ago Nitze noted that one meaning of "winning" is "the comparison between the postwar position of the victor and the defeated" and argued that it was "of the utmost importance that the West maintain a sufficient margin of superior capability so that if general war occurred we could 'win' in [this] sense. The greater the margin (and the more clearly the communists understand that we have a margin), the less likely it is that nuclear war will ever occur."[40] More recently, Nitze has stressed

---

38. Gregg Herken, *Counsels of War* (New York: Knopf, 1985), p. 6; also see p. 47. Also see Steven Rearden, *The Evolution of American Strategic Doctrine: Paul Nitze and the Soviet Challenge*, SAIS Papers in International Affairs no. 4 (Boulder, Colo.: Westview Press, 1984), pp. 3, 23. Nitze was correct as long as atomic bombs remained relatively small and scarce.
39. Paul Nitze, "Is SALT II a Fair Deal for the United States?" (Washington, D.C.: Committee on the Present Danger, 1979), p. 6.
40. Paul Nitze, "Atoms, Strategy and Policy," *Foreign Affairs*, 34 (January 1956), 190–91.

the importance of being able to deny a Soviet leader "the ability or perception that he might successfully prosecute a war-winning strategy and emerge from a war in a predominant military position."[41]

The reasoning behind this position, spelled out by Harold Brown when he was secretary of the Air Force, is that "if the Soviets thought they may be able to recover in some period of time while the U.S. would take three or four times as long, or would never recover, then the Soviets might not be deterred."[42] Thus one of the criteria that Secretary of Defense Melvin Laird held necessary for the essential equivalence of Soviet and American forces was "preventing the Soviet Union from gaining the ability to cause considerable greater urban/industrial destruction than the United States would in a nuclear war."[43] Although noting that this approach could "be carried to absurd lengths," one of his successors argued that under one standard "if the Soviet Union could emerge from [a nuclear war] with superior military power, and could recuperate from the effects more rapidly than the United States, the U.S. capability for assured retaliation would be considered inadequate."[44] A secret White House memorandum in 1972 used a similar formulation when it defined "strategic sufficiency" as the forces necessary "to ensure that the United States would emerge from a nuclear war in discernibly better shape than the Soviet Union."[45]

41. Paul Nitze, "The Objectives of Arms Control," March 28, 1985 (U.S. Department of State, *Current Policy*, no. 667), p. 3. Nitze has expressed slightly different views in "The Relationship of Strategic and Theater Nuclear Forces," *International Security*, 2 (Fall 1977), 124, and in his interview in Michael Charlton, *From Deterrence to Defense*, (Cambridge: Harvard University Press, 1987), pp. 65–66. For how a range of officials and analysts think a nuclear war might be terminated, see the interviews reported in Stephen Kull, *Minds at War: Nuclear Reality and the Inner Conflict of Defense Policymakers* (New York: Basic Books, 1988), chap. 4.

42. U.S. Senate, Preparedness Investigating Subcommittee of the Committee on Armed Services, *Hearings on Status of U.S. Strategic Power*, 90th Cong., 2d sess., April 30, 1968 (Washington, D.C.: Government Printing Office, 1968), p. 186.

43. U.S. House of Representatives, Subcommittee on Department of Defense, *Appropriations for the FY 1973 Defense Budget and FY 1973–1977 Program*, 92d Cong., 2d sess., February 22, 1972 (Washington, D.C.: Government Printing Office 1972), p. 65. At one point, Eisenhower endorsed similar criteria: he told Dulles that the United States must be ready "to inflict greater loss upon the enemy than he could reasonably hope to inflict upon us" (*FRUS, 1952–1954*, vol. 2, pt. 1, p. 461). But this was only a passing formulation and his more considered and frequently-expressed position was very different, as we saw earlier.

44. Donald Rumsfeld, in Department of Defense, *Annual Report for FY 1978* (Washington, D.C.: Government Printing Office, 1977), p. 68.

45. Quoted in Herken, *Counsels of War*, p. 266. As the head of SAC, Gen. Thomas Power was supposed to have said in 1960: "At the end of the war, if there are two Americans and one Russian, we win!" (To which William W. Kaufmann replied: "Well,

This conception leads to measuring the peacetime strategic balance and the projected balance during a hypothetical war by looking at which side has more nuclear capability (amount of megatonnage, number of warheads, numbers of warheads capable of destroying hardened targets, etc.).[46] Similarly, Colin Gray, who shares many of Nitze's views on specific issues of nuclear strategy, argues that nuclear weapons have "*not* effected a revolution in statecraft." Following out the logic, he argues that "the United States [should] take seriously the proposition that deterrence and defense are one and the same," in part because "if the Soviet Union can win a war militarily, it will very likely be able to pick up the somewhat radioactive pieces at home." The goal of denying the Soviets a victory "translates with little difficulty into the requirement for a theory of a victory."[47]

Two linked aspects of this conception of victory reveal a conventionalized perspective. First, it is zero-sum. One side must come out ahead of the other; one or the other must retain more military power and be less slow to recover. Thus every war must have a winner. Second, the judgment involved is a relative one—the position of each side is being compared with that of the other. This stress on relative advantage fits nicely with the normal conception of power in international politics. Starting with Thucydides, scholars have argued that power makes no sense when viewed in absolute terms because the outcome of conflict, especially military conflict, will be determined not by the absolute size of the armies involved but by their relative capabilities. When deterrence by punishment is crucial, however, it is the absolute level of destruction that a state faces and can inflict that controls its behavior.[48]

While the conclusion that military victory is possible follows from

---

you'd better make sure that they're a man and a woman.") Quoted in Fred Kaplan, *The Wizards of Armageddon* (New York: Simon & Schuster, 1983), p. 246.

46. I have discussed the problems with this approach in "Cognition and Political Behavior," in Richard Lau and David Sears, eds., *Political Cognition* (Hillsdale, N.J.: Earlbaum, 1986), pp. 330–33, and "The Drunkard's Search," in Shanto Iyengar and William McGuire, eds., *Current Approaches to Political Psychology* (Urbana: University of Illinois Press, forthcoming).

47. Colin Gray, *Nuclear Strategy and National Style* (Lanham, Md.: Hamilton Press, 1986), pp. ix–x, 318, 117, emphasis in the original. The last step in the reasoning works because defeating the Soviet armed forces would probably mean "political disintegration" in the Soviet Union (p. 118). Also see Gray's *The Geopolitics of Super Power* (Lexington: University Press of Kentucky, 1988), pp. 35–36.

48. Note that the title of the book by Brodie et al. was *The Absolute Weapon*. For further discussion, see Jervis, *Illogic of American Nuclear Strategy*, pp. 59–63. For discussions of the differences in behavior that follow from a concern with relative gains and losses as contrasted with absolute gains and losses, see Arthur Stein, *Dilemmas of Interdependence: Logics of International Cooperation and Conflict* (Ithaca: Cornell University Press, forthcom-

the definition employed, such a conclusion is remarkably apolitical.[49] It does not relate the costs of the war to the objectives and thus ignores the question of whether the destruction would be so great that the winner, as well as the loser, would regret having fought it. Holders of this view, then, fall into the trap that Clausewitz warned about of seeing war as an end in itself instead of as a means to national goals, a point I will return to in the concluding chapter. The only way to rescue this argument would be to assume that the Russians are so highly motivated to expand that they would be willing to accept any level of destruction as long as they ended up ahead of the West and so were able to dominate the postwar world. Indeed, some analysts seem to ascribe this outlook to the Soviet Union, but they have not explicated the argument carefully enough to permit it to be taken seriously.[50] Also crucial and apolitical is the assumption that the state that could recover more quickly could control the adversary. It is hard to have any sense of what the postwar world would look like, but geography alone should caution against believing that either the United States or the Soviet Union could easily dominate the other.

The Stability-Instability Paradox

Before the implications of the nuclear revolution can be explored, we should note the fallacy in the common argument that because military victory is impossible in a nuclear war, nuclear weapons have little utility. At first glance, it would appear that this conclusion follows ineluctably from the premise. That it makes no sense for either side to start a major nuclear war nullifies the threat to strike except in retaliation. The result is what Glenn Snyder has called the stability-

---

ing), and Joseph Grieco, "Anarchy and the Limits of Cooperation," *International Organization*, 42 (Summer 1988), 485-507.

49. This is implicitly acknowledged by Nitze in an interview in Charlton, *From Deterrence to Defense*, pp. 65-66.

50. See the arguments by American officials in U.S. House of Representatives, Subcommittee on Department of Defense, *Appropriations for the FY 1973 Defense Budget and FY 1973-77 Program*, p. 65; U.S. Senate, Committee on Armed Services, *Hearings on FY 1978 Military Procurement, Research and Development, and Personnel Strengths*, pt. 2, 95th Cong., 1st sess. (Washington, D.C.: Government Printing Office, 1977), p. 892; U.S. Senate, Preparedness Investigating Subcommittee of the Committee on Armed Services, *Hearings on Status of U.S. Strategic Power*, p. 186; Francis Hoeber, "How Little Is Enough?" *International Security*, 3 (Winter 1978-79), 67; Nitze, "Atoms, Strategy and Policy," pp. 190-91. Also see Colin Gray, "Nuclear Strategy: A Case for a Theory of Victory," *International Security*, 4 (Summer 1979), 66-67, 76-77. Even George Kennan argued that the United States should ensure that "if cataclysm is unavoidable, [the catastrophe] is at least less than that suffered by our enemies" (*FRUS, 1950*, vol. 1, p. 37).

instability paradox.[51] Strategic stability creates instability by making lower levels of violence relatively safe and undermining "extended deterrence"—that is, the threat to use strategic nuclear weapons to protect allies. Thus, the argument goes, the ability of the Soviet Union to destroy the United States means that the United States cannot credibly threaten to use its strategic nuclear forces in response to a Soviet attack on West Europe or the Persian Gulf.

The point can be put more generally. Kenneth Boulding argues: "If [deterrence] were really stable . . . it would cease to deter. If the probability of nuclear weapons going off were zero, they would not deter anybody."[52] More graphic in tone but similar in content is Khrushchev's account: "When I was appointed First Secretary of the Central Committee and learned all the facts about nuclear power I couldn't sleep for several days. Then I became convinced that we could never possibly use these weapons, and I was able to sleep again. But all the same we must be prepared."[53] In the same vein, Patrick Morgan argues that the normal criticism that deterrence requires complete rationality has things backward. If decisionmakers were completely rational, they would never order the large-scale use of nuclear weapons and so the credibility of the nuclear threat would be very low.[54] This argument implies that each side's nuclear weapons cancel out the influence of the other's. Analysts as politically different as Robert McNamara and Colin Gray agree on this point. In the words of the latter, as long as the United States lacks a plausible means of securing victory, deterrence by punishment "is an idea it would be hard to improve upon were one seeking to minimize the relevance of (American) strategic weapons to world politics."[55] Nuclear weapons, then, have only two consequences, albeit

---

51. Glenn Snyder, "The Balance of Power and the Balance of Terror," in Paul Seabury, ed., *The Balance of Power* (San Francisco: Chandler, 1965), pp. 184–201. Also see Jervis, *Illogic of American Nuclear Strategy*, pp. 29–34.

52. Kenneth Boulding, "Confession of Roots," *International Studies Notes*, 12 (Spring 1986), 32.

53. Quoted in Mohamed Heikal, *The Sphinx and the Commissar: The Rise and Fall of Soviet Influence in the Middle East* (New York: Harper & Row, 1978), p. 129.

54. Patrick Morgan, *Deterrence: A Conceptual Analysis* (Beverly Hills, Calif.: Sage, 1977).

55. Gray, "Nuclear Strategy," p. 70. Robert McNamara's views are parallel: the "sole purpose [of strategic nuclear weapons] . . . is to deter the other side's first use of its strategic forces" ("The Military Role of Nuclear Weapons: Perceptions and Misperceptions," *Foreign Affairs*, 62 [Fall 1983], 68; also see p. 79 and the interview in Michael Charlton, *From Deterrence to Defense*, p. 18, in which McNamara explains the genesis of his views). For further discussion, see Chapter 3 below.

major ones. First, they make it extremely unlikely that either side will directly attack the other and, second, they ensure incredible destruction were an attack to be made.

If this view were correct, the nuclear revolution would not be trivial— these two results are surely significant. But the effect still would be contained to a relatively small sphere. In fact, although the logic is impeccable, the argument is flawed because it is too abstract and ignores crucial aspects of international behavior.

As long as we imagine a world of certainties—one in which decision makers can predict how the other side will react and have complete control over their emotions, subordinates, and military machinery— the argument works fairly well.[56] But this condition, although useful for some kinds of analysis, is not realistic. The outcome that everyone wants to avoid can come about; people have been killed playing Chicken. Even in everyday international politics, national behavior often diverges from that desired by the leaders, and the interaction of the behavior of several nations often produces results none of them foresaw. These effects are compounded in a crisis, especially when military forces are put in motion.[57] As I will discuss in Chapters 3 and 5, crisis management is endangered not only by the competitive moves of the other side but by the inherent difficulties in understanding and controlling a complex situation.

Because escalation can occur although no one wants it to, mutual second-strike capability does not make the world safe for major provocations and limited wars. The common claim to the contrary, says Thomas Schelling, "seems to depend on the clean-cut notion that war results—or is expected to result—only from a deliberate yes-no decision. But if war tends to result from a *process*, a dynamic process in which both sides get more and more deeply involved, more and more expectant, more and more concerned not to be a slow second in case the war starts, it is not a 'credible first strike' that one threatens, but

---

56. See Clausewitz's discussion of how the theory of absolute war needs "modifications in practice" (*On War*, pp. 78–81).

57. See, for example, Scott Sagan, "Nuclear Alerts and Crisis Management," *International Security*, 9 (Spring 1985), 99–139; Alexander George, "Crisis Management: The Interaction of Political and Military Considerations," *Survival*, 26 (September/October 1984), 223–34; George, "Problems of Crisis Management and Crisis Avoidance in U.S.–Soviet Relations," in Øyvind Østerud, ed., *Studies of War and Peace* (Oslo: Norwegian University Press, 1986), pp. 202–26; Richard Ned Lebow, *Nuclear Crisis Management: A Dangerous Illusion* (Ithaca: Cornell University Press, 1987); Ashton Carter, John Steinbruner, and Charles Zraket, *Managing Nuclear Operations* (Washington, D.C.: Brookings Institution, 1987).

just plain war."[58] In other words, states need not threaten an immediate full-scale nuclear attack on the other side in order to deter it. Instead, they can threaten to take actions that could lead to an undesired conflagration by a series of steps that cannot entirely be foreseen.[59] Empirical evidence bears out this argument: Alexander George and Richard Smoke found that one important cause of deterrence failure was the challenger's belief that he could control his risks.[60] But because having a larger nuclear arsenal or more nuclear options than the adversary cannot keep the interaction under control, the outcomes of confrontations are not strongly influenced by the details of the nuclear balance. This does not mean that the influence of nuclear weapons is sharply restricted, however.

The Possibility of Political Victory

Because the specter of devastation is present in any superpower confrontation, the fear of all-out war can deter many adventures even though starting such a war would be irrational. The stability-instability paradox then is not as stark as it is often portrayed: the influence of nuclear weapons on world politics is far-reaching. Although *military* victory is impossible, victory is not: nuclear weapons can help reach many important political goals.[61] Secretary of State Dean Rusk understood this well: "in this confrontation of two great blocs, each side has a capacity to inflict very great damage on the other. Therefore in terms of handling the relationships between the two power blocs, all responsible governments need to take that into account and not act irresponsibly or frivolously or not suppose that they can press in upon the vital interests of the other without incurring very great risks."[62] Herman Kahn also came to appreciate this view, although he is better known for his baroque portrayal of nuclear options. In the mid-1960s

58. Schelling, *Arms and Influence*, pp. 98–99. I have discussed the implications of these dynamics in *Illogic of American Nuclear Strategy*, chap. 5 and 6; see also Chapter 3 below.

59. This is Schelling's "threat that leaves something to chance." Schelling, *The Strategy of Conflict* (Cambridge: Harvard University Press, 1960), pp. 187–204; Schelling, *Arms and Influence*, pp. 92–125.

60. Alexander George and Richard Smoke, *Deterrence in American Foreign Policy* (New York: Columbia University Press, 1974), pp. 527–30.

61. This argument parallels McGeorge Bundy's argument about "existential deterrence," although the implications I draw for extended deterrence differ from his. See Bundy, "The Bishops and the Bomb," pp. 3–8. Also see Brodie, *War and Politics*, pp. 433–96, for the argument summarized in the chapter title "On Nuclear Weapons: Utility in Nonuse."

62. "Secretary Rusk Interviewed on 'Issues and Answers,' " *U.S. Department of State Bulletin*, 45 (November 13, 1961), 802.

he wrote: "Some years ago, I said, with a certain degree of contempt, that 'some . . . seem to view the deterrence of a rational enemy as almost a simple philosophical consequence of the existence of thermonuclear bombs.' I realize today that these people may have been much closer to the truth than I then thought reasonable."[63] The fear of war can lead the Soviet Union and the United States not only to refrain from attacking the other but also to make other concessions. The resulting victories may not be entirely clear-cut, nor is it certain that they will be upheld in the future, but they are real nevertheless. For a status-quo power like the United States the victories that are possible also are of major importance. The United States does not need the ability to win a nuclear war to protect itself and its allies.[64]

EXPECTED CONSEQUENCES OF
THE NUCLEAR REVOLUTION

The arguments so far, like many other writings on nuclear strategy, are more logical than empirical. Such an approach has been subject to legitimate criticism for paying less attention to evidence than to the elaboration of inferences based on unexamined first principles,[65] but it can be turned to an advantage when we treat the nuclear revolution as a theory yielding propositions that can be measured against the historical record. What follows are some first steps in such an attempt. They are limited by the looseness of the connections between the theory and the propositions, the ambiguity of evidence, and the availability of alternative explanations. Nevertheless, they indicate that nuclear weapons have indeed drastically altered the relationships between force and statecraft.

Peace

The first implication of the nuclear revolution is that military victory is not possible. From this it follows that if statesmen are sensible, wars

---

63. Herman Kahn, *On Escalation* (Baltimore: Penguin Books, 1968), p. 246.

64. The argument to the contrary is implicit in many arguments but is put most clearly by Colin Gray. See, for example, his "War Fighting for Deterrence," *Journal of Strategic Studies*, 7 (March 1984), 5–28, and *Nuclear Strategy and National Style*.

65. See, for example, George and Smoke, *Deterrence in American Foreign Policy*, pp. 58–83; Jervis, "Deterrence Theory Revisited," *World Politics*, 31 (January, 1979), pp. 289–301.

[23]

among the great powers should not occur.[66] Indeed, since 1945 they have not. This is significant evidence because the absence of fighting between the main international rivals is rare. Indeed, it seems to be unprecedented. "Since the second century A.D. under the Pax Romana, the Western World has known no long periods of general peace. The modern record was 38 years, 9 months, and five days . . . from the aftermath of Napoleon's defeat at Waterloo to the effective beginning of the Crimean War. . . . That record was broken . . . on May 15, 1984."[67] Joseph Nye's counting rule is a bit less stringent, and yields a previous record of forty-three years of peace (between the Franco-Prussian War and World War I), a record that has just been surpassed.[68]

Of course, contrary to the expectations generated by the theory, war could occur at any time.[69] But logic indicates another important change—if all-out war comes, it can come *only* through preemption, loss of control, and each side's belief that the other is about to strike. Preemption is not new—it played a role, for example, in 1914. But as long as each side maintains a second-strike capability, the highest levels of violence now can be reached through no other path. While all the other historically important causes of war can still yield Soviet-American tension and even limited violence, they cannot lead directly to total war, as they could in the past.

This is not to say that nuclear weapons are the only possible cause of peace. First, bipolarity may have brought peace by providing an easy and unambiguous identification of potential enemies and by diminishing the ability of allies to drag the leading powers into conflict.[70] When there are only two major powers in the system, each knows that only the other one can badly menace it, that it cannot pass the buck to third parties, and also that it need not worry about a dangerous

---

66. See Morgan, *Deterrence*, pp. 401–24 for a discussion of "sensible" as opposed to "rational" decision-making. Of course under some conditions it can be rational for a statesman to start a war even if he is sure his state will lose it. Losing a war could be better than the expected value of the world in the absence of a war or it could be believed that the adversary was about to attack and so peace was not a possiblity. The former path to war (discussed in Jervis, "War and Misperception," *Journal of Interdisciplinary History*, 18 [Spring 1988], 677–79) no longer seems troublesome; the latter still is: see Chapter 5 below.

67. Paul Schroeder, "Does Murphy's Law Apply to History?" *Wilson Quarterly*, 9 (New Year's 1985), 88.

68. Joseph Nye, Jr., "The Long-Term Future of Nuclear Deterrence," in Roman Kolkowicz, ed., *The Logic of Nuclear Terror* (Boston: Allen & Unwin, 1987), p. 234.

69. See, for example, Fred Iklé, "Can Nuclear Deterrence Last Out the Century?" *Foreign Affairs*, 51 (January 1973), 267–85.

70. Kenneth Waltz, *Theory of International Politics* (Reading, Mass.: Addison-Wesley, 1979).

shift in the balance of power if one of its allies should defect. As Kenneth Waltz argues, these changes eliminate three common paths to major war: the first two operated in the 1930s and the third was in part responsible for World War I. But a bipolar world in which military victory was possible might be unstable, as the examples of Athens and Sparta and Rome and Carthage indicate. Furthermore, although the Soviet Union became a superpower before it developed a large nuclear stockpile, it is not clear that, in the absence of nuclear weapons, it would so unequivocally still have that status.

Second, the processes of political and economic modernization might have brought peace even without nuclear weapons.[71] Several converging changes have been at work. As the two world wars and the conflict between Iran and Iraq indicate, modern states are so resilient and difficult to defeat that victory at reasonable cost is hard to obtain. Although blitzkriegs cannot be ruled out, technology and nationalism usually favor the defense. Prolonged wars fought with modern weapons are likely to exact a fearful toll from the victor; statesmen who understand this will risk a major war only for the strongest of motives. Furthermore, nonnuclear explosives are extremely powerful and can be delivered against populations over the heads of defending armies. Thus, deterrence by punishment would play a large role in a nonnuclear world.

As modernization has increased the pain of war, it may have simultaneously decreased the value of what victory brings. Trade, it can be argued, provides many of the economic benefits that previously came with conquest, as Japan's success indicates. Territory, the prime spoil of war, has become at least somewhat devalued. Although territorial disputes are not absent in Eastern Europe, Germans no longer burn to retake Alsace and Lorraine from France, and Frenchmen hardly miss the Saar. Indeed, it even appears that Canada would have been willing to permit Quebec to secede. Thus weapons of mass destruction may not have been needed to produce situations in which the expected costs of fighting outrun the expected gains.

While I would not completely dissent from this view, it seems incomplete and in places misleading.[72] First, the gains from trade can be

---

71. This is one of the themes of the provocative study by John Mueller, *Retreat from Doomsday: The Obsolescence of Major War* (New York: Basic Books, 1989). Also see Klaus Knorr, *On the Uses of Military Power in the Nuclear Age* (Princeton: Princeton University Press, 1966) and Richard Rosecrance, *The Rise of the Trading State* (New York: Basic Books, 1985).

72. This paragraph is drawn from Jervis, "The Political Effect of Nuclear Weapons," *International Security*, 13 (Fall 1988), 83–90.

realized only within a political structure that is supported in part by military power. Second, it is not entirely clear whether the diminished importance of territory is as much a cause as an effect of the unlikelihood of war. If France or Germany believed that war between them were possible, their desire for the previously contested lands might increase. On the cost side of the ledger, while meaningful victory would be difficult with conventional explosives, it could still be possible. As noted earlier, both the scale and the speed of destruction of a nuclear war are much greater than those of a conventional conflict. The former could deter where the latter, although daunting, might appear worth the chance of conquest. Furthermore, states would be likely to search for technologies, forces, and tactics that would permit blitzkreig. The general bias of military establishments toward offensive postures could reinforce the hopes of civilian decision makers and create crisis instability. Without nuclear weapons, war between the superpowers would not, of course, be certain and might not even be likely, but it would be more likely than it is now. The vast increases in the scale of destruction and the speed with which it could be accomplished give contemporary deterrence a potency it might otherwise lack.

Finally, it is easy to overlook the most obvious alternative explanation of Soviet-American peace—neither side has a strong motive to change the status quo. While both would prefer a somewhat different world, they already have what is most important for them. Thus it does not take a great deal of restraint to keep the peace. Much of American theory and practice of deterrence assumes that the adversary will seize on any opportunity to expand, but in fact it is far from clear whether this assumption applies to the USSR.[73] Even without the knowledge that all-out war would bring total destruction, the superpowers probably would refrain from fighting because they have so little reason to do so. The Soviet Union has benefited from the status quo only slightly

---

73. For a discussion of "initiation theory," see George and Smoke, *Deterrence in American Foreign Policy*, pp. 519–33; also see Jervis, "Deterrence Theory Revisited," pp. 322–24. A similar question is raised from a different perspective in George Modelski and Patrick Morgan, "Understanding Global War," *Journal of Conflict Resolution*, 29 (September 1985), 391–417. This argument points to a problem with Kenneth Waltz's argument that proliferation would make the world safer by replicating the Soviet-American nuclear stalemate (*The Spread of Nuclear Weapons: More May Be Better*, Adelphi Paper no. 171 [London: International Institute of Strategic Studies, 1981]). Many of the countries that might develop nuclear weapons are much more strongly motivated to challenge their rivals than are the United States or the USSR. Under these circumstances, coercion or war is a considerable danger.

less than the United States, a situation that has produced what John Mueller calls "general stability."[74]

Again, I think there is much to be said for this argument. But even though neither the United States nor the Soviet Union is strongly driven to expand, they do have important conflicts of interest and clashing security requirements. Furthermore, the basic insight of systems theory is that we cannot equate results with intentions: for wars to occur it is not required that the actors seek such an outcome.[75] Previous wars have broken out even though the major states were not pressing to overturn the status quo; without nuclear weapons these processes could be replicated. John Gaddis's analysis is persuasive:

> Wars, in the past, have started over far lesser provocations than have been present since 1945. World War I itself began as the result of a single political assassination. The Crimean War grew out of a quarrel between France and Russia over the custody of holy places in Palestine. Spain and England went to war in 1739, or so we are told, over the cutting off of a single sailor's ear. One need only compare these trivialities, with all their bloody effects, to such postwar episodes as the Iranian crisis of 1946, the Czechoslovak coup and the Berlin blockage in 1948, the North Korean invasion of South Korea in 1950, the fall of Dienbienphu in 1954, the Quemoy-Matsu incidents of 1954–55 and 1958, the Hungarian uprising and the Suez crisis of 1956, the Berlin confrontations of 1958–59 and 1961, the Cuban missile crisis of 1962, the mining of Haiphong harbor and the bombing of Hanoi in 1972, the Defcon 3 nuclear alert during the 1973 Middle East war, the invasion of Afghanistan in 1979, and the Korean airliner incident in 1983.[76]

In summary, although the "long peace" is consistent with the theory of the nuclear revolution, other explanations pointing to other developments can claim to account for this outcome.[77] But it is not clear that

---

74. Mueller, *Retreat from Doomsday*; also see Waltz, *Theory of International Politics*, p. 190.

75. Kenneth Waltz, *Man, the State, and War* (New York: Columbia University Press, 1955); Waltz, *Theory of International Politics*.

76. John Gaddis, "Nuclear Weapons, Stability, and the Postwar International System" (unpublished paper, Ohio University, Athens), pp. 7–8.

77. The phrase comes from John Gaddis, "The Long Peace: Elements of Stability in the Postwar International System," *International Security*, 10 (Spring 1986), 99–142, who presents a balanced analysis of its causes.

they fully predict the results we have seen. In many cases these developments reinforce effects of nuclear weapons, and it is not easy to apportion the responsibility for peace.

One interesting kind of evidence cuts against our general argument, however. Once we look beyond the Soviet-American case, we can see that force has been used against states with nuclear weapons. Indeed, by some definitions, the territory of these states has been invaded. British nuclear weapons did not stop Argentina from taking the Falklands, although the attack made sense to the Argentines only because they thought the British realized that this territory was not really British.[78] The 1973 Middle East war raises the same challenge more sharply. Even though Israel does not acknowledge having nuclear weapons, it was generally thought to have them. Yet this did not deter Egypt from attacking in Sinai and the Syrians from moving into territory the Israelis considered their own and later annexed. Indeed, it is not clear in retrospect—and certainly was not clear to the Israelis at the time—that Syria would have stopped had its army reached Israel proper.[79] The fighting along the Sino-Soviet border in 1968 constitutes a third case. Although the potential gains and losses of territory were minuscule, they were heavily freighted with political symbolism, and both sides possessed nuclear weapons.

American interests were challenged even when the United States had a nuclear monopoly, or something close to it. Not only did the Russians try to force the United States out of Berlin in 1948, but North Korea attacked South Korea two years later. Of course in the former case violence was not used, and in the latter it seemed that the United States would not resist. But when China joined the Korean War it had to engage American troops directly and could not dismiss the danger of an atomic response.

The ability of nuclear weapons to keep the peace and provide extended deterrence for close allies is also rendered questionable by later

78. Richard Ned Lebow, "Miscalculation in the South Atlantic: The Origins of the Falklands War," in Robert Jervis, Richard Ned Lebow, and Janice Stein, *Psychology and Deterrence* (Baltimore: Johns Hopkins University Press, 1985), pp. 89–124. For a discussion of the role of nuclear weapons in the war, see George Quester, "The Nuclear Implications of the South Atlantic War," in R. B. Byers, ed., *The Denuclearization of the Oceans* (London: Croom Helm, 1986), pp. 119–26.

79. When the situation looked bleakest for Israel, Golda Meir apparently sent President Nixon a message that said that unless the situation was reversed, Israel might have to use "every means" at its disposal (Alan Dowty, *Middle East Crises: U.S. Decision-Making in 1958, 1970, and 1973* [Berkeley: University of California Press, 1984], p. 245; also see Nadav Safran, *Israel: The Embattled Ally* [Cambridge: Harvard University Press, 1978], p. 483).

events in Southeast Asia. Chinese nuclear weapons did not deter Vietnam from conquering China's protégé, Cambodia; Soviet nuclear weapons did not prevent China from responding with a foray into Vietnam. Of course in these cases nuclear weapons may have restrained either or both sides; we cannot tell what they would have done in the absence of the chance of devastation. Furthermore, in some of these conflicts, particularly the 1973 Middle East war, the knowledge that the superpowers would not permit the complete defeat of either side may have provided underlying stability that simultaneously limited the local adventures and made them more safe.

These cases underline the crucial role played by the degree to which the states are highly motivated to act in ways inconsistent with the other's vital interests and remind us that the theory of the nuclear revolution does not imply that the status quo can easily and safely be maintained in the face of an adversary who is willing to run high risks to change it. But it does imply that the risks of trying to do so are higher than they were in the past.

Preservation of the Status Quo

The nuclear revolution can also explain the second most striking characteristic of the postwar world—the absence of peaceful change on issues of most concern to the superpowers. In principle, the fear of war could be used as a lever to change the status quo as well as to preserve it. Nuclear weapons would still have very great influence, but the world would be quite different from what it is. Offense in the sense of altering a situation would be as easy as defense in the sense of protecting it; instability would be greater; states would be quick to exploit any opportunity for nuclear blackmail; the chances of miscalculation and the resulting danger of war would be great.[80]

---

80. My analysis here parallels much of Schelling's argument that deterrence is usually easier than compellence. In the latter, the actor requires the adversary to change his behavior, either to stop doing something he has been doing or to commence behavior he otherwise would not undertake. Deterrence only requires that the other continue to refrain from forbidden acts. Deterrence usually seeks to uphold the status quo and compellence to change it, but Schelling's distinction refers to the adversary's behavior, whereas the status quo refers to a situation. On occasion, the two distinctions will not coincide, for example when one side needs to take new actions in order to maintain the status quo. Thus in 1968 the Soviet Union had to intervene forcibly in Czechoslovakia in order to maintain its hold on that country, and in 1980 the Carter administration made a weak attempt to deter the Soviet Union from sending its armies into Poland to accomplish this objective. After North Vietnam started sending soldiers to the South, the United States sought to compel it to cease these activities, thus facilitating the maintenance of

In fact, however, our argument implies that this lever is not used. The side defending the status quo usually enjoys two kinds of advantages. First, its interest is usually greater than that of the other side. Bargaining theory supports common sense in indicating that the higher the value a state places on prevailing on an issue, the higher the risks it will be willing to run in order to do so. Thus the side that has more of a stake in an issue can make more credible threats to stand firm.[81] As Robert Kennedy explained, "The missiles in Cuba, we felt, vitally concerned our national security, but not that of the Soviet Union."[82] This asymmetry of interests made it both necessary and possible for the United States to prevail on the central issues. Historical, political, and psychological factors conspire to give the defender a strong interest in perpetuating the situation. The distribution of values and territory that constitutes the status quo is no accident; the United States and the Soviet Union have generally achieved dominant influence in the

---

the status quo. Schelling, *Arms and Influence*, pp. 69–91, 99–105, 172–76. Also see David Baldwin, "Bargaining with Airline Hijackers," in I. William Zartman, ed., *The 50% Solution* (Garden City, N.Y.: Doubleday, 1976), pp. 416–21 and Jervis, "Deterrence Theory Revisited," 314–22. Alexander George, David Hall, and William Simons, *The Limits of Coercive Diplomacy* (Boston: Little, Brown, 1971), develop empirical arguments about the conditions under which the superpowers can use threats and limited force to change the status quo. Also see Walter Petersen, "Deterrence and Compellence: A Critical Assessment of Conventional Wisdom," *International Studies Quarterly*, 30 (September 1986), 269–94.

81. See George, Hall, and Simons, *Limits of Coercive Diplomacy*; George and Smoke, *Deterrence in American Foreign Policy*; Glenn Snyder, " 'Prisoner's Dilemma' and 'Chicken' Models in International Politics," *International Studies Quarterly*, 15 (March 1971), 66–103; Robert Jervis, "Bargaining and Bargaining Tactics," in J. Roland Pennock and John Chapman, eds., *Coercion*, NOMOS, vol. 14 (Chicago: Aldine, Atherton, 1972), pp. 272–88; Jervis, "Deterrence Theory Revisited," pp. 314–22. Khrushchev put the point in his typical style when discussing a confrontation in the Middle East: "The real problem is not one of weapons; it's one of peace or war. The situation is highly a dangerous one, and I think that the people with the strongest nerves will be the winners. That is the most important consideration in the power struggle of our time. The people with weak nerves will go to the wall" (quoted in Heikal, *The Sphinx and the Commissar*, pp. 97–98.) Also see the sophisticated modification of this argument: Robert Powell, "Crisis Bargaining, Escalation, and MAD," *American Political Science Review*, 81 (September 1987), 717–27, and Powell, "Nuclear Brinkmanship with Two-Sided Incomplete Information," *American Political Science Review*, 82 (March 1988), 155–78. It should be noted that while the high value the United States places on Western Europe helps protect it against Soviet aggression, these ties also turn the Soviet ability to destroy the Continent into bargaining leverage against the United States. This was particularly important in the years before the Soviets developed second-strike capability. For in this period when the United States itself was relatively invulnerable it may have been restrained by the knowledge that a war with the USSR would entail the loss of territory that it valued only slightly less than its own.

82. Robert Kennedy, *Thirteen Days* (New York: Norton, 1971), p. 104.

areas that are most important to them. This effect is compounded by a psychological one. Ingenious experiments have confirmed what most of us feel by introspection—the hurt of losing a certain amount of a value is usually deeper than the gratification of gaining that same amount of a value.[83] Actors will then go to greater lengths to resist a degradation of their position than they will to better it.

Furthermore, the status quo normally serves as a salient point for a settlement, thus increasing its attraction as a solution to tacit bargaining. Partly for this reason, demands to change the status quo cannot help but raise the question of whether yielding will call up further demands. By contrast, the state that refrains from challenging an existing situation is not likely to lead its adversary to conclude that it will permit encroachments on its interests.[84]

It is then hard for a state to threaten to run high risks to alter the status quo. The defender can plausibly argue that changes would be intolerable; its adversary has in fact tolerated the previous distribution of values. The circumstances under which this handicap can be overcome are fairly restrictive: the revisionist state needs to show either that the balance of capabilities has changed—which is only marginally relevant in an era of nuclear plenty; that the status quo itself has changed to its detriment and that it is merely seeking to reestablish its position; or that what it had been able to live with before now has become impossibly painful (as the increased flow of refugees from East to West Berlin in the early 1960s made the lack of a firm division between the two halves of the city much worse for the Soviet bloc than it had been in the 1950s).

The second general factor at work is that the state that seeks to change the status quo must bear the onus of moving first. The possibility of escalation means that to create a crisis or to use force against the other superpower is to multiply drastically the chance of all-out war. Even a limited and successful aggression which would require the defender to escalate in order to reply adequately would start a journey whose destination neither side could foresee. This is nicely brought out by the exchange between Khrushchev and Averell Harriman about Berlin in 1959. As Harriman later remembered it, the Soviet leader declared

83. For citations and a further discussion of the implication of this phenomenon, see Chapter 5 below.
84. Schelling, *Arms and Influence*, pp. 69–78, 100–5; Morton Kaplan, *The Strategy of Limited Retaliation*, Policy Memorandum no. 19 (Princeton University Center of International Studies, April 1959). Retreats are often believed to be likely to lead to the "domino effect" of producing further losses thereby increasing the incentives to defend the status quo. Actors rarely expect such positive feedback when they make gains.

that America could not maintain its position in Berlin by force: after he signed a peace treaty with East Germany, any attempt to reassert Western access rights would mean that "rockets would fly and the tanks would burn." Harriman's account of what happened next almost seems designed to fit the argument here: "I laughed. He asked, 'What are you laughing about?' I said, 'What you're talking about would lead to war and I know you're too sensible a man to want to have war.' He stopped a minute and looked at me and said, 'You're right.' "[85]

Much of this explanation for the bargaining advantage of the side defending the status quo applies to the prenuclear era as well. But the effect is magnified by mutual vulnerability. In the past, a revisionist power of sufficient strength could either wage war to alter the situation or credibly threaten to do so unless the other side met its demands. But when all-out war is catastrophic and even the limited use of force is very costly and dangerous, brute force will not avail.

This is not to say that threats can always uphold the status quo and never change it. Indeed, the status quo may be ambiguous.[86] Was the United States trying to maintain the status quo during the Cuban missile crisis or to force the return to a previous situation (i.e., one in which there were no missiles or bombers in Cuba)? What was the status quo in Afghanistan in December 1979? To the extent that it was the Soviet domination of that country, the invasion solidified—or sought to solidify—the situation. But of course the status quo could be seen— and was seen by at least some participants—as the absence of either Soviet troops or complete Soviet control, and so in this sense the invasion altered it. Assessments are especially likely to diverge if the actors have different concepts of the idea of the status quo. On a general level, the Soviets may see it not as the frozen situation, but as constant change through the objective "forces of history." In specific clashes, each side may well see itself as defending the status quo. Indeed, because of political dynamics like the security dilemma, it may be hard for a country to consolidate its position without infringing on what the other sees as its established interests. Thus the crises over Berlin, especially in 1948–49, that the United States saw as Soviet attempts to

---

85. Quoted in Glenn Seaborg, with the assistance of Benjamin Loeb, *Kennedy, Khrushchev, and the Test Ban* (Berkeley: University of California Press, 1981), p. 252. This story may be too good to be true. As Marc Trachtenberg has pointed out to me, it does not appear in the contemporary description of the conversation: Owen to State Department, June 26, 1959, President's Office Files, box 126, folder "USSR, Vienna Meeting, Background Documents (D)," John F. Kennedy Library, Boston.

86. For a related discussion, see Edward Kolodziej, "The Limits of Deterrence Theory," *Journal of Social Issues*, 43, no. 4 (1987), 130–1.

make major gains may have been largely driven by the Soviet desire to shore up the East German regime.

A second complicating factor is a broader version of the dynamics just discussed: a state may need to change some part of the status quo if it is to preserve its general outlines. Just as alliance commitments can require a status quo power to take the military offensive, so external ties and internal needs can necessitate coercing the adversary to change some of his positions. To take a hypothetical case, if a West German government began undermining the German Democratic Republic (GDR) by propaganda and force of example, the USSR might have to change the situation to be able to maintain its client.

We also must remember that changes in the status quo can be set in motion by actors other than the superpowers. While many of us think of the Soviet attempt to compel the West to withdraw from West Berlin as the paradigm case of superpower conflict, the Middle East or Angola probably are better models for the future. When the situation is fluid, the idea of the status quo makes little sense. What was the status quo in Angola in 1974–75? Furthermore, forces of change are likely to arise within Third World countries or in conflicts among them. Neither superpower will need to bear the onus of directly challenging the other; neither will be able to gain the bargaining advantages discussed above. Indeed, even if both sides believe that local strife holds greater menace than prospects for gain, they may not be able to prevent it, and when they cannot, defending the status quo will often be as difficult as challenging it—if the two can be distinguished.

Finally, even when there is a clear status quo and the superpowers are the dominant actors, for a number of reasons the balance of incentives may favor change.[87] First, of course, the expansionist may have sufficient power to implement its threats with little cost or danger. Second, the expansionist can have unusually high resolve or the defender unusually low resolve. Thus Hitler differed from normal German statesmen not so much in his aspirations as in his willingness to risk all in order to try to fulfill them. Third, statesmen may see either the domestic or the international situation as precarious enough to merit great risks and costs. They will be strongly motivated to act when they see enormous gains to be had by forcing a change, or, more frequently the case, enormous losses looming if they do not do so.

---

87. An early discussion of bargaining that is extremely useful on this point is David Baldwin, "Inter-Nation Influence Revisited," *Journal of Conflict Resolution*, 15 (December 1971), 471–86. Also see George and Smoke, *Deterrence in American Foreign Policy*, pp. 519–32, and Jervis, "Deterrence Theory Revisited," pp. 317–19.

Thus, states have often contemplated or carried out preventive wars because they believed that they could not otherwise maintain their positions.[88] Dynamics within the state can produce the same result. When political leaders have staked their domestic fortunes on forcing the other side to accommodate to their desires, the incentives to achieve their objective, even at a high cost to the nation as a whole, are very great.[89] In these situations, deterrence is rendered more difficult and, if the defender understands the situation, coercive changes become easier, although rarely easy, to accomplish.

It is clear, then, that under some circumstances the status quo is not a meaningful benchmark and that under others defending it is no easier than altering it. Nevertheless, on the central issues of the Cold War, the side practicing deterrence usually has significant bargaining advantages. Part of the result is that overt challenges are beaten back, but even more, that such challenges will be relatively rare. A state will seek to alter the status quo only when it thinks that its move may succeed; the understanding that its bargaining position is weak is most clearly shown by its reluctant acceptance of the prevailing situation.

The theory of the nuclear revolution, then, predicts that the basic outlines of the status quo will be preserved. Major shifts in territory and spheres of influence usually occur through war or the threat of war. Because of the bargaining advantages held by the defender, these motors of change should be less potent. This expectation is generally borne out. The most important change in world politics—decolonization—was one that neither offended nor was engineered by either superpower. Of course in many parts of the world the superpowers have gained or lost influence, most strikingly in the change of orientation of China, first through a civil war and then through a diplomatic realignment. But neither side has been able to use threats of force to move the other out of the most important positions it established after World War II. We tend to take this situation for granted, but it is unusual for the map of the areas of greatest interest to the major powers to remain almost unchanged for two generations. Although nuclear

88. For a good discussion of the empirical and methodological issues, see Jack Levy, "Declining Power and the Preventive Motivation for War," *World Politics*, 40 (October 1987), 82–108.

89. High international or domestic incentives for change also generate psychological pressures that can lead the state to underestimate the risks it is running. See Richard Ned Lebow, *Between Peace and War* (Baltimore: Johns Hopkins University Press, 1981); Jervis, Lebow, and Stein, *Psychology and Deterrence*; George and Smoke, *Deterrence in American Foreign Policy*, pp. 572–80.

weapons are not the only new factor in world politics, they are the one most easily connected with the new stability.

If the argument here is correct, then, contrary to many claims about the influence of nuclear weapons, the maintenance of mutual second-strike capability permits the superpowers to protect a good deal more than their homelands. If the stability-instability paradox operated strongly, either side should be prepared to use force when the local balance is in its favor. In fact, this situation has occurred only well below the nuclear threshold—for example, in Southeast Asia, Grenada, Afghanistan, and Angola. These events show that nuclear weapons have not put an end to all superpower adventures, but they do not contradict the central argument here. I am not arguing that stability extends throughout the globe but that it does extend to the areas where both powers are deeply concerned. More damaging to my argument are the attempts to alter the status quo in Europe. Thus the Soviets have tried to force the West out of Berlin and have used tactics of intimidation against Western Germany, while the United States made some attempts to deter the Soviets from using force to put down Solidarity in Poland. But these efforts have been infrequent and none has succeeded. The success of extended deterrence is quite striking when compared with the proposition—one that logically follows from conventionalized premises—that the threat of nuclear war cannot protect the status quo beyond the superpowers' borders.

The Infrequency of Crises

A third implication of the nuclear revolution is that once the lines of the status quo are clear and both sides have second-strike capability, crises should not be frequent. Furthermore, those that occur usually should be in peripheral areas and be initiated, not by the superpowers themselves, but by local actors.

In eras when military victory was possible, a state could challenge its adversary in the expectation that if the latter did not retreat, the state could resort to war. Today, the knowledge that war would be suicide coupled with the bargaining advantage possessed by the side defending the status quo means that would-be expansionists should be loath to instigate confrontations. In addition, because in the past the balance of power could be upset if a significant actor shifted from one camp to the other, the major powers' security interests were often deeply involved with those of their allies. The series of pre–World War I confrontations provide obvious examples. The main reason why Britain supported France in the Moroccan crises was the fear that if it did not, France might desert the Entente and leave England dangerously isolated. The same dynamics were at work in July 1914. France had to support Russia and Britain had to support France and Russia because a failure to do so might break up the Entente and leave them exposed to German dominance. Similarly, Germany could not afford to see Austria-Hungary leave the alliance or, more probably, disintegrate. In the nuclear era, by contrast, security is provided by second-strike capability; defections by allies are therefore less damaging. Thus neither France's withdrawal from the military arrangements of NATO nor China's realignment precipitated a superpower crisis. If this argument is correct, the superpowers should not permit their allies to drag them into excessively dangerous situations.[90]

Postwar history supports these hypotheses. Crises have been rare since the advent of mutual second-strike capability; in this period most tensions have been generated by third actors in areas of less than central importance and are driven more by the superpowers' desire to project a general image of high resolve than by any specific stake; allies have less ability than they did before the advent of nuclear weapons to require that the superpowers support them in risky ventures. Crises were most frequent in the late 1940s and early 1950s, a period in which the status quo was not entirely clear and before the United States, let alone the Soviet Union, possessed overwhelming levels of destructive capability.[91] The single most dangerous confrontation—the Cuban missile crisis—not only occurred when the Soviets had weak nuclear forces but was in part motivated by the urgent Soviet need to gain something like parity. In the years since this goal has been reached, there have been no serious crises. The nearest approximation was the 1973 confrontation in the Middle East, which was mild compared with crises that were frequent in the nonnuclear era.

The other disturbing incidents since the mid-1960s have occurred in areas where neither side was deeply involved and in which local actors drew the superpowers in. The clashes in Angola and the Horn of Africa fit this pattern. The status quo was not clear and was changing largely

90. Of course the explanation offered here parallels that for the role of bipolarity. Here, as in several other places, the two influences are similar and it is therefore difficult to determine which theory offers the better explanation. See Waltz, *Theory of International Politics*, and Glenn Snyder and Paul Diesing, *Conflict among Nations* (Princeton: Princeton University Press, 1977), chap. 6.

91. But Richard Betts notes that even in the 1950s American decision makers acted as though the Soviets had second strike capability (*Nuclear Blackmail and Nuclear Balance* [Washington, D.C.: Brookings Institution, 1987], chap. 4).

in response to local forces. Neither superpower sought a major confrontation and, for the United States at least, the main fear was that the adversary would perceive a weakness of will that would be expected to manifest itself in areas of greater importance. This is not to say that these incidents were trivial: they contributed to the decline of detente and in the future ones like them could lead to sharper confrontations. But their infrequency and unimportance, as compared with those in the prenuclear world, is what is most striking and significant. As the theory of the nuclear revolution leads us to expect, as long as neither side is overwhelmingly dissatisfied with the status quo, creating a crisis to try to make competitive gains is unattractive because the prospects for success are not great enough to merit the costs of greater tensions and the increased danger of war.

The expectation that allies lack the bargaining leverage to bring the superpowers to the brink of war also appears to be borne out. The Soviet Union refused to give more than lip service to the PRC's attempt to retake Quemoy and Matsu in the 1950s. Increasing the conflict with China was less costly than increasing the risk of war with the other superpower. Similarly, although the United States paid some heed to the preferences of its German ally during the Berlin crisis, it would not allow itself to be pushed into bold and dangerous policies. Even more strikingly, the transcripts of the meetings at the climax of the Cuban missile crisis reveal that President Kennedy probably would have been willing to offend the NATO allies by trading the missiles in Turkey if this had been necessary to avoid an armed clash with the USSR.[92] The combination of the supreme penalty that war would bring and the diminished importance of allies has made the superpowers more cautious and less willing to challenge each other, especially for the benefit of their weaker partners, than they had been in previous eras.

---

92. See McGeorge Bundy, transcriber, and James Blight, ed., "October 27, 1962: Transcripts of the Meeting of the ExComm," *International Security*, 12 (Winter 1987–88), 32–92, and Dean Rusk's letter printed in James Blight, Joseph Nye, Jr., and David Welch, "The Cuban Missile Crisis Revisited," *Foreign Affairs*, 66 (Fall 1987), 179. For earlier treatments that had stressed Kennedy's caution and willingness to make concessions, see George, Hall, and Simons, *Limits of Coercive Diplomacy*, pp. 86–140, and Arthur Schlesinger, Jr., *Robert F. Kennedy and His Times* (Boston: Houghton Mifflin, 1978), pp. 530–43. Bernard Brodie also noted that in the crisis each superpower was "asking each other: How do we get out of this with the absolute minimum of damage to each other?" Furthermore, consistent with this unusual goal, which was created by the mutual need to avoid war, came a change in method: "From beginning to end the confrontation . . . shows a remarkably different quality from any previous one in history. There is an unprecedented candor, direct personal contact, and at the same time mutual respect between the chief actors" (Brodie, *War and Politics*, p. 426).

[37]

It is often said that crises are the functional substitute for war. War being impossible, crises now take on the roles of determining relative power, recalibrating dominance, and redistributing contested values. There is something to this argument, but a number of amendments are in order. As long as crises can be dangerous and the most important aspects of the status quo are too well entrenched to be easily altered, crises may become even less frequent than wars were in the past. Thus, as I will discuss in Chapter 6, other kinds of demonstration may become prominent. Moreover, nuclear crises are not likely to arise out of differences in judgments about military strength, as they often did in the past, nor will their outcomes be primarily determined by the military balance. They will be triggered by differences in estimates of how likely each side is to stand firm, which in turn will be influenced by judgments about the relative importance of the issue to each side and general assessments of each side's willingness to run risks.

While the paucity of crises could also be deduced from some of the competing theories presented earlier, the propositions about the causes and resolutions of the confrontations cannot be. Thus, if sustained, these propositions give us strong reasons to conclude that the nuclear revolution is real. As usual, the evidence is scarce and ambiguous, but on preliminary inspection the findings seems confirmatory. As I will discuss further below, it is hard to correlate the rise and fall of each superpower's general influence and ability to prevail in crises with its military, let alone its nuclear, power.

Credibility, Chicken, and Bargaining

Since the ultimate sanction is mutual suicide, it is both difficult and important to make threats credible, but nuclear threats may not have to be highly credible in order to be highly effective. Even a slight chance that a provocation could lead to nuclear war will be sufficient to deter all but the most highly motivated adversaries.[93] Furthermore, because a high level of violence could result even if neither side sought that outcome, states need not threaten all-out war in order to have that specter loom large in the adversary's (and their own) mind. For example, while it would be totally irrational to destroy the world in order to try to stop the Soviet Union from conquering Iran, it could make

93. Many arguments about military strategy may really revolve less around the sorts of considerations advanced here and more around the nature of the Soviet Union, its goals, its motivations, and how much credibility is required in order to deter it. See Jervis, *Perception and Misperception in International Politics*, chap. 3, and Robert Levine, *The Arms Debate* (Cambridge: Harvard University Press, 1963).

sense for the United States to respond to a Soviet invasion by taking actions that it believed entailed a significant risk of this result.

The possibility of threats to create dangerous situations does not solve all problems. Each superpower still must be concerned lest the adversary believe that the fear of nuclear war will lead the former to abandon important interests rather than run any risk of destruction. Credibility and resolve are hard to demonstrate, however. Bluffs are always possible and thus valid threats subject to discount. Two implications follow. First, small issues will often loom large, not because of their intrinsic importance, but because they are taken as tests of resolve. What actually happens in many disputes in peripheral areas of world politics is not important; whether the United States and the Soviet Union are seen as having lived up to their commitments in these disputes may be crucial. As superpower tensions in Europe have eased and the focus of Soviet-American conflict has turned to the Third World, what is at stake in most confrontations are not issues of intrinsic value but, rather, each side's image. But the question of how images of resolve are projected and interpreted is plagued with both logical and empirical difficulties, some of which will be discussed in Chapter 6. A careful study of prenuclear crises shows that while states fear that others will draw wide-ranging inferences from cases in which they do not stand firm, in fact statesmen do not examine the other's behavior in this way.[94] Indeed, it may not make a great deal of sense for states to try to decide how others would behave at the brink of war on the basis of what they do when the stakes and dangers are much lower. The costs and risks of fighting a nuclear war or even a major conventional one are so much greater than those involved in any confrontation up to now that behavior in such confrontations probably does not predict what either side would do in unprecedented crises. But, in the absence of better indicators of resolve, it is understandable both that statesmen would see minor conflicts as a way to demonstrate that they would be bold in future crises and that the adversary in fact might not be particularly impressed by this behavior.

A second implication of the need to demonstrate resolve is that states must resort to a variety of bargaining tactics to show that they will

94. Snyder and Diesing, *Conflict among Nations*, p. 187; also see Jervis, "Deterrence Theory Revisited," pp. 317–22. But also see Paul Huth and Bruce Russett, "What Makes Deterrence Work: Cases from 1900 to 1980," *World Politics*, 36 (July 1984), 517, and Paul Huth, *Extended Deterrence and the Prevention of War* (New Haven: Yale University Press, 1988), pp. 55, 68–71, 80–83. For a general discussion, see Robert Jervis, "Domino Beliefs and Strategic Behavior," in Jack Snyder and Robert Jervis, eds., *Dominoes and Bandwagons: Strategic Beliefs and Superpower Competition in the Eurasian Rimland* (New York: Oxford University Press, forthcoming).

stand firm. When the situation resembles a game of Chicken, each side would rather make concessions than go to war or even to enter a situation in which war is likely. But since each side knows that this is the other's preference as well, it can try to use the common interest in avoiding danger to make competitive gains.

Although the details of the tactics that can be used are limited only by statesmen's imaginations, the general outlines can be deduced from the structure of the game.[95] Most obviously, states can try to commit themselves to standing firm. In some cases, commitment can be physical—that is, the state can make it difficult to avoid going to war if the other side takes prohibited actions. Thus by having American troops in Europe, the United States ensures that a Soviet invasion would kill Americans. Furthermore, the presence of American dependents means that not only American soldiers but women and children as well would be killed. While the United States is not physically committed to launching a nuclear attack, it could not avoid bloodshed that could easily escalate.

The second kind of commitment occurs when a state stakes its reputation on resisting the other side's demands. Because commitments are believed to be interdependent, to renege on one is to endanger others. By becoming committed, then, states increase the cost they will pay if they eventually retreat, limit their own freedom of maneuver, and thereby make it less likely that they will back down. A related bargaining tactic is Schelling's "rationality of irrationality."[96] Standing firm may be irrational because it entails excessive costs, but if the state can convince the other side that it is in fact irrational, the other will have no choice but to retreat and the result will be that the state will gain its objective.

These tactics are familiar, and if they are much more common in the nuclear age than they were in the past, the theory of nuclear revolution will be confirmed. As usual, only impressionistic evidence is available and even this is mixed. On the one hand, states seem very reluctant

---

95. See Schelling, *Strategy of Conflict*; Schelling, *Arms and Influence*; Snyder, " 'Prisoner's Dilemma' and 'Chicken' Models in International Politics," pp. 66–103; Jervis, "Bargaining and Bargaining Tactics," pp. 272–88.

96. Schelling, *Strategy of Conflict*, pp. 16–20, and *Arms and Influence*, pp. 36–43, 229; for a good application see Daniel Ellsberg, "The Theory and Practice of Blackmail," in Oran Young, ed., *Bargaining* (Urbana: University of Illinois Press, 1975), pp. 343–64. For recent elaborations of this argument, see George Quester, "Some Thoughts on 'Deterrence Failures,' " in Paul Stern, Robert Axelrod, Robert Jervis, and Roy Radnor, eds., *Perspectives on Deterrence* (New York: Oxford University Press, 1989), and Edward Rhodes, *Rational Deterrence and Irrational Responses: The Logic of Nuclear Coercion* (New York: Columbia University Press, 1989).

to foreclose their future options, let alone to pretend to be irrational.[97] Robert Haldeman reports that President Nixon sought to lead the North Vietnamese to conclude that he was unpredictable and could not be counted on to be sensibly restrained, but even if this story is correct, it seems exceptional.[98] On the other hand, the superpowers—or at least the Americans—do seem more concerned with their bargaining reputations than they were in the past.[99] This is not to say that such considerations were ever absent. But when states could rationally resort to war, concern with credibility and commitment was not as dominant. The realization—or belief—that they must convince others of their willingness to pay a high price to defend their interests has led statesmen routinely to adopt tactics that were used only in extreme cases in the past. Similarly, although it is hard to be sure that the difference is one of national behavior rather than one of scholars' attention, it seems that tactics of commitment are much more common than they were in previous eras. The Chicken model generates expectations that generally are met by superpower behavior in severe crises, for example in October 1962. The United States not only prepared to fight if need be— as would have been the case in prenuclear crises—but pledged its reputation on seeing that missiles were removed. By moving publicly and forcefully, the United States limited its options, increased the cost it would pay if it backed down, and thereby increased its bargaining leverage.

Compromising Knowing that tactics of commitment should be common and the side defending the status quo usually should have the advantage does not tell us the extent to which compromises will be accepted in order to avoid a war. Because Chicken is a game in which each side tries to outguess and outbluff the other, one cannot readily predict each side's choices. Much of the academic discussion has been of tactics that can extract the greatest advantage, and the *flavor* of these treatments implies that at least one side will be willing to run high risks in order to prevail. Indeed, the state gains a bargaining advantage if it can convince its adversary that it is willing to do so.

But moderation, although not following deterministically from the nuclear revolution, certainly is compatible with it. As long as the cost

97. See Oran Young, *The Politics of Force* (Princeton: Princeton University Press, 1968), pp. 217–20; Jervis, "Deterrence Theory Revisited," pp. 303–4.

98. See H. Robert Haldeman, *The Ends of Power* (New York: New York Times Books, 1968), pp. 82–83, 98.

99. See Patrick Morgan, "Saving Face for the Sake of Deterrence," in Jervis, Lebow, and Stein, *Psychology and Deterrence*, pp. 125–52.

of standing firm in the incorrect belief that the other will retreat is enormous, there is reason to expect that both sides will be cautious. The state that has the upper hand will not press its advantage to the limit when the marginal gains for so doing are outweighed by the danger of war. The recent revelations of the Cuban missile crisis fit this pattern. As noted, President Kennedy was open to the idea of trading the missiles in Turkey for those in Cuba even though the price of doing so would have been high. Had the cost of all-out war been lower, the United States might have been more unyielding. Similarly, in the aftermath of the crisis, Kennedy considered allowing the IL-28 bombers to remain in Cuba rather than renew the confrontation if the Soviets proved adamant on this point, which they did not.[100] Although the evidence from other Cold War crises is more ambiguous, it fits the same pattern. McGeorge Bundy reveals that "in the White House at the height of the [1961 Berlin] crisis there was a greater interest in . . . compromise than Kennedy ever chose to show publicly. On August 28 I reported to him the growing belief among those at work on our negotiating position 'that we can and should shift substantially toward the acceptance of the GDR, the Oder-Neisse Line, a non-aggression pact, and even the idea of two peace treaties.' "[101] More speculatively, Bundy reminds us of Anthony Eden's judgment that the fear of nuclear war helps explain why the participants in the Geneva summit in 1954 were willing to compromise and end the Indochina war.[102] Thus it appears that Cuba is not unique in generating a settlement in which a state could have made more gains—at least in the short run—if it had been willing to maintain or increase the risk of war. Nuclear weapons have now made such behavior too dangerous for sensible decision makers to undertake if they can possibly avoid it.

Military Balance, Balance of Resolve, and Political Outcomes

If the arguments about the nuclear revolution are correct, there should be only tenuous links between the details of the military balance and political outcomes. As McGeorge Bundy has put it, what matters

---

100. Raymond Garthoff, *Reflections on the Cuban Missile Crisis* (Washington, D.C.: Brookings Institution, 1987), pp. 67–71. As President, Nixon similarly recognized that "the balance of nuclear power has placed a premium on negotiation rather than confrontation": Richard Nixon, *U.S. Foreign Policy for the 1970s: A New Strategy for Peace:* A report to the Congress, February 18, 1970, p. 133.

101. McGeorge Bundy, *Danger and Survival* (New York: Random House, 1988), p. 385.

102. Ibid., pp. 271–73.

is not nuclear *superiority* or the exact state of the nuclear *balance*, but the nuclear *danger*.[103] Since having more nuclear weapons or more nuclear options than the adversary cannot provide much assistance in terminating the war, this posture should not provide a great peacetime advantage. Were it to be shown that the international political fortunes of the superpowers were significantly correlated with the state of the nuclear balance, this would be important evidence against the validity of the theory of the nuclear revolution.

The evidence is, of course, highly ambiguous and a full canvass of it is beyond the scope of this book.[104] But it is difficult to attribute many political outcomes over the past twenty-five years to changes in the nuclear balance. For example, while there are many possible causes of the Soviet invasion of (and retreat from) Afghanistan and adventures in Africa—probably the most alarming events since the Cuban missile crisis—the superpowers' nuclear postures do not number among them. It is also interesting to note that even changes in the nuclear balance as great as those that have occurred since 1962 have not allowed the Soviets to revise the agreements that ended the Cuban missile crisis, although they have made fitful attempts to do so.[105] Indeed, Kissinger has said that the existence of nuclear parity did not inhibit the Nixon administration in the conflict over the Soviet submarine base at Cienfuegoes in 1970: "We used more or less the same tactics [as Kennedy used in 1962] and we achieved more or less the same result."[106] Similarly, the pleas of Kissinger and others for the Carter administration to take a firmer stand against the Soviets in Africa only make sense if they believed that such a tough stance was not prohibited by the nuclear balance. In this light it is not surprising that Carter administration officials replied in the negative when asked whether they would have advocated taking a harder line in disputes with the Soviet Union if the United States had had greater nuclear strength.[107]

103. Ibid., passim, and especially chap. 8.

104. The best surveys are Betts, *Nuclear Blackmail and Nuclear Balance*, and Bundy, *Danger and Survival*. Also see Richard Betts, "Nuclear Peace and Conventional War," *Journal of Strategic Studies*, 11 (March 1988), 79–95, and Chapter 3 below.

105. Of course the military advantages of putting missiles into Cuba would now be quite slight, but the political gain would be very significant, especially if the Russians actually were pressing hard to expand their influence. Thus their continued acquiesence cannot be explained entirely by the unimportance of the issue to them.

106. Interview in Charlton, *From Deterrence to Defense*, p. 34.

107. Interviews conducted by the author during 1979–83. A few government officials claim that the Soviet adventures in Africa and Afghanistan can be attributed to the nuclear balance, but these assertions are not supported by evidence or careful analysis. Indeed they often fly in the face of the facts. See Chapter 3 below.

Similarly, if the Soviets have been more moderate since 1980, the reason cannot be the state of military balance, because it remains essentially unchanged. In 1978, Kissinger stressed that because of "the vulnerability of our strategic forces . . . [Soviet] willingness to run risks . . . must exponentially increase." The following five years, he argued, were going to be "our period of maximum danger."[108] The logic is impeccable: that subsequent events did not conform indicates that the fallacy lies in the premise.

Those who argue for the powerful operation of the stability-instability paradox agree that the nuclear balance is not crucial but expect the local conventional military balance to strongly influence the outcomes of confrontation. Thus they argue for the importance of the American naval predominance around Cuba in 1962. While this argument seems to make sense, closer examination casts it into doubt. If conventional superiority were crucial in Cuba, why did the parallel Soviet advantage around Berlin not produce a parallel result? A decade later, the increases in the mobility of Soviet forces were a necessary condition for the interventions in Africa. But these increases were a matter of Soviet capabilities, not of the military balance. No Western strength could have removed the transport aircraft from Soviet hands. In fact, the United States could have transported more men and matériel to Africa than the Soviets did or could have forcibly interdicted the Soviet supply lines. The reason the United States did not engage in such a contest was not lack of capability but the belief that the issues were not worth the costs and risks that intervention would have entailed. In 1979 Harold Brown argued, "We now recognize that the strategic nuclear forces can deter only a relatively narrow range of contingencies, much smaller in range than was foreseen only twenty or thirty years ago."[109] Leaving aside the dubious historical recollection, what is striking is that neither superpower has taken advantage of conventional superiority to challenge the other's important interests.

Of course, it would be dangerous if the imbalance of conventional forces were so great that the Soviets could stage a fait accompli and quickly conquer an area of importance to the West.[110] But the large-

108. U.S. Senate, Committee on Foreign Relations, *The SALT II Treaty*, 96th Cong., 1st sess., (Washington, D. C.: Government Printing Office, 1979) pt. 3, pp. 224–25. Paul Nitze took a similar position thirty years earlier: *FRUS, 1950*, vol. 1, p. 147.

109. Department of Defense, *Annual Report for FY 1980* (Washington, D.C.: Government Printing Office, 1979), p. 76.

110. For a discussion of failures of deterrence because of the Soviet ability to carry out a fait accompli, see George and Smoke, *Deterrence in American Foreign Policy*, pp. 536–40.

scale use of conventional force, particularly in areas in which the other side has an established position, carries with it the risk of escalation, especially when the fighting is likely to be prolonged. Thus military capability is not a good predictor of national behavior or international outcomes, and deterrence by denial is not necessary in order to convince the adversary that such moves should not be undertaken. The Soviets have not moved in Europe in spite of their reputed overwhelming conventional advantage (an estimate disputed by articulate critics and, perhaps, by the Soviets). Their increased ability to fight a conventional war in Europe has not made them bolder.[111] (Indeed, the military buildup has been accompanied by political settlements.) While there is no reason to believe that military calculations are central to this Soviet policy, it is likely that what plays at least some role is the realization that the ability to win a conventional war is not synonymous with the ability to keep the war conventional.[112]

The implications of mutual second-strike capability are many and far-reaching. If nuclear weapons have had the influence that the nuclear-revolution theory indicates they should have, then there will be peace between the superpowers, crises will be rare, neither side will be eager to press bargaining advantages to the limit, the status quo will be relatively easy to maintain, and political outcomes will not be closely related to either the nuclear or the conventional balance. Although the evidence is ambiguous, it generally confirms these propositions.

111. The most thorough treatment is Michael MccGwire, *Military Objectives in Soviet Foreign Policy* (Washington, D.C.: Brookings Institution, 1987).

112. Again, the strength of the Soviet motivation to change the status quo may be a crucial factor. Were Soviet dissatisfaction greater—either because of the desire to dominate Western Europe or the fear that they would be attacked if they did not—the Western posture might be inadequate. But, for reasons both rational and psychological, if the Soviet incentives were great enough, they might attack without regard for the military balance.

[45]

[2]

Strategic Theory: What's New and What's True

CONTINUITY IN STRATEGIC THOUGHT—
BRODIE AND BORDEN

Much of the recent debate about nuclear weapons and nuclear strategy was anticipated by the contrasting views set forth by Bernard Brodie and William Liscum Borden more than forty years ago. What Brodie wrote six months after Hiroshima contains a great deal of truth; much of the effort to develop new ideas has been misguided.[1]

The centerpiece of Brodie's position was the claim that nuclear weapons revolutionized military strategy and the relationships between force and foreign policy. I have summarized much of his argument in Chapter 1. Nuclear weapons have severed the links between the ability to protect the state's values; deterrence by punishment has replaced

1. Bernard Brodie et al., *The Absolute Weapon* (New York: Harcourt, Brace, 1946). Of course, I do not mean to imply that Brodie's ideas were consistent and unchanging. See Barry Steiner, "Using the Absolute Weapon: Early Ideas on Atomic Strategy," *Journal of Strategic Studies*, 7 (December 1984), 365–93. For a contemporary argument paralleling Brodie's, see Jacob Viner, "Implications of the Atomic Bomb for International Relations," *Proceedings of the American Philosophical Society*, 90 (January 1946), 53–58. I am grateful to McGeorge Bundy for pointing out to me that in November 1945, *Time* magazine listed twelve points that, like Brodie's argument, have proved to be remarkably prescient. Among them were the following: "Atomic weapons will overshadow peacetime uses of atomic energy," "No military or scientific defense can be expected," "Much larger atom charges are in prospect," "No big secret protects the atom bomb," and most important, "Outproducing the enemy is not much advantage in atomic warfare. Two hundred may be better than 100, but 10,000 is no better than 5,000, because 5,000 would destroy all important targets in a country" (*Time*, November 12, 1945, p. 28).

deterrence by denial because no one could win an all-out nuclear war; levels of absolute capability are now more important than relative power because with nuclear weapons, what is crucial is each side's ability to cripple the other, and this capability is measured by the match between the country's forces and the targets it seeks to destroy, not between the two sides' forces.

For Brodie, military victory in a nuclear war was not possible. Crises and even limited wars could be terminated in ways that are highly advantageous to one side and disavantageous to the other, but as long as both sides remain vulnerable, the balance of military power is not decisive because it cannot protect either side from destruction.[2]

Brodie's views were certainly incorrect when he enunciated them because nuclear weapons were scarce and, by today's standards, small. The first careful study of the utility of atomic bombs—the Harmon Report of 1949—concluded that the American bombs were too few and carried by planes that were too vulnerable to allow the air force to win a war on its own. (Perhaps not surprisingly, the secretary of defense withheld the report from President Truman.)[3] It took the hydrogen bomb to bring about the world Brodie had foreseen. Interestingly enough, Brodie's initial reaction to this development was to stress the need for the ability to fight limited wars on the grounds that the immense destructive power that would soon be available to the superpowers made all-out war impossible, an issue that is a main focus of debate today.

Of course, Brodie was not the only pioneer. Not only were other people working out similar ideas, but William Liscum Borden made counterarguments strikingly similar to those of current American nuclear doctrine. In his little known *There Will Be No Time*, Borden saw nuclear weapons not as revolutionizing strategy but as reinforcing

2. Although I will concentrate in this chapter on ideas about strategic policy rather than on the policy itself, some parallels between the two should be noted. John Gaddis has argued that American policy can be divided into periods characterized by symmetry or asymmetry. By "symmetric policies" he means those that seek to meet the Soviet threat at each level of violence; by "asymmetric policies," those that are built on the premise that nuclear weapons are sufficient to protect a wide range of American values. In other words, symmetric policies seek deterrence by denial, at least for levels of violence below all-out war, while asymmetric policies fully accept the nuclear revolution and utilize deterrence by punishment. Gaddis's explanation for which approach is adopted has little to do with the power of abstract ideas; rather, he sees the cause in the difference in administrations' willingness to support high defense budgets (*Strategies of Containment* [New York: Oxford University Press, 1962]).

3. David Rosenberg, "American Atomic Strategy and the Hydrogen Bomb Decision," *Journal of American History*, 66 (June 1979), 71–77.

many of its traditional elements.[4] Cities indeed were vulnerable, but the result would be that each side would spare the adversary's cities so that the adversary would be similarly restrained; atomic bombs would be used against military installations. Furthermore, defense might be possible, a vision Brodie had denied. Capability therefore still had to be measured in relative terms because, just as in the past, preventing the adversary from gaining a military advantage was essential. For Borden, then, nuclear war could result in a meaningful victory. Destruction would be enormous, but one side could end up ahead, and this possibly could influence peacetime bargaining. It follows that American military strategy must resemble the general outlines of prenuclear strategy. The United States needs to be prepared to fight a nuclear war or, rather, to fight the variety of nuclear wars that might occur. Being prepared does not mean the United States should seek such wars. The purpose of it is deterrence. But deterrence works through the ability to win if need be.

Of course, not all the basic ideas were on the table by the end of 1946. Without trying to give a history of the development of strategic thought, I should note three concepts developed in the 1950s that fleshed out the earlier ideas.[5] Albert Wohlstetter's distinction between first- and second-strike capability, Glenn Snyder's clarification of the stability-instability paradox and the problem of extended deterrence, and Thomas Schelling's discussions of threats that leave something to chance and the reciprocal fear of surprise attack—what is now called crisis instability—were crucial in providing the conceptual tools for our current strategic thinking.[6] These developments added sophistication

4. William Liscum Borden, *There Will Be No Time* (New York: Macmillan, 1946). I am grateful to James King, "The New Strategists" (unpublished manuscript) for stressing the significance of this book. It should be noted that Borden argued that nuclear weapons did bring about a revolution, but the assertion is based on a misinterpretation of crucial aspects of World War II. Although Brodie and Borden differed greatly, Marc Trachtenberg points out that "strategic discourse [in the 1940s and the 1950s] was not sectarian or doctrinaire: the striking thing was that the same people were attracted to both approaches, often at the same time" ("Strategic Thought in America, 1952–1966," *Political Science Quarterly*, forthcoming).

5. For such a history, see Lawrence Freedman, *The Evolution of Nuclear Strategy* (New York: St. Martin's Press, 1981). As Freedman notes, "Much of what is offered today as a profound and new insight was said yesterday; and usually in a more precise and literate manner" (p. xv; also see p. 396).

6. Wohlstetter's ideas grew out of a classified study that is summarized in E. S. Quade, "The Selection and Use of Strategic Air Bases," in Quade, ed., *Analysis for Military Decisions* (Chicago: Rand McNally, 1966), pp. 24–63. The study itself is now printed: A. J. Wohlstetter, F. S. Hoffman, R. J. Lutz, and H. S. Rowen, "Selection and Use of Strategic Air Bases," in Marc Trachtenberg, ed., *The Development of American Strategic Thought:*

and nuance to the positions associated with Brodie and Borden, but they left the basic arguments unchanged.

It is sometimes argued that these ideas can no longer explain national behavior or shape policy because circumstances have changed from those that prevailed when they were developed. As Secretary of Defense Caspar Weinberger asked, "Should ideas formulated in an era of American military predominance apply with equal validity in an era of parity?"[7] A negative answer seems self-evident but is not. Although the 1950s and 1960s may now appear to be eras in which the Soviet military challenge was relatively slight, contemporaries did not hold such a view.[8] Furthermore, the strategic ideas were developed with the configuration of parity in mind. Both Brodie and Borden were writing not for the present but for the inevitable future when both sides would be heavily armed.

Incentives to Innovate

In the realm of ideas, there are great incentives to innovate. Credit goes to those who say something original and interesting. It helps to be right, but this is rarely necessary. Thus academics bemoan "dead" fields: how can one write a book if everything significant has been said? Further pressures to come up with something new arise from the belief that progress, if not inevitable, should certainly be possible.

Policy makers also have incentives to innovate. The military needs rationales for increased budgets, although the fact that the armed services want to continue to perform established missions puts a brake on the development of new ideas. Of special relevance for nuclear strategy, those people who are responsible for war plans feel bureaucratic and psychological pressures to develop new ideas. Officials who have to think of what the state should do in the event of war must consider the widest range of possibilities and, unless they are fooling themselves, will never be satisfied by

---

Writings on Strategy, 1952–1960, vol. 1 (New York: Garland, 1988), pp. 163–589. The importance of threats that leave something to chance is discussed in Chapter 3 below; crisis stability is treated in Chapter 5 below.

7. Caspar Weinberger, *Annual Report to the Congress, FY 1987* (Washington, D.C: Government Printing Office, 1986), p. 73. Also see Samuel Huntington, "The Renewal of Strategy," in Huntington, ed., *The Strategic Imperative: New Policies for American Security* (Cambridge: Ballinger, 1982), p. 49.

8. See Richard Betts, *Nuclear Blackmail and Nuclear Balance* (Washington, D.C.: Brookings Institution, 1987), pp. 144–72.

the responses that are available. Therefore, they will be driven to develop ever more elaborate, complex, and subtle plans. Furthermore, incoming administrations need to distinguish their policies from those of the predecessor and so must announce, if not construct, a policy that is new and different. Thus, Secretary Weinberger began a recent statement on American defense policy by saying, "When the Reagan Administration entered office in 1981, a lengthy debate could have been held on the question: 'Which was in worse shape—U.S. military hardware or U.S. strategic concepts?' "[9] Developing modern ideas, he went on to argue, is as important as developing modern weapons.

The problem, however, is that whereas academics can afford to be original at the expense of being correct, statesmen cannot. Yet, officials have called for a "renaissance in strategic thinking" without much consideration of the fact that originality is not automatically good.[10] We are better off following old good ideas than developing new bad ones. The distinction between what is new and what is true produces a fourfold table which provides a useful way to organize many of the ideas in nuclear strategy.

	VALID	INVALID
Old	nuclear revolution crisis stability	deterrence by denial counterforce
New	deterrence and cooperation psychological factors	complex scenarios overelaborate war plans and target lists

Old, Good Ideas

The major old, good ideas have already been mentioned—that is, the concept of the nuclear revolution with the concomitant implication that many prenuclear ideas are now inappropriate. Perhaps most important is the claim, now bitterly contested, that the state does not need the ability to take militarily meaningful action in order to deter depredations. Because any extreme crisis and, even

9. Weinberger, *Anual Report, FY 1987*, p. 13.
10. Fred Iklé, quoted in Richard Bernstein, "Americans, at Forum in France, Put Forward a Case for 'Star Wars,' " *New York Times*, October 21, 1985, p. B10.

more, any use of force between the superpowers creates a chance of mutual destruction, military advantage loses most of its traditional meaning.

Therefore the United States does not need to meet all Soviet threats on their own terms, as Brodie realized. Armies do not have to be able to win in order to deter. As long as using force to change the status quo sets in motion forces that are hard to control, taking advantage of local military imbalances is extremely dangerous. Thus, although Brodie's initial reaction to the development of the hydrogen bomb was to argue that the United States had to prepare to fight limited wars, by the early 1960s he felt that the Kennedy administration was pushing this idea much too far. The West did not need to be able to mount a full-scale conventional defense of Europe, he argued. There is every reason to believe that the pattern he discerned in past confrontations will continue to hold:

> The essential question was: How much did the strictly local forces affect the Russians' willingness to risk open hostilities with us— or, for that matter, our willingness to get into such hostilities with them? And the answer clearly was, little or none—unless both sides had been completely convinced that a quite considerable shooting war could develop on the spot without its substantially widening and incurring extremely grave risk of nuclear weapons being introduced.[11]

OLD, BAD IDEAS

Most of the ideas that are old but bad start from the belief that mutual vulnerability either can be overcome or need not be of central importance. As Brodie noted in *Strategy in the Missile Age*, the fact that the Soviet Union could destroy the United States has led to a number of attempts to escape from vulnerability and reestablish traditional routes to security.[12] Perhaps the most powerful and lasting ideas of this kind are the politically opposed, but intellectually linked, desires to take our cities out of hostage and to abolish nuclear weapons. Both impulses arise from feelings about what is necessary, not analyses about what

11. Bernard Brodie, *War and Politics* (New York: Macmillan, 1973), p. 412, emphasis omitted.

12. Bernard Brodie, *Strategy in the Missile Age* (Princeton: Princeton University Press, 1959).

is possible. For example, Reagan's ABM program was not derived from a considered judgment that the problem can be solved. Instead, it was driven by the notion that the alternative to defense is unacceptable. The emotion behind Reagan's position comes through in his extemporaneous remark, "To look down an endless future with both of us sitting here with these horrible missiles aimed at each other, and the only thing preventing a holocaust is just so long as no one pulls this trigger, this is unthinkable."[13]

At the other end of the political spectrum, but driven by the same fear, is the call to abolish nuclear weapons. The popularity of two recent books by Jonathan Schell shows the strength of feeling about this issue, and it is interesting that in the second book he argues that ABM systems will make abolition possible.[14] Indeed, at Reykjavik Reagan and Gorbachev reaffirmed their longstanding commitments to doing away eventually with all nuclear weapons, although there are few indications that they or their advisers have thought seriously about the politics of a nonnuclear world.

A second idea that is both old and bad is what Hans Morgenthau called "conventionalization."[15] Many analyses of nuclear weapons use the intellectual framework that was appropriate in an earlier era, when defense by denial was possible and pushing back the other side's army could both reach the state's goals and protect its citizens. Consistent with Borden's point of view, recent administrations have argued that even if cities cannot be removed from hostage, partial security can still be achieved through the ability to prevent the Soviet Union from reaching its military goals in third areas—for example, by being able to defend Europe and the Persian Gulf against nonnuclear attacks. Because nuclear weapons cancel each other out, conventional defense by denial is necessary and possible.[16] But this position would make sense only if lower levels of violence were hermetically sealed off from higher ones. Since they are not, conventionalized perspectives cannot explain past Soviet-

13. "Transcript of Press Interview with President at White House," *New York Times*, March 30, 1983.

14. Jonathan Schell, *The Fate of the Earth* (New York: Knopf, 1982), and Schell, *The Abolition* (New York: Knopf, 1984).

15. Hans Morgenthau, "The Fallacy of Thinking Conventionally about Nuclear Weapons," in David Carlton and Carlo Schaerf, eds., *Arms Control and Technologicial Innovation* (New York: Wiley, 1976), pp. 256–64.

16. See, for example, Robert McNamara, "The Military Role of Nuclear Weapons," *Foreign Affairs*, 62 (Fall 1983), 68.

American interactions or guide effective policies, although they do help explain many aspects of American war planning.[17]

NEW, GOOD IDEAS

Understanding the Security Dilemma

Although the bulk of the ideas, good and bad, that dominate strategic thinking date from the first fifteen years of the nuclear era, some are fairly recent. The first new and good idea is a renewed appreciation of the importance of the security dilemma—the fact that under many circumstances an increase in one state's security will automatically and inadvertently decrease that of others. The idea of the security dilemma is very old—Thucydides saw this dynamic as the root cause of the conflict between Athens and Sparta. It received renewed attention in the late 1940s and early 1950s, but not by people who were specializing in nuclear weapons.[18] Partly because of the understandable self-righteousness of the first years of the Cold War, statesmen and analysts gave little consideration to the impact of U.S. policy on legitimate Soviet security interests. For example, the program devised by Dean Acheson and David Lilienthal for international control of nuclear weapons, let alone the Baruch Plan that the United States finally proposed, was a sufficient threat to Soviet security so that almost any Soviet leader, even if he were neither paranoid nor aggressive, would have rejected it. But few American experts realized this. Although they expected the Soviets to reject the proposal, the basis for this prediction was the belief that the Soviets were aggressive, not that the proposal was unreasonable. Indeed, the Soviet reaction was taken as confirmation of this dark view of the Soviets motives. In the succeeding years, much U.S. policy and many aspects of strategic analysis fit this pattern. In the early 1960s, even after it was known that the missile gap did not exist, few people worried about the effect of the American buildup on Soviet security or the extent to which the policy might lead the Soviets to view the Americans' expressed desire for arms control as hypocrisy.

---

17. Robert Jervis, *The Illogic of American Nuclear Strategy* (Ithaca: Cornell University Press, 1984).

18. Herbert Butterfield, *History and Human Relations* (London: Collins, 1951); John Herz, "Idealist Internationalism and the Security Dilemma," *World Politics*, 2 (January 1950), 157–80.

(The Soviets seem to have had a similar inability to appreciate the unintended consequences of their own actions.)[19]

Scholars, if not decision makers, are now more aware of the security dilemma and thus more sensitive to the possibility that the attempt to gain unilateral security will inadvertently set off spirals of tension and hostility. Unfortunately, it is extremely difficult, even after the fact, to determine each side's motivation and to judge whether more conciliatory policies would have dampened the conflict. For example, scholars still debate whether World War I could have been avoided, and if so, whether firmer or more conciliatory policies would have been required.[20]

The problem is that it is difficult to determine the other side's intentions, and trying to deter a state that is primarily seeking security is likely to create unnecessary conflict. Deterrence should be stressed only in certain situations; applied inappropriately, it can heighten the security dilemma. And, because it is often impossible to be certain of the other side's intentions, statesmen should try to design policies and postures that will protect their security without excessively decreasing the other's security. An understanding of the security dilemma can lead statesmen to seek to ameliorate it.

There are, of course, severe limits on what is possible. Even when technology is most propitious, protecting oneself is likely to menace others at least to some extent. Often there is only a narrow choice as to which technology to employ. For example, it would be difficult for the United States and the USSR to return to a world of invulnerable ICBMS even if they desired to. Furthermore, technology is not the only factor that intervenes between understanding the security dilemma and

---

19. For a discussion of both the American and the Soviet lack of awareness, see Raymond Garthoff, *Détente and Confrontation* (Washington, D.C.: Brookings Institution, 1987). Not surprisingly, those analysts who feel that the Soviets are highly aggressive and who deny the existence of the nuclear revolution usually are the ones who dismiss or fail to understand the security dilemma. Thus in 1951, Borden urged a great increase in the American nuclear capacity in these terms: "If we act to increase our supply of atomic weapons and they turn out to be unnecessary, we may lose a few million dollars. If we fail to produce these weapons and they turn out to be necessary, we may lose our country" (Quoted in Glenn Seaborg with Benjamin Loeb, *Stemming the Tide: Arms Control in the Johnson Years* [Lexington, Mass.: Lexington Books, 1987], p. 30; also see the strikingly similar statement by Richard Perle quoted in Daniel Yergin, " 'Scoop' Jackson Goes for Broke," *Atlantic Monthly*, June 1974, p. 81). The same error is made even more crudely by Secretary of Defense Weinberger in *Annual Report to the Congress, FY 1988* (Washington, D.C.: Government Printing Office, 1987), p. 16.

20. For a discussion of the conditions under which deterrence theory or the spiral model is more appropriate, see Robert Jervis, *Perception and Misperception in International Politics* (Princeton: Princeton University Press, 1976), chap. 3.

designing relatively nonthreatening policies. States' security interests often are extensive and may call for offensive capability. Thus an American policy that requires a credible threat to initiate nuclear war in response to a Soviet conventional attack on Europe or the Persian Gulf must appear to the Soviets to be a posture that might be used to change the status quo to their disadvantage.

But if a purely defensive and nonthreatening posture is rarely possible for a major power, not all possible responses are equally threatening to the other side. For example, making one's missiles less vulnerable threatens the other side less than does increasing their numbers. Similarly, NATO could increase its security without menacing the Warsaw Pact if it were to fortify the East-West border, especially in Germany. (Unfortunately, the realities of German domestic politics make this very difficult.) By contrast, whatever its other merits, a NATO strategy based on a counterattack into Eastern Europe or strikes deep behind Warsaw Pact lines would decrease Soviet security, just as the Soviet offensive doctrine menaces the West and leads to the inference that Soviet intentions are malign.[21]

Four implications follow. First, the state may want its adversary's forces to be invulnerable—especially if its own are—because decreasing the other side's security may make the state less rather than more secure. Few would disagree with this statement in the abstract, but whether one judges it applicable to the current situation depends not only on analyses of nuclear strategy, but on one's beliefs about the Soviet Union, its political objectives and risk-taking propensities, and its military strategy. Also important in this judgment are one's beliefs about whether the United State needs to be able to threaten a large-scale first strike in order to protect its allies.[22] So it is not surprising that American policy has been ambivalent and vacillating on this point.

21. See Richard Ned Lebow, "The Soviet Offensive in Europe: the Schlieffen Plan Revisited?" *International Security,* 9 (Spring 1985), 44–78. For a discussion of the recent thinking of the Soviets that appears to take account of the security dilemma and move away from their offensive strategy in Europe, see Jack Snyder, "Limiting Offensive Conventional Forces: Soviet Proposals and Western Options," *International Security,* 12 (Spring 1988), 48–77. Of course, even fortifications are not entirely defensive because they allow a state to protect its border with a relatively small number of soldiers, thus leaving a large part of its army free to take the offensive. Similarly, states may seek to take the offensive, not because they are aggressive and want to acquire more territory, but because they seek to deter others; see Samuel Huntington, "Conventional Deterrence and Conventional Retaliation in Europe," *International Security,* 8 (Winter 1983–84), 32–56.

22. For further discussion, see Joseph Nye, Jr., "The Future of Strategic Nuclear Systems," *Washington Quarterly,* 11 (Spring 1988), 48–52, and Chapter 5 below.

McNamara spoke of the mutual advantages of mutual second-strike capability, although he did so in the context of attempting to keep a war limited to military targets.[23] But it is not clear that the United States ever meaningfully restrained its ability to destroy Soviet missiles. More recently, the United States several times has shifted its position on whether it prefers Soviet ICBMs to be mobile—and thus almost invulnerable—or not.

Second, if mutual vulnerability is what is most dangerous, then arms control should concentrate on the characteristics of weapons, not on the numbers of them.[24] Increasing one or both sides' arsenals may not be destabilizing; freezing or decreasing levels may not make either side more secure. What is important is that each country's strategic forces be both invulnerable and unable to destroy those of the other side.

Third, stability in a crisis is decreased when the measures each side would take to protect its ability to retaliate would simultaneously increase its ability to strike first. Thus, to the extent that mobilization involves making larger numbers of weapons ready to fire, the state not only increases the forces that are likely to survive an adversary's strike, but also can launch a more effective first strike. Similarly, putting the command, control, and communications (C^3) system on alert would be necessary for launching a first strike as well as for striking back.

In principle, some measures would be purely defensive—for example, moving mobile missiles from known bases to hidden ones. But such measures, rarely taken, are likely to be perceived in the heat of a crisis as evidence of a likely first strike even if they do not actually put the side in a better position to start the war. Nevertheless, postures and weapons systems that look different when they are being manipulated in preparation for a first strike from when they are being made secure against a possible attack enhance crisis stability.

Fourth, although statesmen are fully aware of the need to make their threats credible, they often neglect the need to make credible their willingness to abstain from war and to respect the other's vital interests if the other cooperates. Although Schelling touched on this subject, it has remained largely unexplored.[25] Indeed, decision makers may not see the need at all. For example, even as sophisticated a statesman as

23. Stewart Alsop, "McNamara Thinks about the Unthinkable," *Saturday Evening Post,* Dec. 1, 1962, p. 18.

24. For a nice restatement of this posture, see Thomas Schelling, "What Went Wrong with Arms Control?" *Foreign Affairs,* 64 (Winter 1985–86), 219–33. For a modification of this position, see Chapter 6 below.

25. Thomas Schelling, *Strategy of Conflict* (Cambridge: Harvard University Press, 1960), pp. 43–44, 120, 129, 131–34.

Dean Acheson did not think he had to convince China that a United Nations force on its Yalu border would not menace its security. Similarly, in part because they cannot empathize with the other side and realize that it may fear that the state will strike first, decision makers' reassurances tend to be perfunctory at best. Scholars have not done much better; we do not have sustained analyses of how promises can be made credible, what devices or tactics might be employed, the barriers to the accurate perception of such commitments, and the conditions under which leaders have thought creatively about the problem.[26]

Possibilities of Cooperation

An appreciation of the security dilemma has facilitated the analysis of cooperation. Even if each side's preferred choice is to take advantage of the other, mutual cooperation is possible if big transactions are broken up into a series of small ones, if defensive postures are stronger than and different from offensive ones, if in any single instance exploiting the other does not produce overwhelming gains and being exploited by the other does not inflict overwhelming losses, and if each side can tell what the other is doing.[27] A related approach has been developed by scholars working on the question of international regimes. They argue that even in the absence of formal international institutions with powers of enforcement, the development of common principles, norms, and rules can facilitate cooperation.[28]

There is thus a convergence of two fields of study that usually ignore

26. For a good summary of what is known, see Janice Stein, "Deterrence and Reassurance," in Philip Tetlock et al., eds., *Behavior, Society and Nuclear War*, vol. 2 (New York: Oxford University Press, forthcoming).

27. See Robert Jervis, "Cooperation under the Security Dilemma," *World Politics*, 30 (January 1978), 167–214; Robert Axelrod, *The Evolution of Cooperation* (New York: Basic Books, 1984); Robert Keohane, *After Hegemony* (Princeton: Princeton University Press, 1984); and the special issue of *World Politics*, 38 (October 1985). For criticisms of this perspective, see Harrison Wagner, "The Theory of Games and the Problem of International Cooperation," *American Political Science Review*, 77 (June 1983), 330–46.

28. See the special issue of *International Organization*, 36 (Spring 1982), ed. Stephen Krasner, and Joseph Nye, "Nuclear Learning and U.S.–Soviet Security Regimes," *International Organization*, 41 (Summer 1987), 371–402. Even in domestic society, where centrally imposed sanctions are available, private response is often both efficient and vital. In many instances, collaboration is enforced and maintained because the injured party not only can cease dealing with the other but also can spread the word that the other has acted dishonorably, making it less likely that third parties will be willing to enter into agreements with the other. Much of what is usually called trust is actually the availability of effective sanctions of this type, and communities within which such sanctions can be used will be more efficient than those that lack them because they permit a wide range of bargains and an extensive division of labor.

and implicitly contradict each other—the field of security policy and the field of international organization and international political economy. The former has tended to stress conflict, the latter cooperation; the former has taken a realist perspective, the latter has embodied elements of legalism and idealism. But studies of security that stress the security dilemma and the concomitant concern with unnecessary conflict have much in common with analyses of international political economy that deal with the dilemmas created by the fact that economic cooperation is not automatic even when the actors prefer this outcome to one in which they all pursue highly competitive policies. Students of security see that states must avoid unnecessarily threatening others; students of regimes have come to realize that cooperation can be maintained only if each state is able to retaliate against others' transgressions.[29]

In other words, both fields are concerned with problems of how states can maintain the credibility of threats and promises, protect their interests without setting off a cycle of mutually destructive responses, and determine whether the other side is living up to its agreements. While this does not mean that we can adapt what we know about the workings of the General Agreement on Tariffs and Trade (GATT) to an understanding of Soviet-American arms control, some of the problems are the same, some kinds of explanations apply in both arenas, and there are parallels in the kinds of policies that will be effective.[30]

Making either threats or promises credible is difficult enough; doing both simultaneously is especially demanding. For example, President Carter probably succeeded in convincing the Soviets that he would cooperate, but he also tempted them to exploit him. Reagan convinced them that he would respond to their lack of cooperation by a similar stance of his own, but he left them with grave doubts as to whether he would also reciprocate concessions. Decision makers often fail to appreciate the latter problem. Thus while Reagan often lamented proposed congressional restrictions on arms programs on the legitimate

29. See, for example, the surprise expressed by two economists about the role of retaliation in maintaining trade agreements: Beth Yarbrough and Robert Yarbrough, "Reciprocity, Bilateralism, and Economic 'Hostages': Self-Enforcing Agreements in International Trade," *International Studies Quarterly*, 30 (March 1986), 15.

30. Even though there are important similarities between the two realms, the nature of international security politics means that cooperation is more difficult to achieve in that area than in political economy. See Robert Jervis, "Security Regimes," *International Organization*, 36 (Spring 1982), 358–60, and Charles Lipson, "International Cooperation in Economic and Security Affairs," *World Politics*, 37 (October 1984), 1–23.

grounds that they reduced the Soviets' incentives to negotiate, he never seemed to realize that without such congressional pressure the Soviets might be even less inclined to believe that he would be willing to reach any agreements.[31] Reagan administration officials who were deeply concerned about the credibility of American threats similarily gave little thought to whether what was widely seen as a reinterpretation of the ABM treaty would make its future promises less valuable.

I would propose the hypothesis that American foreign policy toward the USSR has more often suffered from the difficulty of making the Soviets believe its promises than from that of making them believe its threats. Do the Soviets believe that Americans will restrain their defense programs if the Soviets restrain theirs? Do they think that the West will abstain from interventions in the Third World if they do? Do they think that renewed détente would bring economic credits rather than increased pressures for undesired changes in policy? One can, of course, argue that these bargains would be unacceptable to the Soviet Union or should be unacceptable to the United States, but it is difficult to maintain that the Soviets have reason to be confident that the Americans would match their cooperation.

To make one's behavior conditional on that of others requires the ability to determine what others are doing—in other words, intelligence and inspection. Although in the security field most of the discussion of inspection has been connected with arms control agreements, the need is present even without them; indeed, the United States developed satellite surveillance systems before there were any treaties to verify. With or without formal agreements, inspection can increase cooperation and mutual security both by alleviating each side's fear that the other is increasing its arms and by making it unlikely that either could think that it could engage in a buildup without being detected.

The state not only wants to know what its adversary is doing, but under many conditions also wants its adversary to know what it is doing: it then wants the other side to have an effective intelligence system. This is the case when one state seeks mutual restraint and believes that the adversary is more likely to keep its level of arms low if it believes the state is also following this policy. As I will discuss in

31. For example, see Reagan's remarks quoted in Jonathan Fuerbringer, "Reagan Asks House to Yield On Arms-Control Disputes," *New York Times*, October 8, 1986, and Gerald Boyd, "Reagan Rules Out House Compromise on Arms Control," *New York Times*, October 9, 1986.

a later chapter, the most dramatic instance of this need is to show the adversary that the state is not about to attack in a crisis, thus reducing both sides' incentives to preempt. But the requirement is present in less dramatic instances of security cooperation as well.

Similarly, attempts to maintain a relatively open international economic system require that each state know the extent to which others are constructing protectionist barriers. When the main obstacles to trade are tariffs, the relevant information is readily available and unambiguous, thus facilitating cooperation. In recent years, however, nontariff barriers have become more important, and these are difficult to measure. Thus, the international economic realm may no longer be more transparent than the security arena: strategic weapons are usually easy to count, although the vital associated apparatus, like military doctrine and command and control arrangements, are more opaque.

Accurate information will not do the state any good if it is received too late to be acted on; cooperation will be facilitated if each side believes that only limited losses will be suffered before it can put a new policy in place. The notion of timely warning, developed in discussions of the Non-Proliferation Treaty, applies more broadly. States then seek not only to speed the flow of information but also to decrease the time necessary to construct and implement a prophylactic response and to decrease the advantage the adversary will gain in the interim. Thus states may break up large transactions into a series of smaller ones.[32] Similarly, arrangements that lengthen the amount of time between the commencement of noncooperation and the point at which harm would be inflicted on others make it easier for states to cooperate.

Of course timely warning requires that the state be able to act on the basis of the information. If the Reagan administration was correct in its claims that the Soviets are violating various arms control agreements, the problem is not lack of verification but the American inability to develop an appropriate response. In the best of circumstances, these responses would have several characteristics. First, the actions would not be so difficult or expensive that others would find the threat to implement them to be incredible. Students of security policy have been preoccupied with this requirement since 1945; students of cooperative arrangements in international economics are also becoming aware of its importance. A second attribute is even more difficult to attain. The actions should be relatively impervious to misjudgments in two ways: the adversary should be able to tell that they are a response to its failure to cooperate and, if the response itself was based on a mistaken judg-

---

32. Schelling, *Strategy of Conflict*, pp. 134–35.

ment of the adversary's behavior, the adversary should not suffer great damage. This attribute would minimize the danger that the response would set off an unnecessary spiral with each side seeing the other as seeking unilateral advantage. Third, the actions or their effects should be reversible. That is, it should be clear to the other side that co-operation can be restored if it ceases trying to exploit the state. Fourth, it is often not enough that a state be able to protect itself; in order to deter the other side from transgressing, it may need to be able to inflict costs on the other that will more than nullify the illegitimate gains the other had made. Of course, these requirements often are in tension with each other. For example, to the extent that it is cheap for a state to retaliate against the other's refusal to cooperate, it is also likely to be relatively tempting for the state itself to break the cooperative arrangement.

Cooperation is made possible because each side realizes that the other can halt its cooperation if provoked. Each must see that the other is not so devoid of alternatives that it has no choice but to go along. Of major importance, then, is not only accurate perception of the other's behavior but also the attribution of that behavior to causes that both permit future cooperation and rule out the possibility of exploiting the other. Thus the United States probably did not increase the chances of cooperation with the Soviet Union when it held down its spending on strategic arms in the decade from the late 1960s to the late 1970s. The Soviets probably thought the restraint was not voluntary and so on two counts saw little reason to reciprocate (assuming that they desired such an arrangement). First, they did not attribute the American behavior to desire for better relations with the Soviet Union and so had no reason to expect that a regime of mutual restraint was possible. Second, if the American restraint was not responsive to Soviet behavior, there was no incentive for the Soviets to be moderate. Rather, it was safe to seek unilateral advantage. When the Soviets said that detente was irreversible, many Americans were reassured, but this position was disturbing because it implied that the United States had no choice but to maintain the relationship no matter what the Soviet Union did.[33] As deterrence theory has stressed, concessions viewed as stemming from weakness will not be reciprocated but will instead lead to increased pressure.

Equally destructive to the chance of mutual cooperation is the belief

---

33. I have discussed other examples of this pattern in "From Balance to Concert," *World Politics*, 38 (October 1985), 76–78. Also see P. J. V. Rolo, *Entente Cordiale* (New York: St. Martin's Press, 1969), p. 49.

that the other side is already doing all it can to harm the state. Whereas the belief discussed in the previous paragraph removes the state's incentives to be moderate by leading it to conclude that it can make greater gains by exploitation, this belief produces the same effect by undermining the fear that shifting to a noncooperative policy will be met by an undesired response. Thus Assistant Secretary of Defense Richard Perle buttressed his argument for abandoning SALT II by claiming that the Soviets could do no more even if there were no treaty.[34] Similarly, when President Reagan was asked whether the Soviets might increase their arms spending in response to the American increases, he replied: "The Soviets—they're up at full pitch. I doubt if they could expand their military production beyond where it is right now."[35]

Reagan's argument rules out the fear that increases in American spending would be matched by the adversary but leaves open the chance that decreases in American spending would lead to Soviet restraint. Secretary of Defense Weinberger implicitly ruled out both possibilities in the area of missile defense when he claimed, "the Soviet commitment to strategic defense is . . . unswerving."[36] (It should also be noted that people with beliefs like this usually also prefer mutual competition to mutual restraint, as Weinberger does in this instance.) Secretary of Defense Brown's quip about Soviet military programs yields the same implication, although Brown did not act according to it: "When we build, they build; when we don't build, they build." Similar inference processes operate with predictions of other kinds of action. When the British considered their policy toward gas warfare in World War II, their continued restraint was made less likely by their estimate that, in the words of the official history of British intelligence, "in view of the measures [Germany] had taken to protect her civilians, the fear of retaliation was not likely to deter her from using gas if it was likely to be to her military advantage."[37] If the Allies had acted on this belief, they might have used gas when short-run calculations indicated there were gains from doing so because they would not have thought they could keep Germany restrained.

The strategy of tit-for-tat summarizes the need to make threats and promises conditional. The state responds to the other's cooperative

34. Leo Sartori, "Will SALT II Survive?" *International Security*, 10 (Winter 1985–86), 164–165.

35. *New York Times*, May 23, 1984.

36. Weinberger, *Annual Report for FY 1987*, p. 76.

37. F. H. Hinsley, E. E. Thomas, C. F. G. Ransom, and R. C. Knight, *British Intelligence in the Second World War*, vol. 2 (New York: Cambridge University Press, 1981), p. 117.

moves with cooperation of its own and reacts to hostility with hostility. If both sides prefer mutual cooperation to mutual hostility, if they understand each other's strategy, and if they correctly interpret each other's behavior, the result should be sustained cooperation even though each side's first choice would be to take advantage of the other. This argument has many fascinating applications and implications, as Robert Axelrod has so lucidly shown.[38] But states often fail to cooperate because they easily misinterpret each other's behavior. Or, to put it slightly differently, states and their adversaries often differ in their interpretations.[39] Random errors and random differences are possible. Essentially by accident, a state will sometimes see the other as having cooperated when in fact it did not or as having tried to exploit the state when it actually cooperated. Axelrod has shown that a 1 percent error rate does not destroy the efficacy of tit-for-tat, but George Downs and his colleagues have argued that 1 percent is unrealistically low and have demonstrated that even a slightly larger error rate undermines the strategy.[40]

Even more important than random errors are systematic biases. States tend to overestimate others' hostility and underestimate the harm they are doing to others.[41] It often appears to them that they are keeping their end of the bargain but that the other side is not; that they are responding symmetrically whereas their adversary exploits them at every opportunity; that the only way to protect their interests is to increase their own hostility. Perceptions like these probably accelerated the decline of Soviet-American detente in the 1970s and were at work in earlier cases as well, for example in the erosion of the Anglo-French entente in the 1840s.[42]

38. Axelrod, *Evolution of Cooperation*. Also see Anatol Rapoport, "Editorial Comment," *Journal of Conflict Resolution*, 29 (December 1985), 619–22.

39. For the argument that cooperation depends, not on mechanically reciprocating the other's behavior, but on the interpretations of why the other acted as it did, see Deborah Larson, "Game Theory and the Psychology of Reciprocity" (Paper presented at the annual meeting of the American Political Science Association, Chicago, September 2, 1987). Also see Robert Jervis, "Realism, Game Theory, and Cooperation," *World Politics*, 40 (April 1988), 336–40.

40. George Downs, David Rocke, and Randolph Siverson, "Arms Race and Cooperation," *World Politics*, 38 (October 1985), 134–43. Also see Jonathan Bendor, "In Good Times and Bad: Reciprocity in an Uncertain World," *American Journal of Political Science*, 31 (August 1987), 531–58.

41. Jervis, *Perception and Misperception in International Politics*, pp. 68–75, 349–55.

42. Alexander George, *Managing U.S.–Soviet Rivalry* (Boulder, Colo.: Westview Press, 1983); Roger Bullen, *Palmerstone, Guizot and the Collapse of the Entente Cordiale* (London: Athlone, 1974); Gordon Craig, "The System of Alliances and the Balance of Power," in

When states do not intend to harm others, they overlook the security dilemma and think that others understand that their intentions are benign. Almost universal is the belief that the other side understands that the state is willing to leave the other in peace if the other will only adopt a similar stance. Thus the American decision makers failed to realize that in sending troops to the Yalu they decreased Chinese security. When the other responds with hostility, the problem is compounded if the state's leaders believe that the adversary understood that the state intended to cooperate. They will then conclude that the other's action shows that it is highly aggressive, will take advantage of any opportunity to weaken the state, and will not reciprocate cooperation.

Difficulties in interpreting others' behavior and the differences in the two sides' perceptions also complicate a common prescription for maintaining cooperation. Both Axelrod's computer tournaments and some historical cases indicate that states should react quickly to the other's transgressions. "The longer defections are allowed to go unchallenged, the more likely it is that the other player will draw the conclusion that defection can pay. And the more strongly this pattern is established, the harder it will be to break it."[43] Alexander George's conclusion based on the decline of Soviet-American detente is similar:

> The danger of misperception and miscalculation is particularly serious when one superpower—typically the Soviet Union—intervenes cautiously and on a low level in a local situation, probing to test the other superpower's reaction and, when receiving no response, then decides to escalate its involvement. Failure to grasp that the opponent is conducting a carefully controlled probe and is engaged in a subtle asking of a question regarding the other side's intentions can easily abet miscalculation and set into motion escalation leading to confrontation.[44]

Responding quickly is particularly difficult for democraties; determining quickly that the other had defected often is difficult for any state. Although the passage of time, the gathering of more information, and the accumulation of more instances of the other's behavior do not always reveal exactly what the other side is doing, their absence usually

J. T. P. Bury, ed., *New Cambridge Modern History*, vol. 10, *The Zenith of European Power, 1830–70* (New York: Cambridge University Press, 1960), pp. 254–57.

43. Axelrod, *Evolution of Cooperation*, pp. 184–85.

44. Alexander George, "Political Crisis," in Joseph Nye, Jr., ed., *The Making of America's Soviet Policy* (New Haven: Yale University Press, 1984), p. 150.

makes governments hesitant to act because they realize that their estimates can easily be in error.

The fundamental problem resides in the identification and interpretation of the other's behavior, since a policy based on erroneous judgments can produce the result the policy was designed to prevent. Thus statesmen confront a cruel and unavoidable dilemma. Without quick and firm reaction to cases of unprovoked noncooperation, the other may conclude that it can make gains by frequent but minor cheating, but punishment, or even deterrence, can set off a spiral of unnecessary conflict if the other actually was—or believed it was—cooperating or thought its behavior was a response to a previous defection by the state. For example, when the United States received serious but ambiguous evidence that the Soviet Union and its allies were using chemical and biological weapons in Afghanistan and Cambodia, it quickly made the charges public. The United States thereby gained the possibility of discouraging further use, but if the charges were incorrect—as now appears to be the case—the Soviets probably would have concluded that the United States was acting in bad faith, thus reducing their willingness to cooperate with America in the future. Unfortunately, understanding the other's behavior is difficult, the room for differing interpretations is very great, and the appropriate match between provocation and response is fairly rare.[45]

Psychology and Security

As the previous paragraphs indicate, another fruitful new approach is the application of psychology to the problems of deterrence. Although the initial psychological criticisms of deterrence theory were often naive about international politics and the Soviet Union, they correctly stressed that deterrence theory was misguided in focusing most of its attention on the danger that status-quo powers would fail to make clear their resolve to oppose aggression.[46] Four related problems are also troublesome and need parallel consideration. First, statesmen tend to overestimate the hostility of others: Hitlers are perceived more often than they occur. This bias colors the analysis of specific situations as well. In June 1950, American decision makers took the

---

45. For a further discussion, see Jervis, *Perception and Misperception*, pp. 62–84; Michael Nicholson, *Oligopoly and Conflict: A Dynamic Approach* (Toronto: University of Toronto Press, 1972), chap. 6; Michael Taylor, *Anarchy and Cooperation* (London: Wiley, 1976), p. 96; and Joanne Gowa, "Anarchy, Egoism, and Third Image," *International Organization*, 40 (Winter 1986), 182–83.

46. See, for example, Amitai Etzioni, *The Hard Way to Peace* (New York: Collier, 1962);

North Korean invasion as a Soviet probe of American resolve, when in retrospect it seems to have been opportunism that Stalin assented to rather than instigated.[47] In October 1962, American decision makers thought that the Soviet deployment of missiles in Cuba was the prelude to greatly increased pressure on Berlin, whereas it now appears that the motive was primarily to close the missile gap. Second, as a partial consequence of this kind of error, the exchange of threats between states that are actually willing to tolerate the status quo can lead to spirals of tension and conflict. Third, states may be pushed into war by domestic pressures or by the belief that their situation is deteriorating badly. This cause of war is compatible with the rational utility-maximization approach of deterrence. Indeed, deterrence theorists have focused on the dangers caused by military vulnerability and the reciprocal fear of surprise attack.[48] But until recently the broader kind of political vulnerability has not received the attention it deserves.[49]

The fourth problem is related: the psychological processes of people under pressure explain why the credibility of deterrent threats may be greatly overestimated by the state making them or greatly underestimated by the state being threatened.[50] Deterrence involves not abstract decision makers but human beings whose ways of thinking and feeling strongly affect their behavior. Statesmen are prone to underestimate the pressures others feel to change the status quo, pressures that can result in their misperceiving their environment and challenging commitments that are relatively clear, credible, and potent. Two steps are involved here. First, a statesman who is under grave international or domestic pressures may come to feel that a bellicose policy (either of

Jerome Frank, *Sanity and Survival in the Nuclear Age* (New York: Random House, 1967); Charles Osgood, *An Alternative to War or Surrender* (Urbana: University of Illinois Press, 1962); Ralph White, *Nobody Wanted War* (Garden City, N.Y.: Doubleday, 1968). White's more recent book, *Fearful Warriors* (New York: Free Press, 1984), combines the strengths of the earlier work with a good appreciation of the nature of international politics and the danger of agression and failures of deterrence.

47. Alexander George, "American Policy-Making and the North Korean Aggression," *World Politics*, 7 (January 1955), 209–32. The American responses were not necessarily inappropriate but the lessons learned about the nature of the adversary and what might have been done to avoid the clashes were misleading.

48. Schelling, *Strategy of Conflict*, chap. 9.

49. Paul Schroeder, *Austria, Great Britain, and the Crimean War* (Ithaca: Cornell University Press, 1972); Richard Ned Lebow *Between Peace and War* (Baltimore: Johns Hopkins University Press, 1981); Richard Ned Lebow and Janice Stein, "Beyond Deterrence," *Journal of Social Issues*, 43, no. 4 (1987), 5–72; Paul Stern, Robert Axelrod, Robert Jervis, and Roy Radnor, eds., *Perspectives on Deterrence* (New York: Oxford University Press, forthcoming); and Janice Stein, "Deterrence and Reassurance."

50. See the literature in the preceding note.

supporting or challenging the status quo) is necessary. Second, in order to avoid being disturbed by the acute value trade-off that would arise from an appreciation of the dangers inherent in the policy, the person may then come to see his stance as likely to succeed.

Organizational Perspectives

New perspectives have also arisen out of the abandonment of the view that each state could adequately be characterized as not only a rational actor but also a unitary one. Analyses of bureaucratic politics have greatly enriched our knowledge of how American forces are structured. Although we know a good deal less about the projected employment policy for strategic weapons, what we do know is consistent with the powerful influence of the way the military services have come to define their identities.[51]

What may be at least as important, but much less understood, is the unwieldiness of the military forces mobilized during international crises. As John Steinbruner has argued, the superpowers' military organizations are so large and complex that national leaders cannot fully comprehend them, let alone maintain full control.[52] Complex and tightly interconnected systems are prone to fail disastrously, thus leading to Charles Perrow's unsettling concept of "normal accidents," which our thinking about strategy does not readily encompass.[53]

A high state of alert or the movement of military forces in a crisis would entail the implementation of unfamiliar operations that could lead to war through the operation of two linked mechanisms. First, the military forces on either or both sides could get out of control as authority is delegated to operational levels and commanders overreact—or perhaps just react—to the unprecedented and alarming behavior of the forces on the other side. Second, top decision makers may similarly misinterpret the other side's behavior as indicating that the other is about to attack. Since the United States has not gone on alert for years and the Soviets never have (they did not do so during the Cuban missile crisis, perhaps because they feared triggering American preemption), neither side would know how to interpret what the other was doing.

51. See the essays in Desmond Ball and Jeffrey Richelson eds., *Strategic Nuclear Targeting* (Ithaca: Cornell University Press, 1986).
52. John Steinbruner, "Assessment of Nuclear Crises," in Franklyn Griffiths and John Polanyi, eds., *The Dangers of Nuclear War* (Toronto: University of Toronto Press, 1979), pp. 34–49.
53. Charles Perrow, *Normal Accidents* (New York: Basic Books, 1984).

Of course even if alerts were common, major problems of interpretation would remain, especially if the preparations for retaliation closely resembled the preliminaries for launching a first strike. But ambiguity and room for fear-driven perceptions are even greater when the decision maker is confronted with military activities he has never seen before. Furthermore, the fact of being in a crisis means that the other side's actions will be scrutinized especially carefully, and observers are likely to see things they had not noticed previously even if the other's behavior has not changed. The activities will then be seen as unusual and, given the context provided by the alert, as threatening.

That it will be hard for each state to interpret the other's behavior in a crisis is perhaps less surprising than the fact that the decision makers will not understand their own state's behavior. When military forces are put on alert, they will execute all sorts of maneuvers of which the civilian leaders—and even the top generals—will be ignorant. The actions taken in the name of the state may then be more provocative than the leaders realize or desire. Furthermore, the leaders' misinformation means that they will be especially slow to see the other side's action as a reaction to what their state is doing. As a result, they are likely to infer that the other's behavior reflects a settled decision to heighten the crisis if not to attack.[54] Whether war would result would depend in part on whether decision makers believed that technology and tactics favored the offense or the defense; that is, whether they thought there was a significant advantage to striking first.[55]

New, Bad Ideas

Many new and bad ideas are embodied in current American nuclear strategy, especially in the baroque multiplication of options and targets, which, it seems, involves a process of bootstrapping.[56] A particular kind of target is put on the list, often at the initiative of civilians or because of a temporary surplus of warheads; the military accepts the

54. Two case studies of military alerts are presented in Scott Sagan, "Nuclear Alerts and Crisis Management," *International Security*, 9 (Spring 1985), 99–139. For further discussion, see Chapter 5 below; for discussion of similar problems in the prenuclear era, see Jervis, *Perception and Misperception in International Politics*, pp. 329–42.

55. Of course, beliefs and the objective situation can be very different, as we are reminded by the events of July 1914.

56. David Rosenberg, "The Origins of Overkill: Nuclear Weapons and American Strategy, 1945–1960," *International Security*, 7 (Spring 1983), 3–71; Desmond Ball, "U.S. Strategic Forces: How Would They Be Used?" *International Security*, 7 (Winter 1982–83), 31–60.

logic and reports that since the number of targets in the new category is very large, the force is not sufficient to cover them. (The force requirements also increase as the Soviets increase the number of their installations.) The result is both pressures for increased forces and a sense of insecurity as American leaders learn that the new tasks may outrun their resources. Thus current strategy requires the United States to be able to hold at risk not only Soviet conventional forces but the communist party's control of the Soviet Union. The number of warheads required for these tasks is very large—much larger than the forces available, let alone the number that the United States would have if both sides made deep cuts in their strategic arsenals. Indeed, the number of military targets that the United States might want to destroy in conjunction with war in Europe is almost limitless.

Not only has American policy generated the requirement to destroy ever more targets, but the United States has also sought increased selectivity, control, and precision. Starting from the perceived need to deny the other side a military advantage from any possible course of action, more thought leads to more imagined dangers, more limited options that could prove useful, and more ways in which coercion could be parried or employed. With these fears and intellectual tools, the obvious drive is to cover all contingencies, to think of all possible bargaining strategies. Greater and greater sophistication can then take policy farther and farther down a blind and dangerous alley.

As a result, many defense problems are self-generated.[57] Assuming that the Russians draw straightforward inferences from American statements (a dubious assumption, to be sure), claims about what is necessary for deterrence undercut the credibility of threats by establishing standards that are beyond reach. For example, U.S. officials argue that deterrence requires the ability to fight a protracted nuclear war. But the vulnerabilities of command systems, the tremendous stresses on human beings and mechanical systems alike, and the unforeseeable frictions of an unprecedented kind of warfare mean that no country can develop any reasonable confidence that it can do so. A realistic appraisal of the situation, coupled with the unrealistic requirements for deterrence that it has set, could then undercut America's will.

In the past, statesmen often dismissed certain dangerous situations as simply too implausible to be taken seriously. For example, in 1924, Winston Churchill opposed the Admiralty's argument that more ships had to be built to meet the menace from Japan by arguing: "A war with Japan! But why should there be a war with Japan? I do not believe

57. For further discussion, see Chapter 6 below.

there is the slightest chance of it in our lifetime."[58] These judgments are difficult and, as this example shows, may be wrong. They are particularly hard to make today: the knowledge that world war would be a disaster and the limitations on our knowledge of how war might occur combine to defeat attempts to put bounds on our imagination. One can always generate finer and finer tactics of bargaining with nuclear weapons; one can always ask of any means of keeping the adversary in check, What if it fails? Brodie realized this: "All sorts of notions and propositions are churned out, and often presented for consideration with the prefatory words: 'It is conceivable that . . . ' Such words establish their own truth, for the fact that someone has conceived of whatever proposition follows is enough to establish that it is conceivable. Whether it is worth a second thought, however, is another matter."[59] Of course the penalties for an incorrect negative answer are enormous, but bounds must be established if we are not to pursue in ever more elaborate detail the implications of faulty premises.

Why There Has Been So Little Change

The bulk of this chapter has been devoted to arguing that many of the best ideas in nuclear strategy are old and that not all of the new ideas are good. Here, I note three possible sources of change: advancing technology, new knowledge, and our ability to learn from international events.

One might think that changing technology would not only encourage intellectual innovation but require it. Innovation in weapons systems is now the rule rather than the exception. But most of these changes, significant as they are in terms of military hardware and military spending, involve the substitution of one weapon for another, with little change in the projected missions. Furthermore, strategic thinking often anticipates the production of the new weapons. Borden, again, provides marvelous examples: he envisioned ICBMs, sea-launched missiles (he saw them on surface ships, not submarines), complex sensors, terminal guidance, and ABMs. Of course, the development of an ABM system that could protect cities would constitute a true revolution— or, more accurately, a counterrevolution—but there seems to be little chance of such a development in the foreseeable future.

58. Quoted in Martin Gilbert, *Winston S. Churchill*, vol. 5, *1922–1939* (London: Heinemann, 1978), p. 76.
59. Bernard Brodie, "The Development of Nuclear Strategy," *International Security*, 2 (Spring 1978), 83.

A glance backward helps confirm the limited impact of technology. The development of accurate MIRVs, although disturbing to most strategists because they seemed to give incentives to strike first, have had much less influence on either ideas about strategy or policy itself than most of us predicted at the time. The strategic balance has too many components and is too stable to be greatly affected by even as substantial a change as this.[60] By the same token, de-MIRVing, although desirable, would neither make the world much safer nor meet the requirements for deterrence set forth in current U.S. doctrine.

Some have argued that new technology will lead to new concepts and policies by providing a new range of options.[61] The best example is the possibility of extremely accurate warheads, probably using terminal guidance and perhaps being carried by cruise missiles rather than ICBMs. Indeed, if accuracies are sufficiently high, conventional warheads would suffice. It is true that such technologies would allow the superpowers to do things they cannot do now, for example, destroy military or political control targets without doing great collateral damage. But would they drastically alter the current situation? I think not: new options will not alter mutual vulnerability. New technologies could make highly limited strikes possible but not safe. Decision makers would be likely to implement them only if they thought that their use could terminate the war on acceptable terms. But new options cannot eliminate the dangers of escalation, either in the form of the adversary's controlled response or in the form of a mutually undesired explosion to all-out war. (Critics of limited options cannot have it both ways, however. If one argues that these options are useless, one cannot easily claim that statesmen would be quick to resort to them. It is possible, although more than a bit strained, to argue that although threatening or carrying out these options would not have the desired effects, statesmen would place confidence in them and so would behave incautiously.)

A second source of innovation is purely intellectual: new ideas can be developed as analysts probe the problems more deeply. No one would deny that this provides a partial description for what has happened. Obviously I think this book adds to our knowledge. As I noted in the first chapter, the implications of the nuclear revolution have not been fully understood. But we should not mistake significant, but mar-

60. Ibid., pp. 65–83.

61. Henry Rowen and Albert Wohlstetter, "Varying Response with Circumstances," in John Holst and Uwe Nerlich, eds. *Beyond Nuclear Deterrence* (New York: Crane, Russak, 1977), pp. 225–38.

ginal, arguments for fundamental ones. Although we need to discover how statesmen have thought and operated in the strange world of nuclear weapons, explore the full range of the transformations created by mutual vulnerability, and see how states can best combine deterrence and reassurance, analysts and statesmen may have already discovered the essential point: military victory is now not possible.

The third possible source of new knowledge is history. Each year we have a longer period of history from which to learn about nuclear strategies. Furthermore, each year we get new studies of earlier events, some based on new information and declassified documents. These studies constitute a major source of intellectual sustenance. We have learned that war planning often diverged greatly from declaratory policy, and we are beginning to gain a more accurate and complex picture of how statesmen—at least American statesmen—weighed the role of nuclear weapons during confrontations.[62] The latter question, discussed in Chapter 1, is central to the dispute begun by Brodie and Borden. But we should recognize three inescapable limits to the value of history in this regard. First, there are only a few cases in which the use of nuclear weapons have been contemplated or threatened. Indeed, the Cuban missile crisis is probably the only instance in which nuclear war was seen as a real possibility. We also have no cases of such a confrontation when both sides had ample second-strike capability.[63] The lessons from these cases, furthermore, must remain especially ambiguous in the absence of evidence about the causes of Soviet behavior. Soviet documents would not clear up all of the mysteries— with every document declassified we still argue about the origins of World War I—but without them the room for disagreement is especially great.[64] The ambiguity of the information feeds a third limit on our

62. Betts, *Nuclear Blackmail and Nuclear Balance*; Rosenberg, "The Origins of Overkill;" McGeorge Bundy, *Danger and Survival* (New York: Random House, 1988); Roger Dingman, "From Deterrence to Compellence? The Use of Nuclear Weapons in the Korean War, 1950–1953," *International Security*, 13 (Winter 1988–89), 50–91; Rosemary Foot, *The Wrong War* (Ithaca: Cornell University Press, 1985); Foot, "Nuclear Threats and the Ending of the Korean Conflict," *International Security*, 13 (Winter 1988–89), 92–112.

63. The United States may have acted as though the Soviets had such a capability in 1962. See Fred Kaplan, *The Wizards of Armageddon* (New York: Simon & Schuster, 1983), pp. 298–306. Also see Betts, *Nuclear Blackmail and Nuclear Balance*, pp. 144–72.

64. But the Germans seem to have destroyed many of their important—and presumably incriminating—documents: see Holger Holwig, "Clio Deceived: Patriotic Self-Censorship in Germany after the Great War," *International Security*, 12 (Fall 1987), 5–44. Some Soviets are beginning to reminisce about the Cuban missile crisis but, useful as these accounts are, they cannot substitute for fuller and document-based analyses: see James Blight and David Welch, *On the Brink: Americans and Soviets Reexamine the Cuban Missile Crisis* (New York: Farrar, Straus & Giroux, forthcoming).

learning from the past. For scholars as well as decision makers, images of other countries and beliefs about politics are highly resistant to discrepant information. We all tend to assimilate new information into our preexisting beliefs.[65]

Brodie and Borden clearly did not foreshadow all the important ideas in nuclear strategy. But they did anticipate many of the later intellectual developments, incorporating many of the technologies that appeared in the next generation. Three central points stand out. First, although it has become fashionable to dismiss the role of nuclear doctrine, a great many policy preferences and insights are determined by the doctrinal starting point one chooses. It would be better to argue about these fundamentals than to believe that disagreements on smaller issues can be resolved without probing what underlies them. Second, if one adopts a conventionalized perspective and does not come to grips with the implications of mutual vulnerability, one is inevitably led to try to reestablish the central role of military victory. Secretary of Defense Weinberger was so strongly criticized for allowing his secret defense guidance to speak of the need to "prevail" in a nuclear war that he had to retract the word. But the idea follows inevitably from his premises, which have been widely shared with other defense leaders over the past generation. Similarly, the relentless quest for more options and ever-finer gradations of nuclear force is not surprising. Although the drive has been criticized as excessive by some who fostered this policy while in office,[66] it is a consequence of mistaken assumptions, not excessive zeal. Third, as Brodie stressed in his final book, one must not lose sight of Clausewitz's central point that the use of force is senseless if it is divorced from an intelligent appreciation of political goals.[67] As I will discuss in the concluding chapter, it is quite possible for military advantage to be gained at the expense, not only of the adversary, but also of the state's most important objectives. Security and advantage are not synonymous; indeed they may be antithetical.

65. Of course the actors themselves can learn. See Nye, "Nuclear Learning," and Deborah Larson, "Learning to Cooperate: Beliefs, Motives, and Intentions" (unpublished manuscript, Columbia University).
66. See the comments of two former secretaries of defense quoted in Gregg Herken, *Counsels of War* (New York: Knopf, 1985), pp. 301–2.
67. Brodie, *War and Politics*, chap. 1.

[3]

"MAD Is a Fact, Not a Policy":
Getting the Arguments Straight

So much has been written about nuclear doctrine that the issues and arguments, if not the answers, should be clear. But they are not, even—or especially—for the best-known strategy, Mutual Assured Destruction (MAD). Because those who are sympathetic to MAD do not agree on all its details, some confusion is understandable and this attempt at clarification must be in part a personal one.

Not only does MAD mean different things to different people, but the term is used sometimes for description and sometimes for prescription. It may also refer, either descriptively or prescriptively, to different aspects of a policy—to declaratory policy, procurement policy, or war planning. Since these elements are not always consistent, one aspect of policy may be accurately described as MAD while others might not be. We may also need to separate policies by the contingencies they are designed to deter: a country could have a policy of MAD for attacks against its homeland but not for attacks against its allies. Alternatively, it could adopt MAD for nuclear attacks against it or its allies but not against conventional assaults.

These dimensions can be combined to yield a startling number of different meanings, but it seems more useful to concentrate on four alternative conceptions, moving from the least to the most sophisticated. This brings out many of the central issues and reveals that many of the best-known criticisms apply only to the simplest version. This sense of MAD, which we will call MAD-1, denotes a situation in which:

[74]

(a) the state threatens to inflict "unacceptable" damage on the adversary by aiming its nuclear forces at what it believes the other side values—that is, deterrence by punishment rather than deterrence by denial; *(b)* the other's values are believed to be its society and cities; and *(c)* the forces are in an all-or-none configuration—that is, all the nuclear weapons are fired at the same time, none being withheld in the hope of influencing the other side.[1]

Many of the criticisms of MAD are aimed at this version, which is unfortunate because it never characterized American policy and has had few advocates. In some periods in the mid-1950s and mid-1960s, American spokesmen implied that MAD-1 was American policy, but war planning never fit this picture.[2] Although element *(c)* was present until the early or mid-1960s, American strategic forces have always been aimed at counterforce as well as countervalue targets, and procurement has been strongly influenced by the desire to carry out this mission. The fact that it is only in the past decade that American officials have publically argued that the United States must be able to deny the Soviets a military advantage from moves at any level of violence should not mislead us; this objective has never been absent.

MAD-2 separates intention from result. While decision makers might want to keep war limited, they would be unable to do so. Either because of failures in hardware (primarily in C^3 facilities) or as the result of human calculations or emotions, limited nuclear wars are impossible. A weaker version of this argument would be that although limited nuclear wars could be fought as long as no bombs exploded on the superpowers' homelands, limits would be impossible if that firebreak were breached. A stronger version argues that even conventional war between the Soviet Union and the United States would quickly lead to all-out nuclear war. Because it stresses the unintended consequences of actions, this version of MAD obviously could not be a policy. It is an argument that the likely occurrence of disastrous consequences must condition policy. Attempts to create limited nuclear options will be feckless; the choices that would be introduced would be illusory. As Bernard Brodie put it in reply to the claim that the United States has been slow to develop limited nuclear options because of the rigidity of its analysis, "The rigidity lies in the situation, not in the thinking."[3]

1. Here, as in other versions of MAD, the context is one in which the adversary also has a large and secure strategic force.
2. See David Rosenberg, "The Origins of Overkill: Nuclear Weapons and American Strategy, 1945–60," *International Security*, 7 (Spring 1983), 3–71.
3. Bernard Brodie, "The Development of Nuclear Strategy," *International Security*, 2 (Spring 1978), 82.

MAD-3 draws out the implications of MAD-2 in a way that accords with common sense but that I will argue is wrong. It asserts that since nuclear war cannot be kept limited, in an era of parity, "strategic nuclear weapons have lost whatever military utility may once have been attributed to them. Their sole purpose, at present, is to deter the other side's first use of its strategic forces."[4] (The second sentence does not follow from the first and a more politically sensitive version of MAD accepts the first but rejects the second.) Because the use of strategic nuclear weapons would entail national suicide, there is no rational way for either side to threaten or use them against the other. Nuclear weapons, then, are of little direct use for aggression, but unfortunately neither can they be employed to deter aggression against allies (i.e., extended deterrence is not feasible).[5] In the operation of Glenn Snyder's stability-instability paradox, the fact that strategic nuclear war would destroy both sides means that large conventional forces are required to protect other vital American interests.

Critics of MAD usually focus on some combination of these three viewpoints. Since each of them is flawed, it is not surprising that the counterarguments are strong.[6] Critics first note that although nuclear war would be difficult to control, it would not be impossible. Once proper arrangements have been made for C^3, perhaps the most important step would be to educate statesmen to the possibility of limited use. Furthermore, even if analysts and decision makers cannot be certain that nuclear war could be kept limited, it is surely foolish to base a policy on the assumption that limits are impossible. To do so would both ensure that any Soviet-American war would lead to the destruction of American society and leave the United States open to Soviet coercion in peacetime.

Second, MAD's critics argue that it is both more moral and more effective to aim at military targets than at cities. More moral because

4. Robert McNamara, "The Military Role of Nuclear Weapons,"*Foreign Affairs*, 62 (Fall 1983), 68. For his explanation on how he reached this conclusion, see McNamara's interview in Michael Charlton, *From Deterrence to Defense* (Cambridge: Harvard University Press, 1987), p. 18.

5. Recent fears have grown that the vulnerability of C^3 systems renders these statements invalid. I think the arguments for such fears are important but also exaggerated; see Chapter 5 below.

6. I am here drawing on Colin Gray, *Nuclear Strategy and National Style* (Lanham, Md.: Hamilton Press, 1986); Albert Wohlstetter, "Between an Unfree World and None,"*Foreign Affairs*, 63 (Summer 1985) 962–94; Wohlstetter, "Bishops, Statesmen, and Other Strategists on the Bombing of Innocents," *Commentary*, June 1983, pp. 15–35; Wohlstetter's reply to readers' letters in *Commentary*, December, 1983, pp. 13–22; Fred Hoffman, "The SDI in U.S. Nuclear Strategy," *International Security*, 10 (Summer 1985); and official U.S. statements over the past fifteen years. Secretary of Defense Weinberger's recent annual statements to Congress have presented particularly crude versions of these arguments.

innocent casualties are minimized; more effective because Soviet leaders value the power that underpins their world influence and domestic control more than they value civilian lives. Furthermore, if the war is a limited one, deterrence by denial is possible. That is, low-yield nuclear weapons (and even high-yield conventional weapons) directed by precision guidance and knowledge of the location of Soviet forces would permit the United States to prevent a Soviet victory in Europe or the Persian Gulf. At higher levels of violence, the ability to destroy Soviet strategic nuclear forces, coupled with the ability to protect our own, would also deny the Soviets a military advantage from attacking U.S. strategic forces. Thus counterforce targeting would enable the United States to meet Soviet military adventures on their own terms. Such a capability would provide the basis for threats that would be in the American interest to carry out should deterrence fail.[7]

Even if an all-out response retains some credibility against the extremely unlikely—and indeed pointless—possibility of an all-out Soviet attack against the American homeland, it cannot protect our allies or resist the "selective assaults . . . [that] are the main threats that the West must be prepared to deter or counter."[8] Without limited options, many Soviet aggressions would leave the United States with the choice of suicide or surrender. Realizing this and naturally believing that, however unpalatable the latter choice would be, the United States would prefer it to the former, the Russians would be able to increase their influence throughout the world by means of threats and the limited use of force. This point is consistent with the proponents of MAD-3, who urge an increase in conventional capabilities. But the critics go further and note that the argument that nuclear weapons cannot provide extended deterrence is not a matter of geography. Although most attention has been focused on the defense of Europe, one could take the logic of the stability-instability paradox a step further and ask what would deter a Soviet attack on American strategic systems (the "Nitze scenario") if the United States lacked the ability to respond with controlled and militarily effective force.[9]

---

7. When he was secretary of defense, James Schlesinger stressed the need for the United States to develop nuclear options it would not be afraid to implement in a war: see U.S. House of Representatives, Committee on Armed Services, *Hearings on Military Posture*, pt. 1, 93d Cong., 2d sess. (Washington, D.C.: Government Printing Office, 1974), p. 49. Also see his testimony in U.S. Senate, Subcommittee on Arms Control, International Law and Organization of the Committee on Foreign Relations, *Briefing on Counterforce Attacks*, 93d Cong., 2d sess. (Washington, D.C.: Government Printing Office, 1975), p. 44.

8. Wohlstetter, "Between an Unfree World and None," p. 990.

9. Paul Nitze, "Assuring Strategic Stability in an Era of Détente," *Foreign Affairs*, 54

Finally, the rebuttal goes, it is misleading to claim that MAD is a fact, not a policy. We should not overestimate the constraints that nuclear weapons have established. Although cities on both sides can be destroyed, policies can be developed that provide alternatives to doing so. Nothing in the technology of nuclear weapons precludes flexibility and restraint; the basic fallacy of MAD is to confuse the possibility of mutual annihilation with the impossibility of anything else.

These arguments have a good deal of validity, but the position they rebut is not the one that deserves most consideration. To say that MAD is a fact means—or can mean—something that is compatible with many of these points. That something is wrong with the critique is indicated—although certainly not proved—by the fact that nuclear deterrence seems to have worked quite well despite the frequent claims that it should not be able to. It is almost a truism that because of the stability-instability paradox the American threat to respond to a Soviet conventional attack in Europe with strategic nuclear weapons is simply incredible. The obvious question then arises of why the Russians have not even menaced Berlin in the last fifteen years, let alone invaded Europe. (Of course the credibility of the nuclear threat is not the only possible explanation. NATO's conventional strength, the expected political costs, or the Soviet satisfaction with the status quo are alternative, or at least complementary, explanations.) Indeed, neither superpower seems willing to challenge the other's major interests in the face of its nuclear weapons. The very wording of one of Kissinger's arguments betrays a similar difficulty: "For a decade or more it should have been clear that reliance on Mutual Assured Destruction would lead eventually to the demoralization of the West. It is not possible indefinitely to tell democratic publics that their security depends on the mass extermination of civilians, unopposed by either defenses or a mitigating strategy, without sooner or later producing pacifism and unilateral disarmament."[10] But there is little sign of such demoralization. Kissinger says that "it should have been clear" that MAD would produce these effects, but neither Soviet leaders nor Western leaders nor the Western public have responded as his analysis would indicate they should have. Even the Dutch have failed to succumb to "Hollanditis."[11]

(January 1976), 207–33; Nitze, "Deterring Our Deterrent," *Foreign Policy*, no. 25 (Winter 1976–77), 195–210.

10. Henry Kissinger, "After Reykjavik: Current East-West Negotiations," *The San Franciso Meeting of the Trilateral Commission*, March 1987, p. 4; also see p. 7.

11. See Richard Eichenberg, "The Myth of Hollanditis," *International Security*, 8 (Fall 1983), 143–59; Wallace Theis, *The Atlantic Alliance, Nuclear Weapons, and European Attitudes:*

These claims for the consequences of MAD are not illogical; indeed, the conclusions follow quite clearly from the basic premises. Thus the fact that the conclusions have not been borne out by international behavior indicates that this version of MAD has not characterized world politics. To understand why this is so, we need to examine a version of MAD which better captures the role of nuclear weapons.

MAD-4

MAD-4 starts with the familiar argument for the existence of a "nuclear revolution"; established truths about the relationships between force and statecraft have been turned on their heads by the fact that before—and during—a war each side would be vulnerable to destruction.[12] The impossibility of protecting the state should the other seek to destroy it (i.e., the impossibility of deterrence by denial at the highest level) alters the purpose of military options and renders questionable the efficacy of defense by denial at lower levels of violence.

It is important to separate the unalterable effects of nuclear technology from the realm of choice and policy. In doing so MAD-4 gives a picture that is different both from that of MAD-1, 2, and 3 and that provided by the critics. The latter are correct to note that nothing about mutual vulnerability means that cities and other values must be the first or only targets in a war; nothing in it implies that military installations are immune; nothing in it implies that wars must be quick and unlimited. Because these are all questions whose answers depend in part on national decisions and available technologies, we should not expect them to be settled once and for all but to change over time. MAD-4 agrees on these points but also stresses that any superpower conflict would be carried out in the shadow of mutual destruction and that this shadow strongly influences the prewar and, if there is any, the intrawar bargaining. Advances in technology such as more secure C^3 systems and greater precision in the guidance of bombs and warheads—developments that have long been predicted but which seem slow to materialize—will not have a revolutionary effect because they cannot counteract the effect of mutual vulnerability.

The importance of vulnerability is linked to that of escalation, which

---

Reexamining the Conventional Wisdom, Policy Papers in International Affairs no. 19 (Berkeley: University of California at Berkeley, Institute of International Studes, 1983).

12. The relevant literature, starting with Bernard Brodie et al., *The Absolute Weapon* (New York: Harcourt, Brace, 1946), is large and familiar.

cannot be controlled by a state's having a military advantage over its adversary. In earlier eras, states were able to win limited wars primarily because by gaining the upper hand they were able to continue the conflict at reasonable cost. But today, remaining ahead of the adversary in terms of various indicators of military power and multiple options cannot take the state's civilization out of hostage: the side that is "behind" can bring pressure to bear on the side that is "ahead" as easily as the latter can do so to the former. A degree of military flexibility may be necessary to permit the state to fight a limited war, but winning it is neither necessary nor sufficient for deterrence or successful war termination. As Schelling puts it, "Being able to lose a local war in a dangerous and provocative manner may make the risk—not the sure consequences, but the possibility of this act—outweigh the apparent gains to the other side."[13] Thus the frequent arguments that because limited wars are possible MAD does not exist as a situation and is inadequate as a policy simply miss the point of MAD-4.

If escalation is neither impossible nor certain, deterrence by denial at lower levels of violence is neither necessary nor terribly helpful. That a limited war might—but might not—spread seems like mere common sense. The situations under consideration are unprecedented and it is difficult to see how certainty could be possible. But the implications are extremely important: the fact that escalation is possible enhances deterrence, permits the use of risky bargaining tactics, and undercuts the importance of military advantage. In a world of certainty, statesmen could not credibly threaten or rationally carry out actions that they believed would surely lead to all-out war. Either no violence would be possible (if it were believed that any conflict would trigger the holocaust) or the outcome would be determined by whoever was stronger at the level of violence just below the threshold that each side realized could not be crossed. Similarly, if escalation to all-out war were somehow impossible, mutual vulnerability would not influence the outcome. Under either of these conditions, each side's second-strike capability would hold in check and nullify the other's, as both McNamara and the critics of MAD-1, 2, and 3 argue. Decisions on whether to launch a limited war—for example, a conventional attack on Europe or even a nuclear strike against American strategic forces—would be made on the basis of the expected gains and costs of such a move itself.

---

13. Thomas Schelling, *Arms and Influence* (New Haven: Yale University Press, 1966), pp. 104–5. For a detailed discussion of why a state could escalate even though doing so would not reverse the military balance, see Robert Jervis, *The Illogic of American Nuclear Strategy* (Ithaca: Cornell University Press, 1984) pp. 132–37.

If the Soviets believed that they could win such a limited conflict at reasonable cost, they might attack.

But the world does not fit either of these models. On the one hand, decision makers do not see a clear line that, once crossed, would definitely produce total war. Thus the threat to use limited violence has at least some credibility; implementing it is not tantamount to committing mutual suicide. On the other hand, decision makers could not be sure that escalation would not occur. Since actions like fighting a conventional war or using a few nuclear weapons might lead to uncontrolled violence through processes discussed below, the threat to take such actions would be effective if the other side was not willing to accept the risk. Escalation is seen sometimes as an unintended consequence of action that undermines the state's ability to manage violence and sometimes as what the state can threaten to do if its interests are being destroyed at lower levels of fighting.[14] The probabilistic nature of the expansion of violence means that it partakes of both these meanings. Measured escalation can be credible because the threatened step might be the last one; it carries weight far beyond the immediate effects because it can ultimately result in what is most feared.

The ability to win a local war cannot be translated into the ability to fight it safely and therefore cannot provide a firm foundation for either deterrence or coercion. Compare this argument to the analysis by a recent presidential commission: "The outcome of [a Soviet invasion of the Persian Gulf] would probably be determined by air, land, and sea battles, while the nuclear threat would remain in the background, functioning as a distant monitor and reminder to both sides of the need for restraint."[15] The commission's statement would be true only if both sides were confident that the violence could in fact be kept limited while they fought to a finish in the Gulf, as Bernard Brodie noted fifteen years ago.[16] But when escalation is a real possibility, gaining an advantage on the local battlefield is of only limited significance. Of

14. For an excellent discussion of the evolution of the concept of escalation, see Lawrence Freedman, "On the Tiger's Back: The Development of the Concept of Escalation," in Roman Kolkowicz, ed., *The Logic of Nuclear Terror* (Boston: Allen & Unwin, 1987), pp. 109–54. Good discussions of alternative meanings of the concept of escalation are Fred Iklé, "When the Fighting Has to Stop: The Arguments about Escalation," *World Politics*, 19 (July 1967), 692–707; Richard Smoke, *War: Controlling Escalation* (Cambridge: Harvard University Press, 1977), pp. 36–45, and Herman Kahn, *On Escalation: Metaphors and Scenarios*, rev. ed. (Baltimore: Penguin Books, 1968), pp. 275–300.

15. President's Commission on Integrated Long-Term Strategy, *Discriminate Deterrence*, Report (Washington, D.C.: Government Printing Office, 1987), p. 23; a better formulation is presented on p. 26.

16. Bernard Brodie, *War and Politics* (New York: Macmillan, 1973), pp. 412–16.

course the fear that the violence will expand will weigh on both sides. But even if it is felt equally by both, the restraint that the commission notes may be great enough substantially to influence the course of the fighting. Furthermore, in the more likely eventuality that fear is not equally distributed, the side with greater resolve will have an important bargaining advantage.

Two Kinds of Escalation

Escalation can occur either as the result of an unintended explosion to all-out war or in a controlled manner, as one side intensifies the violence to bring pressure to bear on the other.[17] In the former process, neither side desires escalation; in the latter at least one does. The choice of the latter path rests on the improbability of the former; fear of the former precludes the latter. The prime factors in controlled escalation are the willingness of each side to bear pain and its judgments of the other side's willingness to do so. Where fear of explosion dominates, risk rather than cost is wagered. As the confrontation continues, neither side's losses are overwhelming, but each risks total destruction.[18] The determinants of resolve and the bargaining tactics employed can be somewhat different in the two cases, but the essentials are parallel.

Explosions By definition, no one seeks an explosion to total destruction. But it could occur if events got out of hand. Furthermore, states can exploit the fear of such an outcome through what Schelling has called "the threat that leaves something to chance," which makes the "connection between the strategic background and the local foreground."[19] It is often argued that putting forces on alert, engaging in limited violence, or using a small number of nuclear weapons will be ineffective—"mere signaling,"as it is sometimes put—unless it strongly influences the military situation. This argument not only underestimates the importance of communication in crises but ignores the way

17. Morton Halperin, *Limited War in the Nuclear Age* (New York: Wiley, 1963). Also see Phil Williams, *Crisis Management* (New York: Wiley, 1976), p. 149.

18. As Robert Powell has shown in "The Theoretical Foundations of Strategic Nuclear Deterrence," *Political Science Quarterly*, 100 (Spring 1985), 75–96, fear of escalation and willingness to bear costs are different. While this difference can be significant for many questions, it is not of concern here.

19. Thomas Schelling to Bernard Brodie, February 22, 1965, quoted in Marc Trachtenberg, "Strategic Thought in America, 1952–1966," *Political Science Quarterly* (forthcoming). Also see Schelling, "Nuclear Strategy in Europe," *World Politics*, 14 (April 1962), 421–32. Given the costs of an all-out war, it seems unlikely that any explosion would occur if the actors are perfectly rational. See Chapter 5 below.

in which the use and even the mobilization of military forces increase the danger of undesired escalation. When an army is put in motion, the other side has to be concerned not only with the evidence that this provides about the state's willingness to stand firm, but with the risk that, as Kennedy put it to Khrushchev immediately after the climax of the Cuban missile crisis, "developments [are] approaching a point where events could . . . become unmanageable."[20] Indeed it was this fear—"the smell of scorching in the air"—that probably drove Khrushchev to pull back in October 1962.[21] As he put it at the time:

> If you have not lost command of yourself and realize clearly what this could lead to, then, Mr. President, you and I should not now pull on the ends of the rope in which you have tied a knot of war, because the harder you and I pull, the tighter this knot will become. And a time may come when this knot is tied so tight that the person who tied it is no longer capable of untying it, and then the knot will have to be cut. What that would mean I need not explain to you, because you yourself understand perfectly what dread forces our two countries possess.[22]

It was also this fear—more than expectations of when the missiles would become operational—that led Kennedy to press for a speedy conclusion to the crisis. Especially after the shooting down of the U-2 over Cuba, he felt that the chances of the situation's escaping control were so great that it could not be allowed to continue.[23] According to

20. "Message in Reply to a Broadcast by Chairman Khrushchev on the Cuban Crises," in *Public Papers of the Presidents, John F. Kennedy, 1962* (Washington, D.C.: Government Printing Office, 1963), p. 814.
21. Nikita Khrushchev, "The Present International Situation and the Foreign Policy of the Soviet Union," *Current Digest of the Soviet Press*, 14 (January 16, 1963), 7.
22. *Department of State Bulletin*, 69 (November 19, 1973), 645. In his memoirs, Khrushchev reported being especially alarmed because Robert Kennedy had told Ambassador Dobrynin that because the U.S. military was getting out of control "an irreversible chain of events could occur against [the president's] will" (*Khrushchev Remembers*, trans. and ed. Strobe Talbott [Boston: Little Brown, 1970], pp. 497–98). Robert Kennedy more plausibly says he stressed that the situation, not the military, was getting out of control (*Thirteen Days* (New York: Norton, 1971], pp. 42–50), but irrespective of the exact mechanism Khrushchev worried most about, the effect was the same.
23. Alexander George, David Hall, and William Simons, *The Limits of Coercive Diplomacy* (Boston: Little Brown, 1971), pp. 124–26; McGeorge Bundy, *Danger and Survival* (New York: Random House, 1988), chap. 9. The transcript of the Ex Comm meeting at the climax of the crisis reveals a great sense of urgency but not the exact causes of that sense: McGeorge Bundy, transcriber, and James Blight, ed., "October 27, 1962: Transcripts of the Meetings of the ExComm," *International Security*, 12 (Winter 1987–88), 30–92. Indeed, it is doubtful if the participants were able to distinguish among different

Arthur Schlesinger, Kennedy's sense of urgency was "based on fear, not of Khrushchev's intention, but of human error, of something going terribly wrong down the line."[24] Interestingly enough, this dynamic was not anticipated at the start. In his speech announcing the Soviet deployment and the American response, Kennedy said the crisis could last for months, and in the next days American decision makers seemed prepared for prolonged bargaining. But as the pace of events quickened, complexities grew, and the participants became increasingly exhausted, they came to feel that the confrontation simply had to be brought to a head. Those who felt that the United States should have sought additional gains by maintaining if not increasing the pressure believed that people like McNamara who opposed continuing the crisis overestimated these dangers because of their lack of experience.[25] Although I do not think this attribution is correct, it does support the argument that a large part of the difference between the conflicting views about force and nuclear strategy is to be explained by differing beliefs—often implicit—about whether tense situations can readily be kept under control.[26]

We should not believe that the Cuban and later experiences have enabled us to avoid the dangers of the unintended results of putting force into motion. The lastest incident was on July 3, 1988, when an American cruiser shot down an Iranian airliner in the Persian Gulf because of a series of errors on the part of the former's crew, including misreading the airline schedule, the radar scope, and transponder signals. Even though the cruiser's equipment apparently was working flawlessly, the crew's tensions, fears, and expectations led them to see an attack when none was under way.[27] It also appears that the Iranians could not believe that the American action was inadvertent. Indeed, one reason why they agreed to a truce with Iraq shortly thereafter was the belief that if the United States was cruel and desperate enough to destroy an airliner, it might stage even bloodier interventions if the war continued. But in other cases the result could be increased violence.

---

possible specific causes of anxiety. See McNamara's remarks in James Blight and David Welch, *On the Brink: Americans and Soviets Reexamine the Cuban Missile Crisis* (New York: Farrar, Straus & Giroux, forthcoming), chap. 3.

24. Arthur Schlesinger, Jr., *Robert F. Kennedy and His Times* (Boston: Houghton Mifflin, 1978), p. 529.

25. See Douglas Dillon's remarks in Blight and Welch, *On the Brink*, chap. 3.

26. Robert Jervis, "Why Nuclear Superiority Doesn't Matter," *Political Science Quarterly*, 94 (Winter 1979–80), 618–22.

27. Bernard Trainor, "Errors by a Tense U.S. Crew Led to Downing of Iran Jet, Inquiry Is Reported to Find," *New York Times*, August 3, 1988.

Schelling's explanation of the dynamics involved and why they are so powerful, quoted in chapter 1, is important enough to merit repetition here:

The idea . . . that a country cannot plausibly threaten to engage in a general war over anything but a mortal assault on itself unless it has an appreciable capacity to blunt the other side's attack seems to depend on the clean-cut notion that war results—or is expected to result—only from a deliberate yes-no decision. But if war tends to result from a . . . process in which both sides get more and more deeply involved, more and more expectant, more and more concerned not to be a slow second in case the war starts, it is not a "credible first strike" that one threatens, but just plain war. The Soviet Union can indeed threaten us with war: they can even threaten us with a war that we eventually start, by threatening to get involved with us in a process that blows up into war. . . . Any situation that scares one side will scare both sides with the danger of a war that neither wants, and both will have to pick their way carefully through the crisis, never quite sure that the other knows how to avoid stumbling over the brink.[28]

Any action that generates these pressures will of course be dangerous. In some cases, creating risk can be the explicit purpose of the behavior. In others, it is simply the by-product of resisting the adversary's moves. But the state that wants to resist has no choice but to enter into a contest of willingness to run risks, even though it will simultaneously seek to keep them under control. Thus there is often a trade-off between the requirements of crisis bargaining and those of crisis management.[29] The former seeks to maximize pressure on the adversary and so needs to create a significant chance that things will

28. Schelling, *Arms and Influence*, pp. 89–99. Also see Schelling, *The Strategy of Conflict* (Cambridge: Harvard University Press, 1960), pp. 187–203. For further discussion, see Jervis, *Illogic of American Nuclear Strategy*, pp. 126–46. These dynamics are not new: in earlier eras diplomats often said that even though they were not commited to fight in a certain eventuality, events might draw them in because once shooting began, it was difficult to predict the level to which violence would rise or the number of participants who would join. The use of nuclear weapons is especially likely to threaten control because the tempo of war would be rapid, the situation would be novel and complex, and the pressures would be unprecedented. But the dangers arise with the use of threat of other kinds of force and indeed with the use of economic instruments of power; see David Baldwin, *Economic Statecraft* (Princeton: Princeton University Press, 1985), pp. 111–14.
29. George, Hall, and Simons, *Limits of Coercive Diplomacy* , pp. 125–33.

get out of control; the latter seeks to keep these risks to a minimum. But even crisis management, if it is not to abandon all goals other than avoiding immediate war, must involve some dangers.

In many cases, merely being willing to engage in a confrontation will meet this requirement. As King Victor Emanuel of Italy put it when the German gunboat *Panther* sailed into the harbor at Agadir in 1911, leading to the second Moroccan Crisis: "on such occasions canons have a way of going off on their own."[30] What Clausewitz said about war can be extended to severe crises in the modern era: "War is the realm of chance. No other human activity gives it greater scope." "Everything in war is very simple, but the simplest thing is difficult."[31] The Cuban missile crisis again provides an illustration. The proponents of an air strike argued that while the blockade could prevent additional missiles from entering the country, it could not remove those that were there. While this is only common sense—the ships could not drive up on dry land—the argument overlooked the fact that the blockade was dangerous and therefore generated pressures that could—and did—persuade the Soviets to withdraw.

The course of the crisis demonstrated the power and the mechanisms of risk. While both sides went to extraordinary efforts to try to keep the situation under control, neither could be completely confident that they would succeed. President Kennedy sought to supervise even the small details of the way his policy was being implemented, but such efforts could not prevent all untoward incidents, such as the U-2 that strayed over the Soviet Union during the height of the crisis, the navy's harassment of Soviet submarines, covert actions by the CIA-trained exiles, or the SAC commander's unauthorized and unreported decision to send an alerting message to his forces not in the normal encoded form, but "in the clear," which could have been much more provocative.[32] Kennedy understood this pattern. As he put it after the U-2 incident: "There is always some so-and-so [carrying out the policy] who doesn't get the word."[33] It is not surprising that Robert McNamara,

---

30. Quoted in Holger Herwig, *Germany's Vision of Empire in Venezuela, 1871–1914*, (Princeton: Princeton University Press, 1986), p. 231.

31. Carl von Clausewitz, *On War*, ed. and trans. Michael Howard and Peter Paret (Princeton: Princeton University Press, 1976), pp. 101, 119; also see p. 85. A thorough discussion is in Richard Ned Lebow, "Clausewitz and Crisis Stability," *Political Science Quarterly*, 103 (Spring 1988), 81–110.

32. For the latter incidents, see Raymond Garthoff, *Reflections on the Cuban Missile Crisis* (Washington, D.C.: Brookings Institution, 1987), pp. 38 and 78. The navy also engaged in unauthorized harassment of Soviet submarines in a May 1972 incident off Cuba (ibid., pp. 101–2).

33. Quoted in Roger Hilsman, *To Move a Nation* (Garden City, N.Y.: Doubleday, 1964),

having witnessed these events, argues that the most important lesson of the crisis is "McNamara's Law": "It is impossible to predict with a high degree of confidence what effects of the use of military force will be because of the risks of accident, miscalculation, misperception, and inadvertence."[34]

The ways by which control could be lost are numerous and it is not likely that either we or decision makers could think of all of them in advance. But we can specify three categories: control can be undermined by the decision makers' emotions, by their inability to understand what the other side (and, indeed, their own side) is doing, and by the loss of control over their own forces.

To start with the first possibility, decision makers might escalate a conflict more quickly and more violently than rational analysis would suggest is appropriate. When under great pressure, individuals do sometimes commit suicide. Less extreme emotionally based behavior is also possible and dangerous. Today's newspaper carries the following story:

> A pedestrian was stabbed to death on 42nd Street in Manhattan yesterday morning after he accosted a motorist whose van may have grazed him as he tried to cross the intersection. . . . Mr. Louzader was in the middle of the street when a . . . man made a left turn and either grazed him or nearly struck him. Mr. Louzader slapped the van with his hand and yelled at the driver, the police said, and the driver pulled over and got out. Witnesses said the two men exchanged words and the driver punched Mr. Louzader,

---

p. 221. For the interesting memories of SAC leaders' reactions to this incident, see Richard Kohn and Joseph Harahan, eds., "U.S. Strategic Air Power, 1948–1962: Excerpts from an Interview with Generals Curtis E. LeMay, Leon W. Johnson, David A. Burchinal, and Jack L. Catton," *International Security*, 12 (Spring 1988), 95. Luck may have prevented a more serious incident of this kind: "a member of the Ex Comm in his other duties by chance became aware of another routine operation that should have been reconsidered under crisis conditions. A U.S. intelligence-gathering ship for intercepting communications was perilously close to Cuban waters. No one had remembered it until then; it was promptly ordered to move a safe distance away" (Garthoff, *Reflections on the Cuban Missile Crisis*, pp. 56–57.)

34. Quoted in James Blight, Joseph Nye, Jr., and David Welch, "The Cuban Missile Crisis Revisited," *Foreign Affairs*, 66 (Fall 1987), p. 186. Albert Wohlstetter makes a similar remark: "No substantial conflict, nuclear or non-nuclear, is likely to be neat and perfectly controlled. . . . There will always be a substantial chance that violence would climb disastrously beyond any expected bound" ("Swords without Shields," *National Interest*, no. 8 [Summer 1983], 39). This sensible understanding of crises undercuts many of McNamara's arguments about the lack of utility of nuclear weapons and Wohlstetter's arguments for the utility of nuclear options.

who punched back. The driver then pulled a knife and stabbed the victim. . . . "It looks like it just got out of hand," [the police captain] said.[35]

A different kind of emotional arousal explains how the pilot of an F-14 could shoot down another airplane during maneuvers instead of merely simulating the attack, as he was supposed to. As the official report noted, this was "an illogical act."[36]

Of course states are not individuals, statesmen are socialized to keep control of their emotions, and high emotions do not automatically lead to violence. Fear, in particular, can produce restraint as well as lashing out. Indeed it is probably impossible to identify a single war that was unambiguously caused by this sort of loss of control. But a limited war that could end in the destruction of civilization would put unprecedented strain on people's emotions. In more ordinary crises the pressures are sufficiently great to lower the quality of decision making, and in a crisis a number of psychological mechanisms could lead statesmen to overestimate the inevitability of war or the advantages of going first, thus encouraging a preemptive strike.[37] Furthermore, a statesman can act rationally on the basis of the facts as he believes them, but psychological biases may operate to distort his information processing. For example, people are slow to alter incorrect beliefs in the face of discrepant information; historical analogies are applied promiscuously; subtle—and not so subtle—signals rarely are interpreted as the sender intends; and a person who has become committed to a particular course of action may underestimate its risks and overestimate its chances of suc-

35. Todd Purdum, "Man Slain by Motorist in Midtown," *New York Times*, April 29, 1987.
36. "Pilot Faulted for Downing Jet," *New York Times*, September 16, 1988.
37. For summaries of the relevant literature on psychological pressures and decision making, see Ole Holsti and Alexander George, "The Effects of Stress on the Performace of Foreign Policy-Makers," in Cornelius Cotter, ed., *Political Science Annual*, vol. 6, 1975 (Indianapolis: Bobbs-Merrill, 1975), pp. 255–319; Alexander George, "The Impact of Crisis-Induced Stress on Decision Making," in Fredric Solomon and Robert Marston, eds., *The Medical Implications of Nuclear War* (Washington, D.C.: National Academy Press, 1986), pp. 529–52; Ole Holsti, "Theories of Crisis Decision Making," in Paul Gordon Lauren, *Diplomacy* (New York: Free Press, 1979), pp. 99–136; Holsti, "Crisis Decision-Making," in Philip Tetlock et al., eds., *Behavior, Society, and Nuclear War*, vol. 1 (New York: Oxford University Press, forthcoming). The psychological literature is summarized in Richard Lazarus, *Psychological Stress and the Coping Process* (New York: McGraw-Hill, 1966). For a further discussion of factors leading to overzealousness, see Chapter 5 below.

cess.[38] While these effects do not constitute loss of calculated control in the same way that overpowering emotion does, they are ways in which people's behavior is driven by forces they do not recognize, which do not fit with most conceptions of rationality, and which could produce a war that both sides wanted to avoid.

Even if decision makers remained in full control of their cognitive faculties and emotions, it is far from certain that they would be able to understand what was happening well enough to maintain control of the conflict. The situation inevitably would be very confused and ambiguous and, even if all the command, control, communications and intelligence (C³I) systems were working adequately, it could be difficult for statesmen to comprehend the course of events. Even before force was used, too much would be happening for the decision maker to be fully informed. Thus only much later was it discovered that, by coincidence, the Jupiter missiles were turned over to Turkey (the warheads remained in American control) on the very day that Kennedy announced the blockade of Cuba.[39] American decision makers were similarly unaware of the fact that during the negotiations over whether the Soviets would remove the IL-28 bombers as well as the missiles, "a Cuban covert action team dispatched from the United States successfully blew up a Cuban industrial facility."[40] In wartime it would be still more likely that, not knowing what the situation was, decision makers' actions would erode the tacit bargains required to keep the conflict limited. Statesmen do not understand what their state's armed forces do when they go on alert.[41] They have little sense for what the "rules of engagement" authorize their military to do in specific situations, and it is not likely that they would know exactly what had transpired in a limited war. Technical advances may not have reduced, and certainly have not eliminated, the "fog of war."[42] It is crucial but

38. Richard Ned Lebow, *Between Peace and War* (Baltimore: Johns Hopkins University Press, 1981); Jack Snyder, *The Ideology of the Offensive* (Ithaca: Cornell University Press, 1984); Robert Jervis, Richard Ned Lebow, and Janice Stein, *Psychology and Deterrence* (Baltimore: Johns Hopkins University Press, 1986); Irving Janis and Leon Mann, *Decision Making* (New York: Free Press, 1977).

39. Garthoff, *Reflections on the Cuban Missile Crisis*, p. 43.

40. Ibid., p. 78.

41. See Scott Sagan, "Nuclear Alerts and Crisis Management," *International Security*, 9 (Spring 1985), 99–139, and Bruce Blair, "Alerting in Crisis and Conventional War," in Ashton Carter, John Steinbruner, and Charles Zraket, eds., *Managing Nuclear Operations* (Washington, D.C.: Brookings Institution, 1987), pp. 75–120. For a further discussion, see Chapter 5 below.

42. See, for example, the discussion of the Israeli civilian and military leaders' misunderstanding of what was happening in the first week of the 1973 war in Martin van Creveld, *Command in War* (Cambridge: Harvard University Press, 1985), pp. 185–231.

[89]

difficult for statesmen to know where their forces are, what they have done, what damage they have sustained, and (important in this context) what restraints they have maintained. Furthermore, decision makers are as likely to be misinformed as to be uninformed, an even more dangerous situation. If they seek to maintain limits, they will usually believe that their forces are being restrained. Any undesired expansion of the violence will be attributed to the other side's actions, and indeed to the other's intentions.

Since their focus would be on the other side, statesmen might have greater factual knowledge of what it was doing. Their interpretations of this behavior probably would be distorted, however. Actors tend to see their own behavior as benign and to see the same behavior when undertaken by others as hostile. They tend to see what others do as part of a plan and fail to credit accidents, disunity, and lack of coordination. Thus the two sides could easily develop very different pictures of what was going on, with each believing that it was more restrained than its adversary. Under the most propitious conditions, these propensities can be counterbalanced or overridden. But the conditions of a limited war of unprecedented nature—and quite possibly of unprecedented ferocity—would not encourage a disinterested appreciation of both side's behavior.

The actions of third parties can further increase the chances of misinterpretation. Each superpower is likely to view local adversaries as the other's clients, if not its puppets. For example, during the Cuban missile crisis the United States underestimated Castro's independent role. In another Arab-Israeli war, the Soviet Union would be likely to view Israel's behavior as reflecting American intentions, and American decision makers would probably see Arab actions as at least having been approved if not ordered by Moscow. The result could be undesired escalation as each superpower matches the provocative behavior of the other's ally in the mistaken belief that it is responding to the other superpower.

The disturbing third parties can even be private individuals, as recent revelations about the missile crisis also remind us. The day that Kennedy announced the blockade, the Soviets arrested Colonel Penkovsky, who they had previously suspected was an American spy. What happened next could have had grave consequences. According to Raymond Garthoff, whose source was the CIA officer in charge,

---

For a discussion of possible inadvertent escalation in the Persian Gulf caused by related problems, see Joshua Epstein, *Strategy and Force Planning* (Washington, D.C.: Brookings Institution, 1987), pp. 24–27.

"Penkovsky [had been] given a few standard coded telephonic signals for use in emergencies, including one to be used if he was about to be arrested, and also one to be used in the ultimate contingency: imminent war. When he was being arrested, at his apartment, he had time to send a telephonic signal—but chose to use the signal for an imminent Soviet attack!"[43] Western intelligence officials decided that the signal had to be false and suppressed it. "Not even the higher reaches of the CIA were informed."[44] One can easily imagine a different ending to such a story. It also now appears that the famous proposal by the Russian official Aleksander Fomin that the Soviets would be willing to remove the missiles from Cuba in return for an American promise not to invade the island actually was not a Soviet probe at all, as the Americans were certain it was, but instead was his own personal initiative. This strange "Soviet" behavior and the American error helped resolve the crisis, but misinterpreted personal interventions have often produced less happy results.[45]

The discussion so far has assumed that the key decision makers are a handful of national leaders and that C³I systems would remain intact in the event of war. But these assumptions are heroic ones.[46] Even if the communication system continues to function well, limited wars require significant delegation to field commanders. This was true even in Korea and Vietnam; it would be true to a greater extent in quicker and more intense combat, which would require greater flexibility to take advantage of opportunities and to parry expected enemy thrusts. Washington and Moscow can set guidelines and retain what the leaders

43. Garthoff, *Reflections on the Cuban Missile Crisis*, p. 40.

44. Ibid., p. 41.

45. Raymond Garthoff, "The Cuban Missile Crisis: The Soviet Story," *Foreign Policy*, no. 72 (Fall 1988), 77–78. Similar misinterpretations have occurred in the past, often because agents have misrepresented themselves and the sources of their proposals. For such incidents in Japanese-American relations before World War II, see Robert Butow, *The John Doe Associates* (Stanford: Stanford University Press, 1974), passim; for similar problems in Anglo-German relations about the turn of the century, see J. A. S. Grenville, *Lord Salisbury and Foreign Policy* (London: Athlone Press, 1964), pp. 175, 355–69, and George Monger, *The End of Isolation* (London: Nelson and Sons, 1963), p. 32.

46. See Desmond Ball, *Can Nuclear War Be Controlled?* Adelphi Paper no. 169 (London: International Institute for Strategic Studes, 1981); Congressional Budget Office, *Strategic Command, Control, and Communications: Alternative Approaches for Modernization* (Washington, D.C.: Congress of the United States, 1981); Frank Klotz, "The U.S. President and the Control of Strategic Nuclear Weapons" (Ph.D. diss., Oxford University, 1980); John Steinbruner, "Launch under Attack," *Scientific American*, January 1984, pp. 37–47; Bruce Blair, *Strategic Command and Control* (Washington, D.C.: Brookings Institution, 1985); Carter, Steinbruner, and Zraket, *Managing Nuclear Operations*. A good discussion of NATO command systems can be found in Paul Bracken, *The Command and Control of Nuclear Forces* (New Haven: Yale University Press, 1983).

think are the critical decisions, but even if the military commanders try to act as they think their civilian superiors would want them to, their perspectives will be different. Commanders will feel strong pressures to use all weapons at their disposal, to take the initiative, and to hit the enemy hard before the enemy can do the same to them. Furthermore, anything that increases the number of individuals who can initiate the use of greater force increases the chance of escalation. For example, Soviet officials have recently acknowledged that the decision to shoot down the American U-2 over Cuba was made, not at the highest levels in Moscow, but by the military on the scene.[47] At the time this possibility never crossed the Americans' minds. Indeed, "Washington reasoned, the Soviets must have realized that shooting down U-2s would force the United States to take direct action against the SAMs, and their action therefore seemed to mean that they had decided on a showdown."[48] Ironically, the result turned out for the best: convinced that the crisis was escaping control, Kennedy brought it to a head by giving the Soviets something very much like an ultimatum, which in turn led to an agreement. But the shooting could easily have produced further violence and unpredictable consequences. Indeed, Kennedy had previously decided that if American reconnaissance planes were fired upon, the United States would bomb the antiaircraft sites. He finally decided not to do so, but only at the last minute remembered to convey the new orders to the air force, which was about to carry out the preplanned strike.[49]

In a crisis, and even more in a war, these problems would be com-

47. Richard Bernstein, "Meeting Sheds New Light on Cuban Missile Crisis," *New York Times*, October 14, 1987. Alexander George noted this possibility years ago (George, Hall, and Simons, *Limits of Coercive Diplomacy*, p. 124).

48. Hilsman, *To Move a Nation*, p. 220. At one point during the NSC deliberations, Vice-President Lyndon Johnson said, "You could have an undisciplined anti-aircraft—Cuban anti-aircraft fire, but to have a SAM-site and a Russian crew fire is not an accident." Later, however, he mused on the reconnaissance flights: "I've been afraid of these damned flyers ever since they mentioned them. Just an ordinary plane goin' in there at two or three hundred feet without arms or an announcement. . . . Imagine some crazy Russian captain. . . . He might just pull a trigger. Looks like we're playing Fourth of July over there or something. I'm scared of that, and I don't see—I don't see what you get for that photograph that's so much more important than what you—you know they're working at night; you see them working at night. Now what do you do? Psychologically you scare them. Well, Hell, it's like the fellow telling me in Congress, 'Go on and put the monkey on his back.' Every time I tried to put a monkey on somebody else's back I *got* one. If you're going to try to psychologically scare them with a flare you're liable to get your bottom shot at" (Bundy and Blight, "October 27, 1962: Transcripts," pp. 71, 80).

49. Garthoff, *Reflections on the Cuban Missile Crisis*, pp. 62–63, and interviews with members of the Kennedy administration.

pounded because C³I systems would degrade, thus further reducing the decision makers' ability to tell what is happening and to maintain control of military forces. As information from the field becomes even more clouded, the room for misleading inferences of the kind discussed earlier grows. And as the links to the field loosen, the scope for local decisions increases. Of course we cannot be sure what military commanders would do if and when they lost contact with higher authorities, but there is clearly a chance—and probably a large one—that the result would be much greater escalation than was desired by either side's leaders.

Furthermore, decision makers' anticipation that they would lose the ability to fight a war in a coordinated manner could lead them to escalate while they could still do so effectively. Compounding this, the expectation that the same pressures were operating on the other side could lead them to preempt. These processes could be accelerated if a limited war began to degrade the systems essential for fighting at a higher level of violence. Barry Posen has shown how a conventional war on the northern flank of Europe would have this effect and there is no reason to believe that this geographical area is unique.[50] Limited attacks on strategic C³ systems would in all likelihood produce even stronger reasons to escalate. The pressures on the state to relax the limits on its endangered systems while they could still be used would be great, especially if, as is likely to be the case, each side sees the other's actions as an attempt to gain unilateral advantage.

Any war in Europe would also have to cope with British and French nuclear forces. At the start of the American policy of limited nuclear options, Secretary of Defense McNamara pointed out the incompatibility between this approach and independent national nuclear forces, but the failure of his efforts to control the latter have not led to an abandonment of the former. Instead, almost without exception, analysts and government officials have adopted the somewhat academic approach of assuming away the allied forces. But even though the targeting of British, and perhaps French, weapons is coordinated with the Americans, it is far from certain that American restraints in wartime would be matched by its allies or that the Soviets would anticipate such behavior. The Soviets would surely be tempted to strike the allied forces, and the fear of this outcome would feed the latter's hesitancy to hold back. These forces are too small to be used effectively for counterforce. But it would not take many

50. Barry Posen, "Inadvertent Nuclear War? Escalation and NATO's Northern Flank," *International Security*, 7 (Fall 1982), 28–54.

[93]

bombs on Moscow to produce an explosion; indeed the French justified building their weapons in part in terms of their function as a "detonator."[51]

In summary, the limited use of force can easily get out of hand. As a menacing policy is implemented by the state's agents and interpreted by its adversary, it can produce effects very different from those desired and expected by its architects. Most American and Soviet decision makers, furthermore, are well aware of these ominous possibilities. The result can be to enhance deterrence. A state can credibly threaten to take actions that might result in unwanted escalation because escalation is not certain. An adversary can find this prospect sufficiently daunting that it will retreat or refrain from a challenge even if it has sufficient military force to be able to prevail at reasonable cost if the war is kept limited.

Controlled Escalation The explosive processes discussed so far can be contrasted with the possibility of a more controlled, step-by-step, escalation. Indeed, if the violence stayed at the same level rather than increasing, the result would still be a form of escalation because the damage would be cumulative. Indeed, states could destroy each other piecemeal in a process that had no upper limit. Each side could believe that with the infliction of a bit more pain and the running of a bit more risk, the other side would back down. The relevant model is the dollar bill auction in which players have to forfeit their last bid whether they win or not and so the value of what is at stake does not set a ceiling on how much they might pay.[52] Thus even a purely rational decision maker could participate in a cycle of destruction and counter-destruction.

The pressures for such escalation would be increased by two factors relating to losses the states had already suffered. First, people often try to recoup sunk costs even if rationality dictates ignoring them. Suffering in vain is not easily accepted.[53] Second, sunk costs have

---

51. For discussions of British and French targeting, see the chapters by Lawrence Freedman and David Yost in Desmond Ball and Jeffrey Richelson, eds., *Strategic Nuclear Targeting* (Ithaca: Cornell University Press, 1986).

52. Martin Shubik, "The Dollar Option Game: A Paradox in Noncooperative Behavior and Escalation," *Journal of Conflict Resolution*, 15 (March 1971), 109–11; Barry O'Neill, "International Escalation and the Dollar Auction," *Journal of Conflict Resolution*, 30 (March 1986), 33–50.

53. Recent psychological research has stressed the extent to which which people will run high risks in order to try to avoid losses. See Daniel Kahneman and Amos Tversky, "Prospect Theory: An Analysis of Decision under Risk," *Econometrica*, 47 (March 1979), 263–91; Tversky and Kahneman, "The Framing of Decisions and the Psychology of

important political effects: to lose after entering the fray usually harms the state's reputation more than not having contested the issue at all. Thus many of those who favored continuing the war in Vietnam agreed that the United States would have been better off had it allowed the Communists to win without any American involvement.

Limited War

MAD-1, 2, and 3 assume that nuclear war would have to be total. The critics, arguing that control is possible, point to the role of limited and protracted conflicts. MAD-4 disagrees with both these positions by building on the argument just sketched. Although escalation is not automatic, advances in technology still leave a large danger of explosion remaining. The difficulties of controlling emotions and military forces, of knowing what one's own side is doing and of correctly interpreting the other's actions, are enormous. As Martin Van Creveld's studies of wartime command have shown, technical advances do not automatically increase the ability of military leaders to direct their forces.[54] The effects of smaller warheads and more survivable C³I should not be exaggerated; we should not be too quick to assume that new developments that promise greater civilian manipulation of a war would actually work as planned. This is especially true because American— and probably Soviet—armed forces are more prepared for all-out than for limited nuclear war. As Leon Sigal argues, "limited nuclear war requires organizations that have been trained for large-scale retaliation or preemption to conduct nuclear strikes with pinpoint accuracy and minimum collateral damage. . . . These organizations are not likely to."[55] At the very best, enormous uncertainties would remain: it is almost inconceivable that either superpower could be confident that control would be maintained. From this it follows that the United States and USSR will be extremely reluctant to resort to a limited war and that, if they do, the fear of mutually undesired escalation to all-out violence will never be far from their minds.

Furthermore, the risks of explosion are especially great if the war is counterforce. In such a conflict C³I systems would be such lucrative

---

Choice," *Science*, January 30, 1981, 453–58; Kahneman and Tversky, "Choices, Values, and Frames," *American Psychologist*, 39 (April 1984), 341–50; Tversky and Kahneman, "Rational Choice and the Framing of Decisions," *Journal of Business*, 59 (October 1986), S251–78.

54. Van Creveld, *Command in War*.

55. Leon Sigal, *Fighting to a Finish: The Politics of War Termination in the United States and Japan, 1945* (Ithaca: Cornell University Press, 1988), p. 299.

targets that it is highly unlikely that they would remain immune; it is equally unlikely that restraint could be maintained once they were attacked. Even nuclear war at sea, once believed to be an arena in which war could be controlled, on closer examination appears to be highly prone to escalation.[56]

MAD-4 is further supported by the fact that if technology reduced the danger of explosions, the superpower that wanted to bring pressure to bear on the other could engage in still riskier operations—for example, selected attacks against C^3I facilities—that previously would have been prohibitively dangerous. Creating a situation in which total war can result although neither side wants it is an important tool of statecraft in an era in which military victory is impossible. Technology cannot remove this option. Just as improving the brakes on a car would not make playing Chicken safer, but only would allow the players—and indeed force them—to drive faster in order to produce the same level of intimidation, so raising the threshold below which an explosion would not occur could lead both sides to adjust their behavior to produce the desired level of danger in order to prevail.[57]

We should also realize that any reduction in the danger of explosion would increase the possibility of wars in which each side destroyed each other's values piecemeal. Schelling has likened this kind of war to the way rich men in nineteenth-century San Francisco reportedly settled their rivalries: each threw gold coins into the bay one by one and the loser was the one who could not bear the loss and so withdrew.[58] In the same way, limited wars need not be counterforce; states could selectively attack each other's cities or other sources of value. Again, such a war strains the imagination. But to the extent that nuclear war could be controlled, such unprecedented ways of waging it would become possible.

The point is that while the capability of limiting a war might alter the balance between the two kinds of escalation, it would leave unchanged the ability of each side to destroy the other. This ability, furthermore, is not altered by gaining or denying the other side a military advantage in the limited war. With victory at the highest levels

56. Desmond Ball, "Nuclear War at Sea," *International Security*, 10 (Winter 1985–86), 3–31.

57. For a rigorous analysis along similar lines, see Barry Nalebuff, "Brinkmanship and Deterrence: The Neutrality of Escalation," *Conflict Management and Peace Science*, 9 (Spring 1986), 19–30.

58. Schelling, "Comment," in Klaus Knorr and Thorton Read, eds., *Limited Strategic War* (New York: Praeger, 1962), pp. 241–58. Also see Schelling, "Nuclear Strategy in Europe," pp. 428–31.

of violence impossible, the capability to win at lower levels is neither necessary nor sufficient for deterrence. For example, in a conventional war in Europe or in a counterforce nuclear war, the state that was falling behind would have the option of attacking the other's values. Indeed, a state that is desperate—because its ally is losing territory, because it fears the war cannot be controlled much longer, or because its military force is becoming degraded—has strong incentives to escalate and try to end the war on decent terms because the alternative to doing so is bleak. Thus even if the United States lacked the ability to contain Soviet threats at lower levels of violence, the USSR could not be confident that it could wage war without courting destruction. On the other hand, even if the United States was able to meet limited thrusts on their own terms, it would not be protected against Soviet threats to destroy American cities. To fight the Soviets anywhere in the globe is to risk the destruction of American society: limited options that would be militarily effective do not automatically provide the basis for credible threats.

But the danger of escalation does not mean that nuclear weapons lack utility, as is so often claimed. A recent presidential commission argued that MAD asserts that "nuclear weapons [are] inherently unusable," but Brodie much earlier correctly stressed their "utility in non-use."[59] The danger of nuclear war has far-reaching effects. It is the details of the nuclear balance and the presence or absence of limited counterforce options, not nuclear weapons themselves, that fail to influence foreign policy.

We are misled by the normal formulation of the question, Can the United States credibly threaten to resort to all-out war if the Soviets attack its allies? What more accurately captures the dynamics of international politics is the question, Could the Soviet Union be so confident that a war could be kept limited that it would start one? A negative answer to the first question does not imply a positive answer to the second one, and so is largely irrelevant. What Schelling argued twenty years ago is still true: "The credibility of a massive American response [to a Soviet invasion of Europe] is often depreciated [because the U.S. would be foolish to engage in] anything as 'suicidal' as general war. But this is a simple-minded notion of what makes general war credible. What can make it exceedingly credible to the Russians . . . is that the triggering of a general war can occur whether we intend it or not."[60]

59. President's Commission, *Discriminate Deterrence*, p. 35; Brodie, *War and Politics*, chap. 9.
60. Schelling, "Nuclear Strategy in Europe," p. 422, emphasis omitted. Also see

As long as statesmen doubt that they can control the course of a crisis or, even more, the direct clash of Soviet and American arms, they will not find it easy to translate military advantages into political leverage. Thus second-strike capability can protect Europe and the Persian Gulf because the Soviets realize that even a conventional, let alone a nuclear, war could easily escalate, but escalation is not so certain as to make the Soviets confident that the West would not dare use force to resist their predations.

CONDITIONS AND POLICIES

Mutual vulnerability exists and casts an enormous shadow. This condition is not subtle nor does it depend on the details of the strategic balance or targeting that may loom large to academics or war planners; such details are dwarfed in the eyes of decision makers by the danger of overwhelming destruction. The policy choice is whether or not to try to develop limited options. At the present time, neither the United States nor the USSR seems to have much faith that nuclear war or even a large-scale conventional conflict could be kept limited. Even MAD-1 is quite robust as each superpower has shown a healthy inclination to respect the other's vital interests. At least so far, the possibilities of limited use of nuclear force seem simply irrelevant to international politics.

It seems improbable that the fear of explosion to all-out war could ever be reduced enough to permit controlled countervalue contests like Schelling's rich San Fransiscans throwing coins into the Bay. Even if it could, such a transformation might not be in the American interest. While the United States would find it easier to contemplate limited nuclear options in response to Soviet aggression, the Soviets would also be able to threaten or use force in this manner. Indeed, Alexander George and Richard Smoke have noted that deterrence has failed when the Soviets have believed that they could launch a "limited probe" that would allow them to draw back if the costs and dangers proved to be too high.[61] Although it is tempting to imagine what the United States

---

Bernard Brodie, *Escalation and Nuclear Option* (Princeton: Princeton University Press, 1966).

61. Alexander George and Richard Smoke, *Deterrence in American Foreign Policy* (New York: Columbia University Press, 1974), pp. 540–47. This provides empirical support for Nathan Leites's argument that the Bolshevik operational code stresses the importance

could do with a wider range of options, it is obviously an error to neglect what the Soviet Union could do with them as well.

But MAD-4 does not claim that mutual second-strike capability excludes the possibility that limited nuclear options might permit acceptable war termination. Furthermore, nothing in MAD-4 says that only cities would be appropriate targets.[62] The function of counterforce attacks would be different from that in the past, however, because such attacks could not protect the state. The use of limited nuclear options would increase costs and risks. Even counterforce attacks would inflict pain because the military is a valued instrument of Soviet control. But this effect would probably be dwarfed by the increased risk, especially if either side believed it might lose its ability to keep the other's values in hostage.

The argument that MAD is flawed because it can threaten only an unlimited response to any Soviet aggression is incorrect. MAD-4 foresees that limited wars, even limited nuclear wars, might be possible. But more options would not reduce American vulnerability, and it is the knowledge that it would be destroyed in an all-out war rather than the lack of carefully crafted options that inhibits the United States. To show that the condition of mutual vulnerability is not the major concern, critics would have to demonstrate, not that superpower wars need not be total, but that the fear of escalation would not dominate the bargaining and war termination processes.

REBUTTALS

Two related lines of rebuttal to the arguments for MAD-4 accept the chain of reasoning developed here but argue that because others do not, the United States must adjust its policy accordingly. The first argument is that the Soviets believe that nuclear superiority is meaningful. In its crudest form, the argument says that the more that various indicators of nuclear power are in the Soviets favor, the more likely they are to undertake a range of adventures. A more subtle variant of this argument asserts that this effect would follow, not from gross

---

of maintaining control and permits even bold action under circumstances in which a safe retreat is possible. Leites, *A Study of Bolshevism* (Glencoe, Ill.: Free Press, 1953).

62. For further discussion, see Schelling, *Arms and Influence*, pp. 182–83; Robert Art, "Between Assured Destruction and Nuclear Victory: The Case for the 'MAD-plus' Posture," *Ethics*, 95 (April 1985), 514–15; and Morton Halperin, *Nuclear Fallacy* (Cambridge: Ballinger, 1987), pp. 77–79.

disparities in such factors as numbers of warheads or throwweight, but from the lack of an American ability to meet Soviet military challenges at the level of violence at which they could be launched. For several reasons, starting with the dominance of military officers rather than civilian defense intellectuals in establishing military doctrine, the Soviets deny that nuclear weapons have produced revolutionary effects. Since their framework of beliefs is what Hans Morgenthau called "conventionalized"—that is, based on and appropriate to eras in which military victory was possible—then American strategy must also be conventionalized in order to deter them.[63] If the Soviets fail to recognize that limited force between the superpowers would create a significant risk of all-out war and that limited nuclear options could destroy values piecemeal, they might believe that military advantage is crucial. In support of this analysis, it can be argued that unfavorable political trends and Soviet venturesomeness over the past fifteen years can be attributed in significant measure to the Soviet belief that they, but not the United States, possess what James Schlesinger called "implementable threats."[64]

But this argument is not convincing. First, although there is a great deal of room for dispute about the Soviets' strategy, it does not appear that even before Gorbachev they have placed much faith in limited nuclear options.[65] The Soviets might try to fight a war in Europe without using nuclear weapons, and there is some evidence that they believe that a tactical nuclear war could be kept limited to that continent, but they do not seem to think that nuclear exchanges between the homelands of the superpowers could be kept controlled.[66] While apparently they would not seek the destruction of American values as an end in itself, neither would they forgo hit-

---

63. Hans Morgenthau, "The Fallacy of Thinking Conventionally about Nuclear Weapons," in David Carlton and Carlo Schaerf, eds. *Arms Control and Technological Innovation* (New York: Wiley, 1976), pp. 256–64. Also see Morgenthau, "The Four Paradoxes of Nuclear Strategy," *American Political Science Review*, 58 (March 1964), 25–35.

64. See the sources listed in notes 6 and 7 above.

65. As Stephen Meyer puts it in analyzing a possible Soviet preemptive strike, "although this is not a spasm attack, it is hardly consistent with the rather flippant discussions of limited nuclear war one often encounters in Western writings" ("Soviet Nuclear Operations," in Carter, Steinbruner, and Zraket, eds., *Managing Nuclear Operations*, p. 512). For a different view, see Albert Wohlstetter and Richard Brody, "Continuing Control as a Requirement for Deterrence," in ibid., pp. 142–96.

66. The most thorough treatment of the Soviets launching a nonnuclear war in Europe is Michael MccGwire, *Military Objectives in Soviet Foreign Policy* (Washington, D.C.: Brookings Institution, 1987).

ting the targets dictated by military necessity in order to try to keep the war limited. In the event of war they would try to limit damage to themselves to the extent possible—which seems to be slight—by fighting as best they could, not by intrawar bargaining. As one Soviet commentator puts it: "The idea of introducing rules and games and artificial restrictions by agreements seems illusory and untenable. It is difficult to visualize that a nuclear war, unleashed, could be kept within the framework of rules and would not develop into an all-out war. In fact, such proposals are a demagogic trick."[67] Another asks, how "is it possible to set the rules of the game, say to agree not to bomb peaceful towns, to limit the power of the bombs to 10 kilotons, and use them in battlefield only, to ban all explosions except airbursts with no radioactive aftermath, etc.?"[68]

As these quotations indicate, the Soviets are fully aware of the difficulties of keeping military confrontations in control and know that the use of force can lead to unintended and unforeseen outcomes.[69]

67. Quoted in Roman Kolkowicz, "Intellectuals and the Nuclear Deterrence System," in Kolkowicz, ed., *The Logic of Nuclear Terror*, p. 31. It can be argued that such statements are only "disinformation" designed to frighten or mislead the West: see, for example, Wohlstetter, "Between an Unfree World and None," pp. 981–92. But if so, the effect would be to deprive the Soviets of the ability to coerce the West by threatening limited use.

68. Quoted in Kolkowicz, "Intellectuals and the Nuclear Deterrence System," p. 31. Also see the argument of Evgeny Velekhov and Andrei Kokoshin, quoted in Gray, *Nuclear Strategy and National Style*, p. 190, and the summary in Mary FitzGerald, "Marshal Ogarkov and the New Revolution in Soviet Military Affairs," *Defense Analysis*, 3 (March 1987), 4–7. The strongest arguments for a Soviet policy of limited nuclear options have been made by Notra Trulock III, "Soviet Perspectives on Limited Nuclear Warfare," in Fred Hoffman, Albert Wohlstetter, and David Yost, eds., *Swords and Shields; NATO, the USSR, and New Choices for Long-Range Offense and Defense* (Lexington, Mass.: Lexington Books, 1987), pp. 53–85; and "Weapons of Mass Destruction in Soviet Strategy" (paper presented at the conference on Soviet military strategy in Oxfordshire, England, September 24–25, 1984). But the evidentiary base is small, alternative explanations are ignored, and the argument is not carefully developed. Trulock relies heavily on notes summarizing a series of lectures on Soviet nuclear doctrine held at Voroshilov Academy of the General Staff in the mid-1970s, material that has only recently been made generally available. The best treatments of Soviet ideas on limited nuclear war present a more balanced treatment of this material and combine it with evidence from other sources: Edward Warner III, "Soviet Concepts and Capabilities for Limited Nuclear War: What We Know and How We Know It," and Raymond Garthoff, "Soviet Military Doctrine and the Prevention of Nuclear War," both in Cynthia Roberts, Warner Schilling, and Jack Snyder, eds., *Soviet Military Policy: Issues and Approaches* (forthcoming).

69. For a further discussion, see Benjamin Lambeth, "Uncertainties for the Soviet War Planner," *International Security*, 7 (Winter 1982–83), 139–66; also see Allen Lynch, "The Soviet Study of International Relations, 1968–82" (Ph.D. diss., Columbia University, 1984), pp. 310–26; Douglas Hart, "Soviet Approaches to Conflict Management: The

They do not publicly analyze in detail such specific factors as misperception, loss of control of military forces, and the incentives for preemption, but their conclusions do not differ from those reached here. The Soviets do not welcome mutual vulnerability and, like the United States, have devoted significant resources to trying to limit the damage that would befall them in the event of war. But they have recognized that mutual vulnerability is a fact that, if it cannot be altered, must be the basis for policy.[70]

Soviet behavior is consistent with their statements: few instances can be found in which the Soviets were bold because they believed that the United States would be restrained by its lack of nuclear options. Indeed, many of those who criticize MAD for neglecting such options also attribute Soviet adventures to American timidity caused by the Vietnam trauma. Although both factors could have been at work, if the latter was so powerful, was the former operating at all? It probably was not; at minimum, links between the state of the strategic balance and Soviet maneuvers in Africa, the invasion of Afghanistan, or the pressure on Europe in the INF controversy are difficult to detect.

A parallel reply is that if the strategic nuclear balance and limited nuclear options were crucial to the Soviets, then their behavior toward Reagan should not have differed from that toward his predecessors: the balance and the availability of options have not changed much since 1980.[71] Indeed, in 1979 Kissinger predicted that because of American nuclear weakness Soviet risk-taking "must exponentially in-

---

Military Dimension," *Survival*, 26 (September–October 1984), 214–22; and the report of Soviet attitudes in Gerard Smith, *Doubletalk* (Garden City, N.Y.: Doubleday, 1980), p. 210.

70. Even Richard Pipes acknowledges that the Soviets understand the significance of their vulnerability ("Why the Russians Think They Could Fight and Win a Nuclear War," *Commentary*, July 1977, p. 29). Furthermore, Stephen Meyer's research indicates that some Soviet measures of military effectiveness have shifted from stressing relative advantage to emphasizing absolute damage (Meyer, *Soviet Theatre Nuclear Forces*, Part 1: *Development of Doctrine and Objectives*, Adelphi Paper no. 187 [London: International Institute for Strategic Studies, 1984], pp. 34–44). I am grateful to Jack Snyder for discussion on this point.

71. Weinberger asserts the opposite: "We have to think that [the] change in [the] pattern of decreased [Soviet] activity is related to the correct perception that the United States is regaining military strength" (quoted in Brad Knickerbocker, "Weinberger on A-Weapons," *Christian Science Monitor*, October 10, 1984). But he gives no evidence and of the two examples of Soviet restraint he cites, one—Poland—is foolish and the other—Afghanistan—seems best explained by the local factors. Moreover, most of the increases in U.S. nuclear strength that he cites were projected for the future and so could hardly explain Soviet behavior in the 1980–84 period.

crease."[72] In fact, the opposite proved to be the case even before Gorbachev's succession. Several factors have been at work; domestic considerations (especially under Gorbachev) and the inutility if not disutility of the apparent previous gains in the Third World are clearly important. The essential point here, however, is that if, as many of Carter's critics argue, American security increased under Reagan, the explanation cannot lie with the military factors whose importance they stress. If the United States is in part responsible for the change, it appears that, as MAD-4 leads one to expect, what is different is the judgment of American resolve and willingness to run risks. Ronald Reagan did not add much to America's nuclear arsenal, but he did act in a more bellicose manner.

The second general counterargument to MAD-4 asserts that American rather than Soviet decision makers do not understand the implications of mutual vulnerability and therefore act on the basis of conventionalized beliefs. American leaders may ignore the uses and dangers of escalation, overlook the extent to which Soviet vulnerability provides leverage, and concomitantly fail to see that gaining military advantages in a conflict with the Soviet Union will not meet the problems posed by American vulnerability. Indeed, on some of the occasions at which the use of nuclear weapons was contemplated—for example, during the Korean War—Americans focused primarily on the direct military effectiveness of the weapons.[73] But this was before both sides had large stockpiles. On later occasions, such as during the Cuban missile crisis, fear of escalation played a large role even though the United States had superiority at every level of violence, including the highest. In the Berlin confrontation of 1958–62, President Kennedy and his advisers were more concerned about the paucity of limited nuclear options than the previous administration had been. But what is most striking is that the possibility of casualties that were extremely low by today's standards was enough to induce caution. Furthermore, the lack of options did not, in the final analysis, prevent Kennedy from running what he thought were significant risks in order to protect the city.

72. U.S. Senate, Committee on Foreign Relations, *The SALT II Treaty*, 96th Cong., 1st sess. (Washington, D.C.: Government Printing Office, 1979), pt. 3, p. 224.

73. See Rosemary Foot, *The Wrong War* (Ithaca: Cornell University Press, 1985); Foot, "Nuclear Threats and the Ending of the Korean Conflict," *International Security*, 13 (Winter 1988–89), 92–112; Roger Dingman, "From Deterrence to Compellence? The Uses of Nuclear Weapons in the Korean War, 1950–1953," *International Security*, 13 (Winter 1988–89), 50–91; Edward Keefer, "President Dwight D. Eisenhower and the End of the Korean War," *Diplomatic History*, 10 (Summer 1986), 267–89.

Interestingly enough, in the era of parity there has been only one Soviet-American conflict that might be called a crisis—the Middle-East defense alert of 1973—and in this case American decision makers did not pay much attention to the state of the nuclear balance or to the possibilities of nuclear options. Indeed, although Henry Kissinger had endorsed the notion that only militarily meaningful threats could be useful, when he had to act in this situation he chose not to follow his theory—for example, by preparing to shoot down Soviet planes—but instead called a nuclear alert, which was just the sort of gesture that MAD-4 would expect and call for but which Kissinger's abstract views had implied would be feckless.

The supposedly adverse state of the nuclear balance and the lack of nuclear options similarly cannot account for the American restraint in the mid-1970s. Indeed, neither can a lack of conventional strength. The United States had the military force to interdict Soviet flights into Angola and Ethiopia. It did not use it because it was unwilling to create a confrontation that seemed more dangerous than the stakes warranted. It seems improbable that a greater number of limited nuclear options would have helped in this or any other past case. Thus it is not surprising that Carter administration officials replied in the negative when they were asked whether greater nuclear strength would have permitted the United States to take a harder line in disputes with the Soviet Union.[74] Similarly, when Henry Kissinger and others criticize the Carter administration for not standing up to the Soviets, they imply that the absence of strategic power and nuclear options were not controlling constraints. Consistent with these positions is the finding that the opinion of American experts on how the United States should respond to a hypothetical Soviet invasion of Iran is not influenced by the state of the strategic nuclear balance.[75] But it is at least possible that future American statesmen would focus on the gaining or losing of military advantage and lose sight of the implications of mutual vulnerability. If this happened, then while MAD-4 might be correct prescriptively, it would not provide an accurate prediction of how such statesmen would behave.

Many arguments about nuclear strategy cannot be verified, at least in the absence of a nuclear war. But one of them lends itself to empirical investigation, although the evidence is not likely to be either easy to

74. Interviews with author, 1979–83.
75. Cheryl Koopman with Jack Snyder and Robert Jervis, "American Elite Views of Relations with the Soviet Union," *Journal of Social Issues*, forthcoming.

gather or unambiguous. MAD-4 would be damaged if an examination of previous crises revealed that decision makers were strongly influenced by the presence or absence of militarily efficacious options and paid little attention to the danger of explosive escalation or to the chance that values would be destroyed bit by bit as each side inflicted increasing costs on the other in the expectation that eventually the other would back down.

Put more generally, it may be possible to discover the extent to which and the circumstances under which statesmen are influenced by the strategic nuclear balance, the local balance of forces in the immediate area of the dispute, and the balance of interest or resolve.[76] MAD-4 argues that, short of huge advantages leading to a first strike capability, the details of the strategic nuclear balance should not have much influence. Similarly, unless the local imbalance is so great that one side thinks it can present the other with a fait accompli, the ability to gain an advantage on a local battlefield should be less important than the balance of interest and resolve, which affects states' behavior through their fear of devastation. Thus the existence of nuclear weapons and nuclear danger exerts great influence, largely of a deterrent nature, while the details of the nuclear balance are relatively unimportant.[77]

The paucity of confrontations, especially since the mid-1960s, makes the research difficult, which may be the most important point of all. In our preoccupation with the danger of "deep crises" and situations in which the primary values of both sides are at stake, we may lose sight of the fact that both sides have managed their conflicts quite well and have stayed far from the brink of war. The United States has indeed contemplated using nuclear weapons during some confrontations, but most of these have been with China, not the Soviet Union. Further-

---

76. See Richard Betts, *Nuclear Blackmail and Nuclear Balance* (Washington, D.C.: Brookings Institution, 1987); Paul Huth and Bruce Russett, "Deterrence Failure and Crisis Escalation," *International Studies Quarterly*, 32 (March 1988), 22–46; Barry Blechman and Stephen Kaplan, *Force without War* (Washington, D.C.: Brookings Institution, 1978); Hannes Adomeit, "Soviet Crisis Prevention and Management," *Orbis*, 30 (Spring 1986), 42–64. These findings generally support the argument here: "Our data do not support a hypothesis that the strategic weapons balance between the United States and the USSR influences outcomes" (Blechman and Kaplan, *Force without War*, p. 132); there is "scant reason to assume . . . that the nuclear balance would be a prime consideration in a decision to resort to nuclear coercion" (Betts, *Nuclear Blackmail*, pp. 218–19); there is "no congruence between increased Soviet military capabilities and enhanced Soviet propensities to take risks" (Adomeit, "Soviet Crisis Prevention," pp. 42–43). Also see Jack Snyder, "Science and Sovietology," *World Politics*, 40 (January 1988), 183–86.

77. See Bundy, *Danger and Survival*, passim, and especially chap. 7.

more, Soviet-American crises have decreased fairly steadily over time: they were plentiful in the late 1940s and early 1950s, and recurred over Berlin in the late 1950s and early 1960s, but since the Cuban crisis of 1962 the only incident worth mentioning occurred in 1973. Even the demise of detente did not bring a return of conflicts in which the strategic nuclear balance might be relevant. Indeed, the issue that was primarily responsible for much of the intensity of the Cold War now seems settled: the 1971 agreements on Germany and Berlin ratified the territorial status quo in Europe. Of course these are only scraps of paper and can be challenged at any time, but it is interesting that neither side has displayed any inclination to do so, even—or especially—during periods when relations were strained. Perhaps, then, the United States and the Soviet Union have been more successful at ameliorating their underlying political disputes than they have been at managing their military policies. The latter, designed to preserve the peace and other national values, have become a problem rather than a solution, an independent source of friction and conflict.

[4]

Morality and
International Strategy

In the Realist tradition of international politics, questions of morality are put aside. The spirit of this approach was well put by the Athenian response to the Melian plea for justice: "The standard of justice depends on the equality of power to compel and . . . the strong do what they have the power to do and the weak accept what they have to accept."[1] Zbigniew Brzezinski put it a bit less sharply in explaining the positions he took during the Carter administration: when the U.S. had to choose "between projecting U.S. power or enhancing human rights . . . I felt that power had to come first."[2] In the same vein, when some of the nastier activities of the CIA were challenged, Henry Kissinger is said to have replied, "Covert action is not to be confused with missionary work." Metternich would have agreed. Of the Greek war of independence he said: "Over there, beyond our frontiers, three or four hundred thousand individuals hanged, impaled or with their throats cut, hardly count."[3] Morality applies only to individuals within domestic society. It neither has nor should have (a normative statement, which presumably is based on moral values) a role in the relations among nations.

1. Thucydides, *The Peloponnesian War*, trans. Rex Warner (Harmondsworth, Engl.: Penguin Books, 1954), p. 360.
2. Zbigniew Brzezinski, *Power and Principle* (New York: Farrar, Straus & Giroux, 1983), p. 49. Indeed, it is no accident that the title of his book is not *Principle and Power*.
3. Quoted in Alan Sked, "Introduction," in Sked, ed., *Europe's Balance of Power, 1815–1848* (London: Macmillan, 1979), p. 7.

This conclusion is based on the central tenet of Realism—lacking a sovereign, international politics is the realm of compulsion, not choice, and morality has no role (and perhaps no meaning) where there is no choice.[4] Statesmen must act as they do because the external environment is such a harsh one. Since there is no international government to make or enforce laws, the guiding principle is self-help, and national leaders must think only of the good of their nation. Others will be behaving in this way; any attempt to take nonnational or supranational interests into account will only weaken the state and endanger its security. Under these circumstances, statesmen who ease their private consciences by acting morally do so at the cost of crucial national values. Personal morality, then, is actually evil, or at least selfish. (Realism's view of the good statesman shows an interesting tension here. Such a person must commit all manner of crimes for his country, but must place his country's well-being above his own and must not be tempted by the desire for personal power, wealth, or salvation. One wonders whether such creatures can exist.)

This exposition immediately raises three questions, although only the last will be discussed here. First, is the international environment really so harsh and dominated by compulsion that morally based choice usually threatens national security? Second, to what extent is Realism an ideology that serves functions other than describing the world? Does it blind both the general public and statesmen themselves to alternative patterns of behavior? The very fact that denying a possible role for morality enables statesmen to shield themselves from painful criticism should make us suspicious of the validity of the approach. Third, are decision makers in fact guided by moral principles? They often claim to be. Even such a Realist as Kissinger justified his policy by the justice of his goals and used forms of discourse—terms like "obligation" and "right"—that make sense only if morality is to be heeded. Today some officials who normally avoid discussion of ethics defend their favored nuclear strategy by arguing that missile defense "is perhaps the most morally right, and indeed I might say the most noble of the enterprises in which we are engaged."[5]

4. For arguments that the existence of international anarchy does not justify an abandonment of morality, see Charles Beitz, *Political Theory and International Relations* (Princeton: Princeton University Press, 1979). Hans Morgenthau also rejects the notion that morality is irrelevant in international politics (*Scientific Man versus Power Politics* [Chicago: University of Chicago Press, 1946], chap. 7). Also see Friedrich Kratochwil, *Rules, Norms, and Decisions: On the Conditions of Practical and Legal Reasoning in International Relations and Domestic Affairs* (Cambridge: Cambridge University Press, forthcoming).

5. Secretary of Defense Caspar Weinberger, in Department of Defense news release no. 564-84, October 30, 1984, p. 2.

Indeed, it seems clear that morality—in the broadest sense of the term—must play a major role in setting the general goals that states seek. The values of societies and decision makers strongly influence what they desire and the type of world they seek to create. The security of the state itself, beyond question to Realists is sought because individuals see it as the means to reach other objectives. Thus states have given up at least some degree of sovereignty to bring unification with co-nationals, greater wealth, or an increased ability to influence world politics. In making the vague concept of the "national interest" the basis for action, people must be guided by more specific values. Sometimes the role of morality is clear, as it was in Jimmy Carter's concern for human rights. It has also been argued that the American sanctions against the Soviet invasion of Afghanistan can be explained largely in terms of elite and mass feelings of moral repugnance and moral responsibility.[6] Even more clearly, peace in Korea was delayed for eighteen months because the United States insisted that it would not force Chinese and North Korean prisoners to return to their homelands. As the secretaries of state and defense put it in a memorandum to the president: "The decision involves the basic moral and humanitarian principles which underlie our entire action in Korea."[7] In other cases, morality may be a crucial part of the attempt to build a world based on principles foreign to Realism. This was one motivation for the British policy of appeasement, and while the policy was misguided we should neither fail to appreciate the significance of the attempt nor scorn the considerations that were involved. Nevile Henderson, the British ambassador to Berlin, was not alone in arguing for "basing one's policy toward [German claims on Czechoslovakia] on moral grounds and not allowing oneself to be influenced by consideration about the balance of power or even the Versailles Treaty. We cannot win the battle for the rule of right versus might until our moral position is unassailable. I feel this very strongly about the Sudeten question." "One may be sorry for the Czechs; . . . one may hate to see Germany encouraged; yet the moral principle [of self-determination] is in the end of far greater importance."[8]

6. William Odom, *The Strategic Significance of Afghanistan's Struggle for Freedom*, Occasional Papers Series, vol. 2, no. 2 (Miami: University of Miami, Graduate School of International Studies, 1988), pp. 2–3.

7. U.S. Department of State, *Foreign Relations of the United States, 1952–1954*, vol. 15, *Korea* (Washington, D.C.: Government Printing Office, 1984), 1, p. 35 (hereafter cited as *FRUS*); for arguments, usually by military officers, that "if Washington would only give up its altruistic concern for a lot of worthless Chinese, there wouldn't be any problem about POWs," ibid., pp. 103–4; also see p. 42.

8. Quoted in Williamson Murray, *The Change in the European Balance of Power, 1938–39* (Princeton: Princeton University Press, 1984), p. 167; E. L. Woodward, Rohan Butler,

cause a concern with anything other than power and security
lly seen as soft-headed if not illegitimate, statesmen often try
ie the sources of their own conduct. By justifying their actions
ιιι terms of national security, they not only can smuggle in personal
or partisan objectives, as President Nixon did, but can also render
obscure to others—and to themselves—some goals and motives that
are more noble than those they profess. Thus America may have fought
in Vietnam less because of threats to its security than because of the
desire to see that society develop with at least a modicum of freedom
and decency. Even at the time it seemed improbable that the fate of
South Vietnam would determine the course of events in India, let alone
West Berlin. But it was easy to believe—as indeed turned out to be
true—that a northern victory would be disastrous for the people of
South Vietnam. Concern over the latter consequence, however, was
too altruistic to provide an acceptable justification of the policy. To take
a smaller example, when Winston Churchill questioned the area bombing campaign immediately after having been shown reports of the
destruction of Dresden, he stressed that he was concerned only about
"our own interests," not morality. But one may wonder whether this
was his driving motive: earlier, when viewing a film taken from bombing raids, he "suddenly sat bolt upright and said . . . 'Are we beasts?
Are we taking this too far?' "[9]

MORALITY, RESTRAINT, AND SELF-INTEREST

In the rest of this chapter I will be concerned about the role of
morality, not in setting national goals, but in influencing the means
states employ, although of course the two can blur together. Furthermore, I will largely be concerned with morality as a restraint—with
cases of and arguments for doing less harm to others at some cost to
the state's short-run interest. Morality is not the only reason to inflict
less harm on others than would be called for if considerations of power
dominated. Thus John Nef argues that during the Middle Ages the
construction of more effective firearms was restrained by the prevailing

---

and Margaret Lambert, eds., *Documents on British Foreign Policy, 1919–1939*, 3d series,
vol. 2, *1938* (London: Her Majesty's Stationery Office, 1949), p. 59; also see pp. 84–85.
Others made the opposite argument: giving in to Hitler's demands might be expedient,
but definitely was immoral

9. Martin Gilbert, *Winston S. Churchill*, vol. 7, *Road to Victory, 1941–45* (Boston: Houghton Mifflin, 1986), pp. 1257, 437.

sense of aesthetics.[10] The conduct of warfare also was influenced by the code of chivalry, and throughout history many kinds of weapons and tactics were resisted because they were seen as incompatible with "manly" or soldierly conduct. Indeed, violating these norms may be believed to endanger the broader structures of the military profession or even the society as a whole. While restraints like these are rooted in a larger set of values, they are quite different from prohibitions against injuring certain kinds of people, or injuring them in certain ways, that flow from general principles of the way people should act.

It is not entirely easy to define morality—presumably we mean living by values that are not strictly self-interested, although of course morality can also influence how people define their self-interests. Doing things to benefit others, suffering so that others will gain (or will not have to suffer), not taking advantage of others' weakness: these are the sorts of things that fall under this heading. In international politics the most obvious examples would be spending the lives of one's own people—and perhaps increasing the chance of losing a war—in order to save the lives of people (usually civilians) on the other side. The simplest prescription would be to choose the policy that would minimize the loss of life, irrespective of whether those lives were those of one's countrymen or one's adversary's. This is different from pacifism because killing people on the other side might save an even larger number of lives of one's own nationals. Of course values other than life can be stressed—to the extent that Secretary of War Henry Stimson decided to spare Kyoto from atomic attack because he valued the Japanese cultural heritage, he was acting on a kind of morality.

Is morality an effective restraint? Perhaps because of the hold of Realism, scholars have not carried out sufficient research to venture an answer. In its absence, three points seem likely to be true. First, the most effective restraints are those in which certain actions are literally unthinkable—statesmen do not consider taking the actions and do not get to the stage of calculating what they would gain by doing so. Instead, the thought never enters their minds. Obviously, we cannot find these cases by the normal method of looking at contested decisions; instead we would have to think of what awful policies were possible but never contemplated. Because scholars are rarely motivated to think through this exercise, we do not know if there are many cases. But some current restraints seem to be of this kind, for example, the civilized treatment of prisoners in most modern wars. Once a position

10. John Nef, *War and Human Progress* (Cambridge: Harvard University Press, 1950).

needs to be explicitly defended in moral terms, it probably will not prevail.

Second, Realists probably are correct when they argue that moral standards will not be obeyed (and perhaps not even be seen as moral) if they conflict too much with self-interest. Thus as technology has come to favor surprise attack, declarations of war have ceased. We may have regarded December 7 as a "day of infamy," but there was little reason for us to have done so. States just do not endanger their vital interests for the sake of upholding general principles. The view that Geoffrey Best attributes to the Royal Navy in the late nineteenth and early twentieth centuries applies more widely: "International law was . . . not to be observed beyond the point of serious strategic disadvantage."[11] While Robert Kennedy argued that during the first five days of the Cuban missile crisis, decision makers "spent more time on . . . moral questions . . . than on any other single matter," the available records do not give this impression.[12] Furthermore, Kennedy limits his claim to the beginning of the crisis, not the period when the danger was felt to be at its highest. It is true that American leaders worried about the precedents they were setting and that when they considered Khrushchev's offer to trade the missiles in Cuba for the American ones in Turkey, the president showed his deep concern with its perceived fairness.[13] While these facts do not sit entirely well with Realism, the United States was able to square its desired actions with the precedents that others might use, and the president's interest in fairness was largely prompted by his expectation about how third parties might react.

Third, war itself tends to erode moral restraints by simultaneously increasing the stakes and reducing the identification between the states. In 1914 none of the combatants thought they would soon be bombing civilians and sinking ships without warning. In 1911 Julian Corbett had said, "No power will incur the odium of sinking a prize

---

11. Geoffrey Best, *Humanity in Warfare* (London: Weidenfeld & Nicolson, 1980), p. 250.

12. Robert Kennedy, *Thirteen Days* (New York: Norton, 1971) p. 17; (also see Arthur Schlesinger, Jr., *Robert F. Kennedy and His Times* [Boston: Houghton Mifflin, 1978], p. 508); Marc Trachtenberg, ed., "Documentation: White House Tapes and Minutes of the Cuban Missile Crisis," *International Security*, 10 (Summer 1985), 164–203.

13. Abram Chayes, *The Cuban Missile Crisis* (New York: Oxford University Press, 1974); McGeorge Bundy, transcriber, and James Blight, ed., "October 27, 1962: Transcripts of the Meetings of the ExComm," *International Security*, 12 (Winter 1987–88), 30–92. For evidence that, contrary to standard economic theory, fairness does play a role in the marketplace, see Daniel Kahneman, Jack Knetsch, and Richard Thaler, "Fairness and the Assumptions of Economics," *Journal of Business*, 59 (October 1986), S285–300.

with all hands," and no one disagreed.[14] And while revulsion
against unrestricted submarine warfare was a major cause of American entry into World War I, the United States adopted this policy
within hours of the attack on Pearl Harbor.[15] At the start of World
War II, neither the United States nor Britain sought to level enemy
cities, but once Britain found that it had no alternative, it quickly
shifted to area bombing. Resistance by the United States to area
bombing owed more to better capabilities than to a stronger morality, as was shown by its adoption of the British approach in the Far
East when precision bombardment proved impractical. By 1945, only
lip-service remained of the old restraint when Truman noted in his
diary that he had instructed Stimson to make sure "that military objectives and soldiers and sailors are the targets [of the atom bombs]
and not women and children."[16] Although poison gas was not used
in Europe (Japan occasionally employed it against China), as casualties from the V–1 and V–2 rocket attacks mounted, Churchill told
his military chiefs: "I should be prepared to do anything that would
hit the enemy in a murderous place. I may certainly have to ask you
to support me in using poison gas. . . . I do not see why we should
always have all the disadvantages of being the gentlemen while they

14. Quoted in Best, *Humanity in Warfare*, p. 255. One British scientist recorded his
thoughts on his own involvement in the process of the expansion of the bombing during
World War II: "In [the] final weeks [of the war] I began to look backward and to ask
myself how it happened that I let myself become involved in this crazy game of murder.
Since the beginning of the war I had been retreating step by step from one moral position
to another, until at the end I had no moral position at all. At the beginning of the war
I believed fiercely in the brotherhood of man, called myself a follower of Gandhi, and
was morally opposed to all violence. After a year of war I retreated and said, Unfortunately nonviolent resistance against Hitler is impracticable, but I am still morally opposed
to bombing. A few years later I said, Unfortunately it seems that bombing is necessary
in order to win the war, and so I am willing to go to work for Bomber Command, but
I am still morally opposed to bombing cities indiscriminately. After I arrived at Bomber
Command I said, Unfortunately it turns out that we are after all bombing cities indiscriminately, but this is morally justified as it is helping to win the war" (Freeman Dyson,
Disturbing the Universe [New York: Harper & Row, 1979], pp. 30–31).
15. Ronald Spector, *Eagle against the Sun* (New York: Free Press, 1985), pp. 179–80.
16. Robert Ferrell, ed., *Off the Record: The Private Journals of Harry S. Truman* (New
York: Norton, 1980), p. 55. One counterexample seems true, although it is hard to believe.
During the height of the war the British refrained from interfering with German instructions to their fighter pilots that were broadcast over "a system which . . . purported to
be a German Forces Programme . . . because legal objections were raised against the
jamming of this kind of programme" (F. H. Hinsley, E. E. Thomas, C. F. G. Ransom,
and R. C. Knight, *British Intelligence in the Second World War*, vol. 3, pt. 1 [New York:
Cambridge University Press, 1984], p. 555).

have all the advantages of being the cad."[17] If what now seems like relatively primitive technology could so cripple traditional moral standards, what would nuclear weapons do?[18]

THE NUCLEAR REVOLUTION

Like many other students of the subject, I have argued that the mutual vulnerability created by nuclear weapons has brought about a revolution in statecraft. The superpowers can no longer deter by denial. Instead they must deter by punishment. Such a radical change affects not only strategy, but also morality. Just as a prenuclear conceptual framework (Hans Morgenthau's "conventionalization") is misleading for empirical analysis, so is it inadequate for questions of ethics. But even a better understanding of the situation will not alter the fact that unless only those who are guilty are being hurt (an alluring possibility discussed below), punishment always involves immorality. Thus the basic facts of the nuclear age may be irreconcilable with our moral impulses.

Non-Combatant Immunity in the Nuclear Age

Because deterrence by punishment is unavoidable and deterrence by denial cannot work, the possibility of noncombatant immunity—one of the basic principles in all conceptions of a just war—is undermined. According to what the American Catholic bishops call a "universally binding principle," it is acceptable to attack only those engaged in fighting and perhaps those directly engaged in supporting the war

---

17. Quoted in Gilbert, *Churchill*, p. 841. One of his other remarks on this subject is also noteworthy: "It is absurd to consider morality on this topic when everybody used gas in the last war without a word of complaint from the moralists or the Church. On the other hand, in the last war the bombing of open cities was regarded as forbidden. Now everybody does it as a matter of course. It is simply a question of fashion changing as she does between long and short skirts for women" (ibid., pp. 840–41). Vietnam does not seem to have followed this pattern of restraints eroding throughout the war. Indeed, even in the bombing of Hanoi at the end of the war, the United States at least marginally increased its expected casualties in order to try to reduce civilian deaths. See William O'Brien, *The Conduct of Just and Limited War* (New York: Praeger, 1981), pp. 311–12. Also see Gunther Lewy, *America in Vietnam* (New York: Oxford University Press, 1978).

18. See James Turner Johnson, *Just War Tradition and the Restraint of War* (Princeton: Princeton University Press, 1981), chap. 6, for a somewhat parallel discussion of the impact of technology on morality in earlier eras.

industries (e.g., munitions workers).[19] Of course as more and more civilian sectors have become involved in the war efforts, this distinction has tended to erode, although some lines can still be drawn. Indeed, since a nuclear war would be fought with the stock of weapons on hand, in theory it might be possible to return to a fairly strict separation between combatants and noncombatants, although attacking the former without killing many of the latter might not be practical.[20] Let us remember the original reason for trying to make the separation, however: attacking civilians could not be reasonably related to the legitimate goals of the conflict. Killing civilians would inflict pain on them and the state as a whole, but in most of the prenuclear era, it could not determine the outcome of the war. The only path to victory was through defeating the other side's army. The principle was thus rooted in the nature of the warfare.

But the nature of warfare—or rather of potential warfare—between the superpowers is very different from what it was in the past. The existence of mutual second-strike capability means that gaining a military advantage does not provide the kind of leverage that it previously did. Because it cannot take cities out of hostage, it cannot bring military victory; it cannot force termination of a war on acceptable terms. Why, then, is it moral to kill soldiers? If they are volunteers, we can say that they have agreed to make themselves targets. But this is not true for the bulk of the Red Army and, given the inequality of income and opportunity in this country, is of only doubtful validity for the United States. Why, then, is it moral to kill a nineteen-year-old who is wearing a uniform but not one who is not?[21]

The principle of civilian immunity is often used as the basis for arguing that morality requires us to avoid the indiscriminate targeting of population implied by Mutual Assured Destruction and to return to

19. National Conference of Catholic Bishops, *The Challenge of Peace: God's Promise and Our Response* (Washington, D.C.: United States Catholic Conference, 1983), p. 4. This general rule obviously leaves open important questions, such as the moral status of the bombing of cities in World War II, whether civilian casualties are proscribed if they are the adjunct to operations aimed at the other side's armed forces, and whether operations known to kill civilians are justified only under certain conditions—e.g., if precautions are taken to minimize such casualties, and if the military necessity for undertaking the operation is great. For a discussion of the genesis of noncombatant immunity, see Paul Ramsey, *War and the Christian Conscience* (Durham, N.C.: Duke University Press, 1961), chap. 3.

20. Robert W. Tucker, "The Rationale of Force," in Robert E. Osgood and Robert W. Tucker, *Force, Order, and Justice* (Baltimore: Johns Hopkins University Press, 1967), p. 209.

21. For an analysis that shares my view of noncombatant immunity but reaches conventionalized conclusions, see David Fisher, *Morality and the Bomb* (London: Croom Helm, 1985), pp. 26–29.

the older ideas of limiting our fire to the enemy's military. Thus William Stanmeyer reaches three conclusions:

> First, the Mutual Assured Destruction strategy is probably immoral, if we grant the usual distinction between "innocent" civilians and "non-innocent" military.... Second, the Counterforce strategy is moral, since one wills the destruction only of combatants and only permits collateral harm to civilians. A corollary is that limited nuclear war is, morally, permissible if one respects the injunction not to will directly the destruction of innocent civilians. Third, an ABM defensive strategy ... is undoubtedly moral. Indeed, it is to be preferred.[22]

I will come back to the assumptions about what is practical and the interesting consistency between people's moral and strategic judgments. But here I want to argue that the call for civilian immunity, while attractive at first glance, fails because it assumes that nuclear weapons help reach political goals in the same manner as do conventional weapons. Since this is not true, the morality, like the logic, no longer works. As long as escalation is possible, crises and even the use of force between the superpowers will function as generators of risk. The outcome of a nuclear confrontation would depend heavily on which side was most willing to risk destruction and each side's perception of how much risk the other was willing to run. The targets threatened might well be military, as they were in the past, but pressure would be brought to bear on the adversary not through weakening its military capability but through the increased threat of all-out war.[23] Once a major military clash between the superpowers started, the

---

22. William Stanmeyer, "Toward a Moral Nuclear Strategy," *Policy Review*, no. 21 (Summer 1982), 65–66. For more thorough discussions of the morality of counterforce war, see Paul Ramsey, *The Just War* (New York: Scribner's, 1968). It should be noted that while American decision makers often talked as though American targeting policy was based on retaliation against cities, it never has been. See, for example, David Rosenberg, "The Origins of Overkill: Nuclear Weapons and American Strategy, 1945–1960," *International Security*, 7 (Spring 1983), 4–71; Desmond Ball, "U.S. Strategic Forces: How Would They Be Used?" *International Security*, 7 (Winter 1982–83), 31–60.

23. For an elaboration of the argument for the central role of risk, see Robert Jervis, *The Illogic of American Nuclear Strategy* (Ithaca: Cornell University Press, 1984), chap. 5. Ramsey reaches a different conclusion because he sees immorality and irrationality as resulting "when war is regarded as primarily or exclusively a trial of wills or a test of resolve" (*The Just War*, pp. 221–22). But he never explains how the alternative—a test of strength—can determine the outcome of conflict in which counterforce advantage cannot protect the state's values. Also see Tucker, "The Rationale of Force," pp. 314–20.

soldiers would be harmless—they would be like prisoners of war in the past—and civilians could not claim a privileged position. Indeed, because states are deterred by the fear that their societies will be destroyed, it is credible threats to civilians that provide bargaining leverage before and even during a war.

A Counterargument—Threatening What the Soviets Value

Perhaps we are being ethnocentric. Many analysts have argued that while Americans value cities and civilians, Soviet leaders do not and so the threat to destroy these targets is pointless. What Soviet rulers value, this argument goes, are the sinews of Soviet power—the Red Army, KGB headquarters, party cadres, internal security forces, and the top leadership itself. Nicely enough, none of these people are "innocent" and so morality and effectiveness are joined, as they often were in earlier eras. There is something to be said for this argument, but while it is plausible to believe that the Soviet leaders value Communist power and not civilian lives, there is little evidence on this point. That it fits with the image of an evil adversary and so is psychologically satisfying does not make it correct. Would the Soviet leaders consider as a victory a war in which the party survived but, say, eighty million civilians did not? I find this unlikely, if for no other reason than because widespread civilian devastation could not but eviscerate Soviet power.[24]

Even if killing civilians is sufficient for deterrence, it may not be required for it. On what strategic or moral grounds could one object to threatening to destroy the sources of Soviet power while killing as few civilians as possible? There are several problems with this attempt to return to a more familiar and comfortable stance, however. The most obvious is one of practicality. We cannot destroy most of the Soviet strategic forces because they are too numerous, hardened, or difficult to find. We cannot, in other words, return to a world of deterrence by denial. Even if we concentrate on other forms of Soviet power, the practicality of the strategy is questionable. Many important targets lie within cities. Small warheads with terminal guidance might be able to destroy the KGB headquarters without touching the surrounding buildings, but we do not yet have the required weapons. Furthermore, while buildings cannot move, people can. The party cadres and members of

24. Robert Art, "Between Assured Destruction and Nuclear Victory: The Case for the 'MAD-Plus' Posture," *Ethics*, 95 (April 1985), 509.

the KGB are not likely to be sitting there, waiting to be killed, especially after we have told them they are targets. Top leadership can do more than move, they can get to protected shelters whose locations we probably cannot know and which we would have trouble destroying. Internal security forces and the Red Army are harder to camouflage or protect, but they are not easy to find. Even limited mobility is quite effective unless the United States has real-time (i.e., immediate and current) intelligence during a war, which is extremely unlikely. Thus to destroy Soviet power, we would have to attack large parts of the country. The distinction between a pure city-busting strategy and one that sought to spare civilians as much as possible while destroying Soviet power would be much smaller in practice than in theory.

Even if much greater discrimination were possible, the strategy of targeting Soviet power and leadership would be more moral than attacking civilian society only if it kept the war limited. But the pressures for and dangers of escalation are very great. Neither side has the C^3 capability to fight a prolonged limited nuclear war. Indeed it would be hard to keep the forces under control even if both sides tried to do so.[25] Furthermore, there is no reason to think that the Soviets would cooperate with our strategy even if they could. While the Soviets do not seem to target American cities for the purposes of revenge, they do not seem to be willing to spare them either. As far as we can tell, their strategy most closely resembles that held by the U.S. Strategic Air Command in the late 1950s. (I say SAC rather than the US government because at that time war planning was done by SAC with little control by the Pentagon, let alone the White House.)[26] Thus in the event of a nuclear war, the Soviets would seek to destroy US military, economic, and political power. Many targets would be in or near cities and so the United States could not hope to limit damage to itself by limiting the damage it was doing to the Soviet Union. Therefore, while trying to spare Soviet cities might save Soviet lives, it would not protect Americans; and, unless American leaders blinded themselves to this reality, the credibility of the threat to implement this strategy would be undermined by Soviet knowledge that the resulting war would destroy what we value.

A final objection to the strategy of targeting Soviet power is that if it were to be implemented, it would fail. Were the United States to

25. For good discussions of C^3 see Desmond Ball, *Can Nuclear War Be Controlled?* Adelphi Paper no. 169 (London: International Institute for Strategic Studies, 1981), and Bruce Blair, *Strategic Command and Control* (Washington, D.C.: Brookings Institution, 1985). For further discussion, see Chapter 5 below.
26. Rosenberg, "The Origins of Overkill."

destroy Soviet power and political control, the remaining leaders would have no reason—other than morality—to refrain from destroying the United States. If the Soviets value their power, then we must spare it if the war is to remain limited. The basic logic of the criticism of attacking cities applies here—the threat to destroy what the Soviets value is not credible because it would trigger an unrestrained Soviet response.

Proportionality

If the nuclear revolution has undermined the rationale for noncombatant immunity, what has it done to the rule of proportionality? Has mutual vulnerability altered the principle that, in the words of the American bishops, "the damage to be inflicted and the costs incurred by war must be proportionate to the good expected by taking up arms"?[27] An all-out war would set civilization back for generations, if not for centuries. This clear violation of the rule of proportionality raises two questions. The first is whether it can be rational or moral to intend to retaliate when doing so would be immoral and pointless. I think David Lewis is correct to respond that the question of the morality of making threats which, if effective, would reach moral goals but which, if they were implemented, would be immoral is largely a nonproblem, the modern equivalent of how many angels can fit on the head of a pin.[28] No statesman can know how he or she would behave in the awful moment of decision.

More to the point is the question, Could anything be worth the price of all-out war? No matter how much we value liberty, would it not be better—both more expedient and more moral—to submit and then struggle to overthrow the tyranny than to fight World War III? There is much to be said for this, but the familiar reply also has great merit. The policy of deterrence allows us to have the best of both worlds—to be neither Red nor dead—and to protect not only the United States, but also close allies.[29] Nevertheless, the obvious challenge is the uncertainty of deterrence. Here the objection branches into two directions. The dovish branch argues that because deterrence can fail with catastrophic results we must look for radical alternatives, such as drastic

---

27. National Conference of Catholic Bishops, *The Challenge of Peace*, p. 31.
28. David Lewis, "Devil's Bargains and the Real World," in Douglas MacLean, ed., *The Security Gamble: Deterrence Dilemmas in the Nuclear Age* (Totowa, N.J.: Rowman & Allanheld, 1984), pp. 141–54. Also see Paul Kattenburg, "MAD Is the Moral Position," in Charles Kegley and Eugene Wittkopf, eds., *The Nuclear Reader* (New York: St. Martin's Press, 1985), pp. 82–83.
29. See Jervis, *The Illogic of American Nuclear Strategy*, pp. 153–62.

and perhaps unilateral disarmament. But this argument does not answer the question of what the United States should do if the alternative to fighting seemed to be the loss of American or allied liberty.

The hawkish branch of the objection argues that the credibility of deterrent threats must be enhanced, preferably by a posture that would also maximize our chances of surviving a nuclear war if one were forced on us. At best this would be done by returning to deterrence by denial via an ABM system. Lacking such a system or to supplement one, we must develop the capacity to respond to less than total attacks with a spectrum of less than total measures—that is, a strategy of flexible response. The result would be to reinstate both credibility and morality through the mechanism of proportionality—we would adjust our military means to the magnitude of the issue at stake. But this line of argument is fundamentally misleading because it is conventionalized and so fails to deal with the fact that meeting a limited threat on its own terms does not take American cities out of hostage.

The implications for proportionality are twofold. First, flexible response, even if supported by military superiority, cannot guarantee that the violence will be kept limited. Both sides have sufficient explosives to destroy the other, and escalation, either as a calculated policy or through inadvertence, is a looming possibiity. Second, because a confrontation or a limited war resembles a game of Chicken, it is the willingness to run risks that is both dangerous and crucial. If proportionality is to be maintained, it must be through states limiting themselves to running risks that are roughly proportional to the stakes. The military requirements for such a policy are quite different from those called for by the policy of flexible response—one needs the ability to take actions that increase the chance of total war but do not make escalation certain. What is less clear, however, is whether proportionality is meaningfully reestablished when what statesmen seek to adjust are the chances of total destruction. While any policy, especially in a crisis, must be chosen in part because of estimates as to how dangerous it (and the alternatives) will be, congratulating ourselves that this way of behaving is moral may be an attempt to rationalize an unpleasant necessity.

Proportionality was easier to maintain in the past because a state had to defeat the other state's armies before it could do great damage to civilians, and once the armies were defeated there was no point to doing this damage. Now either superpower can do harm from the start, and military success cannot prevent the other from doing so. This ability yields great leverage; I do not see how morality can tame it any more than it could tame unrestricted submarine warfare in World

War I or bombing in World War II. If not the trump card, it is at least the weapon of last resort. For this reason the nuclear revolution has created insoluble moral dilemmas. Because the possibility of total destruction is inherent in a world with nuclear weapons, no policy can meet all our moral standards.

Nuclear Weapons, Freedom of Action, and Morality

Nuclear weapons have implications for morality not only through military strategies but also through general foreign policy. In most previous eras, the major states faced a highly constraining environment. If they were to maintain their position, they had to enter many undesired conflicts, sometimes to defend their own interests, sometimes to side with allies who, if deserted, would in turn desert the state and leave it isolated. The nuclear revolution and the associated bipolarity have altered this situation. As Kenneth Waltz has persuasively argued, because the superpowers are so strong, their allies count for much less and so the United States and the USSR have unprecedented freedom to engage in or abstain from conflicts.[30] It follows that the basic argument made by Realists as to why leading states are not bound by morality applies less today than it did in the past. The superpowers cannot easily dismiss moral judgments because they cannot readily claim to have no alternatives.

Their freedom may be least in the military arena. Thus it may be no accident that both superpowers have followed similar ambivalent patterns of war plans and weapons procurement. On the one hand, both have sought to be in the best possible position to fight if war should be forced on them; on the other hand, while neither has welcomed mutual vulnerability, both have realized that it exists as a fact. In broader questions of foreign policy, however, each side's behavior is more diverse, both compared with the behavior of the other superpower and compared with their own behavior at previous times. Thus although some American and Soviet acts mirror each other as those required by their position in the system, many others have to be traced to their values and choices. There is then a great deal of freedom for the United States to decide to support human rights or to stand aside, to provide humanitarian aid or to withhold it, to get involved in Third World conflicts or stay out of them. This is not to argue that the dictates

---

30. Kenneth Waltz, *Theory of International Politics* (Reading, Mass.: Addison-Wesley, 1979), chap. 8. Also see Glenn Snyder and Paul Diesing, *Conflict among Nations* (Princeton: Princeton University Press, 1977), chap. 6.

of morality are clear. But the familiar claim that the United States has no choice but to act in ways that violate or ignore moral principles is another example of the use of an intellectual framework that was appropriate to earlier eras but that serves us less well under current conditions.

HESITANCY TO PERCEIVE TRADE-OFFS

If the concept of morality is to be useful for either analysis or prescription, it cannot be equated with prudent self-interest. But when we look at people's views on important issues, we notice a suspicious consistency—people who see a policy as immoral also tend to see it as ineffective. This is an aspect of the tendency of people to avoid value trade-offs, which I have discussed elsewhere.[31] To summarize this general argument, when people think that a policy is better than the alternatives on one value dimension, they are likely to see it as also superior on other, logically unrelated, dimensions. Yet, unless we believe in a benign God there is no reason why nature should be arranged so conveniently. For example, in the late 1950s and early 1960s, those people who favored a nuclear test ban believed that such an agreement was verifiable, that it would contribute to U.S. foreign and military policy, and that atmospheric testing was a significant hazard to public health. Those who opposed an agreement disagreed *on all three points.* Logically, all that was required was that people on different sides of the issue reach different conclusions as to the total gains and costs of a test ban. There is no reason why they should disagree on each specific—and logically independent—issue. But in fact they did—almost no one said that while testing was medically harmless it was bad for our foreign policy; few argued that testing was a military necessity even though it killed thousands of innocent civilians.

The reasons for this configuration of beliefs are psychological, not logical. Not all the mental processes are entirely clear, but two factors appear to be at work. First, trade-offs are avoided because they are difficult. People's cognitive capacities are limited and so they need to simplify the problems they are facing. It would take a great deal of thought to reduce all the values to a common yardstick. Thus people may instead reach a decision based on the consideration of only one value and then bring other perceptions into line with this judgment.

31. *Perception and Misperception in International Politics* (Princeton: Princeton University Press, 1976), pp. 128–42.

Second, and particularly important in the context of morality, trade-offs are avoided because they are painful. This is clearly true in the previous example—to say that testing must be continued even though it kills people is to admit a willingness to sacrifice innocent lives for foreign policy goals. Much more comfortable is the belief that testing is not only necessary but also harmless.

The same pattern holds with questions of war and morality, for example, with views about strategic bombing during World War II. The Royal Air Force, which throughout much of the war could not bomb with much precision, not only thought that destroying German cities was making a major contribution to the war effort but had no doubts as to its morality. The American air force had both more faith in its ability to hit specific targets and more questions about the moral justification for indiscriminate bombardment. (It should be noted that the American air force in the Far East had no such scruples, or lost them when precision bombing was found to be ineffective.)

The same pattern is seen in disputes about Cold War strategy. For example, many of those who opposed the development of the H-bomb were largely moved by moral and political considerations but bolstered their view with arguments that building the Super, as it was called, might be beyond our capabilities, that it could have little military role, and that the scarce fissionable materials and scientific talent could be better employed on various forms of atomic weapons. Those who wanted to proceed not only were preoccupied with the fear that the Soviets might develop the H-bomb first and saw real military utility in the new weapon, but they also denied any moral difference between the large atomic bombs that were being developed and the Super.

Turning to the current period, it is more than a coincidence that most people who favor the countervailing strategy on grounds of foreign policy also see it as more moral than Mutually Assured Destruction. Similarly, those who attack the morality of doctrines that seek deterrence through the ability to fight nuclear wars also question their strategic value. Those who say, like the pope, that deterrence may be morally acceptable, "but [only] as a step on the way toward a progressive disarmament," also believe that disarmament would make peace more and not less likely.[32] The connections here are not entirely psychological—one logical reason for a person to see MAD as immoral is the belief that it is not capable of preventing wars and Soviet aggression. Doctrines of deterrence through the ability to fight limited war

---

32. Quoted in Bruce Russett, "Ethical Dilemmas of Nuclear Deterrence," *International Security*, 8 (Spring 1984), 41.

are seen as immoral by their critics in part because they are thought to increase the chance of a war—a war, furthermore, that in fact could not be kept limited. The pope presumably sees disarmament as more moral than continued deterrence because he thinks that weapons contribute to international tensions and that war cannot be indefinitely avoided as long as nations rely on nuclear threats.

Thus this consistency makes some sense. It would be odd if moral judgments were entirely divorced from estimates of the consequences of alternative actions. Indeed, for the utilitarians, the former must follow the latter. (I might add that this makes their writings of little interest to strategists. Since they try to do the same sort of things that strategists do, they do not provide new perspectives.) Even for deontologists, who search for moral standards different from the greatest good for the greatest number, estimates of the effects of alternative strategies must also play some role.[33]

But the result is that arguments about morality are difficult to separate from arguments about empirical questions (if one can so classify questions such as what deters the USSR and whether nuclear war could be kept limited). This leads to three related difficulties. First, in many cases it is not clear whether disagreements are over moral or empirical judgments. Are the disputes between those who say that MAD is moral and those who deny this proposition really based on different conceptions of morality? If people could agree on their estimates of the consequences of adopting various policies, would any disagreements remain? To put this another way, is there any point in discussing morality? The moral dialogue cannot lead anyone to change her mind or even to see the issues more clearly if it is really the strategic judgments that are in dispute.

A second and related question is how much moral verdicts are based on hidden empirical assumptions. Much of the moral objection to counterforce doctrines rests on the belief that war cannot be kept limited. Thus Bruce Russett joins the American bishops in arguing, "Limitation of nuclear war fails a third principle of the just war tradition: reasonable chance of success."[34] Here the assumption is explicit, which aids analysis, but it still raises the question of whether morality is relevant to the conclusion being drawn. Even more troublesome are the numerous

---

33. It is often believed or implied that utilitarians will defend deterrence because it has proved effective, while its moral critics will be deontologists, but, as Joseph Nye has shown, this is not true (*Nuclear Ethics* [New York: Free Press, 1986], pp. 59–60). For a position that combines both approaches, see John Finnis, Joseph Boyle, Jr., and Germain Grisez, *Nuclear Deterrence, Morality and Realism* (Oxford: Clarendon Press, 1987).

34. Russett, "Ethical Dilemmas of Nuclear Deterrence," p. 46.

occasions in which the assumptions lie further beneath the surface. For example, the American bishops argue, "If deterrence is our goal, 'sufficiency' to deter is an adequate strategy; the quest for nuclear superiority must be rejected."[35] But if the proponents of the counter-force are correct, then something like superiority is needed for deterring limited nuclear wars. On this point the question of whether war actually could be kept limited is irrelevant: if the Soviets can be deterred only if they believe that the United States is ready to fight a certain kind of war, then the United States is compelled to convince the Soviets that the United States can and will fight such a war. Similarly, the argument for the moral superiority of a disarmed world makes some convenient assumptions about the USSR and the connections between arms and the chance of wars. Unpacking these beliefs can point to questionable strategic judgments and possible clashes among values.

The close connection between empirical and moral judgments also raises the question of whether views on one of these subjects leads to conclusions on the other in a way that is psychologically comfortable but logically—and morally—illegitimate. For some people, moral judg-ments are a handy stick with which to beat their adversaries about the head. Few of the proponents of counterforce targeting were originally preoccupied with considerations of morality. Rather they were seeking the best way to deter war and protect American interests. These are not minor values, and to say that they motivated views on war planning is not to slander the people involved. Only recently, as concern about morality has grown, has counterforce and deterrence by denial been strongly defended on moral grounds. It seems clear that the moral evaluation is not really an independent one but instead merely ratifies the strategic judgment previously arrived at. No one who favored coun-terforce on strategic grounds reacted to the new concern with morality by saying, "Why yes, now that I think of it, my policy is immoral." Similarly, the new interest in morality has not prompted those who had come to favor MAD on the grounds that it was most likely to prevent war to say, "MAD may be effective; but it is also immoral." Indeed, cynical readers might note that my argument that the nuclear revolution undermines the rationale for civilian immunity nicely re-inforces my opposition to extensive counterforce options.

In still other cases a moral judgment does come first and leads to conveniently supporting strategic views. This probably is true for most of the clerics and philosophers who have joined the strategic debate. I doubt that the pope has reached his preference for disarmament by

35. National Conference of Catholic Bishops, *The Challenge of Peace*, p. 59.

a thorough examination of the military and political arguments. More likely, the moral imperative for this position leads to the belief that it is also justified on grounds of strategy. But no matter which value is the motivating one, few people on either side of the debate see a trade-off between national interest and morality.

In part, this happy consistency in people's views is a reflection of the unwillingness to face the possibility of conflicts between decreasing the chance of any superpower war and minimizing casualties if such a war should occur. Proponents of MAD escape from the dilemma by arguing that a limited war would automatically escalate; proponents of limited options escape by arguing that their approach would both save lives during a war and bolster deterrence because the Russians will find the threats particularly credible. Thus our beliefs are psychologically and morally reassuring, but it is unlikely that an independent judgment has been reached at each point. Perhaps the first step toward taking morality seriously would be to understand that doing so would often complicate our lives, making us less rather than more comfortable. Morality should make us face difficult choices and often alter, not reinforce, our behavior.

MORALITY AND PRUDENCE

Although prudent self-interest and morality cannot always coincide if the latter is to have any independent meaning, there are links between them. Most conceptions of morality enjoin a concern with others' lives and well-being: people and nations should be willing to sacrifice at least some of what directly benefits them to help others. In a parallel manner, most scholars argue that a policy that is too selfish and greedy is likely to harm the state, although it may yield advantages in the short run. (I will return to the question of long- versus short-run considerations in the next section). To act only on what gives one's country competitive advantage—to interpret the prescriptions of Realism crudely—is to court great dangers. David Calleo shows that German expansionism led to isolation and ruin in part because the conception of Europe held not only by Hitler but also by the kaiser left little role for the ideals and interests of the other powers.[36] Balance-of-power theory predicts and prescribes that states band together to prevent anyone from dominating. But the speed, cohesiveness, and vehemence

36. David Calleo, *The German Problem Reconsidered* (Cambridge: Cambridge University Press, 1978).

of these efforts are influenced by the character of the would-be hegemon. Germany brought on its own doom by paying so little heed to others' interests that few could see a place for them in Germany's world. Symptomatic was the fact that the Soviets who had welcomed Hitler's troops as liberators were soon supporting the resistance movement. Heinrich Himmler told a group of SS generals: "Whether nations live in prosperity or starve to death interests me only in so far as we need them as slaves for our Kultur: otherwise, it is of no interest to me. Whether 10,000 Russian females fall down from exhaustion while digging an anti-tank ditch interests me only in so far as the anti-tank ditch for Germany is finished."[37] Such a stance is not only immoral but self-defeating. As the British analyst James Headlam-Morley put it, a bit too smugly but not too inaccurately, "What in international affairs is morally indefensible generally turns out in the long run to have been politically inept."[38]

The obsession with power and narrow self-interest—what might be called pseudo-Realism—leads to the dissipation of power and eventually undermines self-interest. As Hans Morgenthau warned, it is common but not wise for statesmen to be contemptuous of others' values and insensitive to their reactions.[39] It is all too easy for the strong to see only their own concerns and so to endanger first others and then themselves as the others' power, skill, and willingness to suffer are underestimated. Thus Michael Walzer argues that it is no accident that the Athenians' refusal to heed the Melians' plea for considering justice as well as power was followed a year later by their overreaching themselves by the dispatch of the expedition to Sicily.[40] Interestingly enough, the conduct of this adventure reveals the same flaw in microcosm. Donald Kagan argues that the expedition might have succeeded had it been smaller, which was the original plan. But when the Athenians enlarged the force, their potential allies on the island feared that they would be the next targets and so stayed neutral or opposed Athens.[41] That the Athenians failed to anticipate this reaction is due at least in part to the arrogance of power. The egoism of pseudo-Realism

37. Quoted in Geoffrey Best, *War and Society in Revolutionary Europe, 1870–1970* (London: Fontana, 1982), p. 181.

38. Quoted in Martin Kitchen, *British Policy towards the Soviet Union during the Second World War* (London: Macmillan, 1986), p. 184.

39. Hans Morgenthau, *Politics among Nations*, 5th ed. rev. (New York: Knopf, 1978), pp. 553–54.

40. Michael Walzer, *Just and Unjust Wars* (New York: Basic Books, 1977), p. 7.

41. Donald Kagan, *The Peace of Nicias and the Sicilian Expedition* (Ithaca: Cornell University Press, 1981), p. 214.

leads statesmen to consider others as instruments, if not as puppets, and to overestimate their own ability to control events.

The failure to consider the other's perspective often leads statesmen to ignore an important tool for deterrence. The preoccupation with the perceived evil of the other side, the resulting over-reliance on threats, and the failure to realize that the adversary may fear unprovoked attack combine to render the statesman insensitive to the importance of giving the adversary reassurances. The other's decision on whether to challenge the status quo depends not only on the gains and costs it expects from doing so but also on what it thinks the future will bring if it is restrained. Thus the state should try to convince the adversary that a future without war is not terribly bleak. If the other side believes that the alternative to attack or expansion is the loss of its influence and values, it may decide to strike even in the face of credible threats of retaliation. Janice Stein has shown how the Egyptian decisions for peace or war in the early 1970s were strongly influenced by their evaluations of what would happen if they did not use force; Richard Ned Lebow has shown the operation of similar calculations in Argentina before the invasion of the Falklands; and McGeorge Bundy and I have argued that American statesmen often neglect the utility of reassurance in dealing with the Soviet Union.[42] The failure to consider the other side's alternatives is shortsighted because it often leads to unnecessary conflicts; it also is immoral in that it treats others as though they had no legitimate interests, as though they had no hopes and fears, as though there was no way to build common interests.

Pseudo-Realism also violates the standards of both morality and prudence by leading statesmen to ignore "the decent respect for the opinions of mankind."[43] "How many divisions has the pope?" Stalin is supposed to have asked, and many of those who abhor the questioner agree with his position. In fact, while it is hard to tell what the answer is, it surely is not zero. Grossly offending moral standards incurs a cost—often a high one. The state sacrifices international sympathy and creates fear that, while perhaps cowing opposition in the short run, is likely to turn to resistance before too long. Others will wonder if a state

---

42. See the essays by Stein and Lebow in Robert Jervis, Richard Ned Lebow, and Janice Stein, *Psychology and Deterrence* (Baltimore: Johns Hopkins University Press, 1985); Bundy, "The Bishops and the Bomb," *New York Review of Books*, January 16, 1983, p. 6; Jervis, *The Illogic of American Nuclear Strategy*, pp. 165–67; and Janice Stein, "Deterrence and Reassurance," in Philip Tetlock et al., eds., *Behavior, Society, and Nuclear War*, vol. 2 (New York: Oxford University Press, forthcoming).

43. The classic discussion is E. H. Carr, *The Twenty Years' Crisis, 1919–1939* (New York: Harper & Row, 1964).

that acts immorally in one situation can be trusted in the future and are likely to infer that it is a menace that needs to be contained if not eliminated. Thus President Reagan is not alone in believing that the Soviet destruction of the Korean airliner revealed antihumanitarian values that must be thwarted for reasons of both morality and national interest. As Reagan put it, "What can be the scope of legitimate mutual discourse with a state whose values permit such atrocities?"[44] The Soviets reasoned similarly after the American invasion of Grenada when they questioned the utility of arms-control negotiations: "If one is a bandit, liar, and murderer, one could not be different on the shores of Lake Geneva."[45] The same kind of considerations explain why oppressive domestic practices usually harm the state internationally. Even though pseudo-Realists argue that what a regime does within its borders is its own business, in fact the whole world does watch and judge. Some of the opposition to Hitler and to the USSR was based on moral revulsion against their internal affairs and Soviet-American relations eased under Gorbachev partly because of the domestic liberalization he initiated. While international moral standards are not enforceable by a central authority, they cannot be disregarded without paying a price.

[margin handwriting: Iranian airliner]

Morality, Prudence, and the Prisoner's Dilemma

"War is cruelty and you cannot refine it," said General William T. Sherman.[46] The major reason for this is the competitive nature of the fighting—if you refrain from using a nasty tactic but your opponent does not, you have lost an advantage, and perhaps the war. This kind of situation can be analyzed in terms of the problem of how to avoid mutual defection (DD) in the Prisoner's Dilemma (PD), a task in which morality and prudence may be joined. In political situations that resemble PD (and it is often hard to determine whether they do), each

---

44. "Transcript of Reagan's Statement on Airliner," *New York Times*, September 3, 1983. It now appears not only that the Soviets believed the airliner was an American spy plane but that American decision makers were so informed by parts of the intelligence community. See Seymour Hersh, *"The Target Is Destroyed"* (New York: Random House, 1986). The Russian failure to take more steps to verify their beliefs about the identity of the plane—which was leaving Soviet airspace and so was no longer posing a threat—nevertheless at best constituted a gross indifference to human life. The American reaction might have been a bit different if this incident had followed rather than preceded the American shooting down of the Iranian airliner.
45. "Soviet Says U.S. Fired at Its Grenada Embassy," *New York Times*, October 29, 1983.
46. Quoted in Walzer, *Just and Unjust Wars*, p. 32.

state's first choice is to exploit the other and gain unilateral advantage—that is, not to cooperate with the other (to defect) although the other is cooperating (DC). The second choice is mutual cooperation (CC), the third choice is mutual competition or defection (DD), and the worst outcome is to be exploited, to cooperate while the other defects (CD). In such situtions there are both offensive and defensive motives for disregarding restraints and the result can be that adversaries are un-restrained (DD) when they would have preferred a situation in which they both cooperated (CC). (I am putting aside cases in which the state would prefer to be restrained no matter what the other does, as may be the case, for example, with the humane treatment of prisoners of war.) This configuration of preferences characterizes not only most limited wars, but many peacetime international interactions as well. It is a basic characteristic of collective action in the context of anarchy.

There are a number of ways of increasing the chance of coopera-tion under these conditions. One is to develop habits and rules of reciprocal restraint. Each side then may be restrained in the expec-tation that the other will behave similarly. Under some circumstan-ces, such mutual cooperation based only on self-interest can thrive.[47] But high conflict and misperception tend to erode this happy pattern. As noted earlier, violence tends to expand during wars partly because states tend to overestimate the degree to which they are cooperating with others and the extent to which others are defecting.[48] Each sees itself as being exploited and believes that its own defections are justified—and will be seen as justified—by the need to respond to the other's previous defections. If restaints are to be maintained, then, self-interest may need to be reinforced by norms rooted in morality.

Before elaborating this argument, I want to note the perverse pos-sibility that moral restraints may undermine, rather than bolster, re-straints. Two forces can be at work here. First, morality can operate on the ends as well as the means. To the extent that the conflict is imbued with moral fervor, either or both sides can believe that what is at stake is nothing less than supreme values. The war will then be total—it will be a zero-sum game, no interest will be seen as common,

---

47. See *International Organization*, 36 (Spring 1982), special issue on regimes, ed. Ste-phen Krasner, and *World Politics*, 38 (October 1985), special issue on cooperation under anarchy, ed. Kenneth Oye.

48. Jervis, *Perception and Misperception in International Politics*, pp. 67–76, 319–27, 338–42, 349–55; Jervis, "Realism, Game Theory, and Cooperation," *World Politics*, 40 (April 1988), 336–40.

and so cooperation will be impossible.[49] Second, even if it remains a PD, cooperation will be less likely if either or both sides believe that the other has no choice but to continue cooperating. CC requires not only the desire to avoid DD but also the realization that unilateral defection (DC) is not a long-term possibility. Thus if the state thinks that the other's morality is so constraining that it will not retaliate even if the state exploits it, then only morality, and not self-interest, will keep the state restrained. But high conflict usually leads each state to see its adversary as immoral, so this possibility is not likely to be more than theoretical.

More often, morality can play an important role in maintaining restraints. With only self-interest operating, fear, temptation, and misperception often suffice to prevent cooperation. Morality can supply additional reasons for restraint that will inhibit defection and thus lead to a cooperative solution that is in each side's long-run interest.[50] Doing good can lead to doing well. Furthermore, if the state believes that its adversary lives by the same morality, it will have reason to expect it to obey the restraint also.[51] This expectation will usually increase the incentives for the state to be restrained. The system of cooperation will be even more stable if the particular restraint not only is supported by moral judgments but also is embedded in a whole framework of ethics.[52]

One can only wish that morality played a greater role in maintaining restraints. Although one cannot assume that any particular situation is a PD, it is striking that statesmen often overlook the possibility of mutual cooperative solutions.[53] At many crucial points since 1945, leaders have failed even to think seriously about the possibility of reaching CC or to contemplate the long-run implications of their lack of re-

49. For further discussion, see Tucker, "The Rationale of Force," p. 198.

50. For a related argument, see ibid., pp. 205–6.

51. Of course this requirement is met only infrequently in periods of high international conflict. Thus in 1952, NSC-135/1 declared that "the directing group of the Soviet Government and of international communism is totally uninhibited by any consideration of a humanitarian, moral or ethical nature" (Department of State, *FRUS, 1952–1954*, vol. 2, *National Security Policy*, pt. 1 [Washington, D.C.: Government Printing Office, 1984], p. 89; also see p. 380).

52. The importance of embedding specific norms and rules in a wider supporting framework is stressed by Vinod Aggarwal, "Textiles: International Negotiations," *International Organization*, 37 (Autumn 1983), 617–45.

53. For an example of the error of assuming a PD, see Douglas Lackey, "Missiles and Morals: A Utilitarian Look at Nuclear Deterrence," *Philosophy and Public Affairs*, 11 (Summer 1982), 199. For further discussion of how common morality can increase cooperation when the situation is PD, see Jervis, "Realism, Game Theory, and Cooperation."

straint.[54] For example, although the United States thought about alternatives to dropping the atomic bomb on a Japanese city in 1945, all choices were evaluated in terms of whether they would bring the war to a quick end. Some people thought of the moral questions (although they had not been raised with the even more destructive fire raids), but no one in a position of responsibility asked whether dropping the bomb would increase or decrease the chances of postwar control of nuclear weapons.[55]

Similarly, when the American leaders were deciding whether to proceed with the development of the hydrogen bomb, little thought was given to the possibility of long-run cooperation, especially via a test ban. Those who called for development argued that the Russians would move ahead no matter what we did—a familiar (and perhaps accurate) assumption—and few of those who urged holding back, although (or perhaps because) they were strongly influenced by morality, called for conditioning American restraint on similar Soviet behavior.[56] The development of MIRVs provides another dreary but instructive example. It should have been clear from the start that the only choices were CC and DD. Although the United States could gain DC in the immediate future, it was foolish to act as though the Soviets would fail to develop MIRVs of their own. If the United States preferred CC to DD, the only way to reach its goal was by formal agreement or tactic bargaining. (In fact, at the time—but probably not now—America decision makers may have preferred DD, in part because of domestic considerations in the form of the Joint Chiefs of Staff's opposition to arms control.) But in the SALT talks the subject came up only in a half-hearted manner, the choice of CC versus DD was never explicitly faced, and the resulting question of how to maintain cooperation was never seriously addressed.[57] Morality may, then, produce prudence by bolstering national restraint and leading statesmen to take others' interests into account. Such an outlook may be best for the state in the long run even if this is not the interest that is motivating the behavior.

54. My thoughts on this point owe much to reading McGeorge Bundy, *Danger and Survival* (New York: Random House, 1988).
55. Ibid., chap. 2. The question was raised in one report, but it was not taken up by the panel of senior scientists, let alone by the political leaders.
56. Ibid., chap. 5; Herbert York, *The Advisors: Oppenheimer, Teller, and the Superbomb* (San Francisco: Freeman, 1976).
57. It is interesting that Henry Kissinger says, "the age of MIRVs has doomed the SALT approach," when he deserves much of the credit for the latter and blame for the former. See "A New Approach to Arms Control," *Time*, March 21, 1983, p. 25.

Anthropologists have argued that taboos can serve important functions by helping to protect society against the temptations of short-run self-interest.[58] Thus if Hindus were guided by immediate individual calculations, they would kill their cattle during severe droughts. But the effect would be devastating over the longer run; when the rains returned they would be unable to reestablish a flourishing agriculture, which depends on the use of these animals. To tell people to ignore their immediate hunger in order to protect their future would not be effective. A rational self-interested person would not heed the plea but would kill his oxen and hope to buy, borrow, or steal someone else's after the drought. The Hindus avoid this disastrous outcome because to them killing cattle is not seen as a matter for such calculations. Instead, it is flatly prohibited by religion. Some people starve as a result, but the society continues. If morality could play the same role in the world as a whole, most of the people and states in it might be better off. Perhaps a kind of irrationality—or at least nonrationality—is necessary if nations are not to act on the fears and temptations that are so strong and that can be so self-defeating.

If analysis of morality and international politics is difficult, firm conclusions are even more so. Thus I will be both brief and tentative. As Bruce Russett has said: "There is *no* perfect practical solution to the problem of nuclear deterrence. Moral considerations further complicate the problem. Every possibility contains practical and moral dangers."[59] Any way of gaining security involves a chance of killing millions of innocents. As the previous discussion indicates, in some situations morality can help ameliorate problems of security by helping decision makers to reach a solution acceptable to both sides. But to imagine that it could solve our most pressing international conflicts is unrealistic. Even if Soviet and American aims are compatible over the long run, the problems remain of how this compatibility is to be recognized and how the greater role for morality is going to be put in place.

I would suggest several more modest functions for morality. First, as Stanley Hoffmann notes, "It is good to remind statesmen that the ends do not justify all means, that restraints should be observed even in an angry war, that humanity must somehow be preserved."[60] The temptation to believe that the environment is so extreme as to compel

58. Marvin Harris, *Cows, Pigs, Wars, and Witches: The Riddles of Culture* (New York: Random House, 1979).

59. Russett, "Ethical Dilemmas of Nuclear Deterrence," pp. 51, 54.

60. Stanley Hoffmann, *Duties beyond Borders: On the Limits and Possibilities of Ethical International Politics* (Syracuse: Syracuse University Press, 1981), p. 81.

the most awful actions and the statemen's hubris of thinking that their acts are beyond judging are terribly strong and must be constantly resisted. Resistance may not alter behavior or even provide detailed guidance, but at least it serves to keep before us the criteria and standards we as human beings must strive for. Although it may be impossible to run a foreign policy along Gladstonian principles—indeed Gladstone was not able to do so—we should not forget the question he raised during the Balkan crisis of 1877: "What is to be the consequence to civilization and humanity, to public order, if British interests are to be the rule for British agents all over the world, and are to be for them the measure of right or wrong?"[61]

Perhaps as shocking as the calculated violations of moral standards are the many cases in which statesmen do not even think of what their acts will cost in terms of innocent lives, deplorable precedents, and values sullied. In extreme circumstances—and such occasions are not uncommon in international politics—states have to break moral standards in order that other values may survive. But at least decision makers should be aware of the crimes that they are committing.[62] Thus Walzer argues that Britain was right to engage in area bombing in the most desperate hours of World War II, but also was right not to honor the airmen involved after the war.[63] Cruel as it was to the men of the Bomber Command, the snub constituted a national admission that the country had, under grave duress, acted immorally, an admission that paid homage to the moral standards and values for which the British had fought.

Morality can also help statesmen avoid pseudo-Realism—the preoccupation with power and interest narrowly conceived that so often is not only evil but self-defeating. It is too easy for decision makers to act without regard for others' values. This self-centered perspective also makes calculation easy and spares decision makers the need to try to understand how others may see the situation and their nation. But while it may seem that self-interested actors should rationally look after only their own interest, in a world of powerful and autonomous states such behavior is not likely to yield long-run benefits. When others can help or harm the state, their acquiescence if not support is needed. This can rarely be obtained unless their interests are understood, taken into account, and at least partially satisfied.

61. Quoted in R. W. Seton-Watson, *Disraeli, Gladstone, and the Eastern Question* (New York: Norton, 1972), p. 69.
62. See, for example, the discussion in Michael Sherry, *The Rise of American Air Power* (New Haven: Yale University Press, 1987), pp. 287–88.
63. Walzer, *Just and Unjust Wars*, pp. 323–25.

Acting on the basis of narrow and immediate interest also can give decision makers a comforting sense of confidence. But uncertainty, which is so important in nuclear strategy, is present in most other international situations as well. Even though they may not recognize it, only rarely can statesmen predict with certainty the consequences of their acts. They must act nevertheless, but since they cannot be sure what will be effective they should perhaps more often care about acting morally. When consequences are hard to judge, as they so often are, statesmen might take more guidance from principles of ethics.

The clash between morality and self-interest will often remain, however. Hans Morgenthau's conclusion that "political ethics is indeed the ethics of doing evil" is particularly true when threats and force come into play.[64] Clausewitz unfortunately was correct: "Kind-hearted people might . . . think there was some ingenious way to disarm or defeat an enemy without too much bloodshed, and might imagine this is the true goal of the art of war. Pleasant as it sounds, it is a fallacy that must be exposed."[65] The difficulties are even greater in the nuclear era. Unless only those who are guilty are being hurt (an alluring but impractical idea), punishment always involves an element of immorality. It is hard to fit our best impulses to the basic facts of nuclear weapons. Morality seeks to limit harm; international coercion seeks to threaten if not inflict it. The two can never be entirely reconciled.

64. Hans Morgenthau, *Scientific Man versus Power Politics*, p. 202.
65. Carl von Clausewitz, *On War*, ed. and trans. Michael Howard and Peter Paret (Princeton: Princeton University Press, 1976), p. 75.

[5]

Psychological Aspects
of Crisis Stability

PSYCHOLOGY AND CRISIS STABILITY

A wide variety of issues and chains of events could lead to all-out nuclear war, but the last step in almost all of them would be preemption. Total war could not occur in the absence of the belief that war is imminent and inevitable and that, as terrible as striking first would be, receiving the first blow would be even worse.[1] These twin beliefs are

---

1. For similar formulations, see Alexander George, "Crisis Management: The Interaction of Political and Military Considerations," *Survival*, 26 (September/October, 1984), 223–34; George, "Problems of Crisis Management and Crisis Avoidance in U.S.–Soviet Relations," in Øyvind Østerud, ed., *Studies of War and Peace* (Oslo: Norwegian University Press, 1986), pp. 202–26; Warner Schilling, William T. R. Fox, Catherine Kelleher, and Donald Puchala, *American Arms and a Changing Europe* (New York: Columbia University Press, 1973), pp. 172–74; and Richard Ned Lebow, *Between Peace and War* (Baltimore: Johns Hopkins University Press, 1981), pp. 254–63. Conversely, statesmen often share the analysis of Alexander Cadogan, permanent undersecretary of the U.K. Foreign Office in 1938: "I certainly feel that it would be very difficult to choose any course of action that might plunge Europe into war now to avert what might be a war later on" (Quoted in Telford Taylor, *Munich* [Garden City, N.Y.: Doubleday, 1979], p. 625).

For a general review of the topic of inadvertent nuclear war, see Daniel Frei, *Risks of Unintended Nuclear War* (Totowa, N.J.: Rowman & Allanheld, 1983), chap. 5. The classic historical case occurred in 1914, when both sides believed that the nature of military technology and tactics gave a great advantage to the offense and that the state that was able to strike first would be able to increase its chance of victory. For an excellent game theoretic treatment that argues that under reasonable assumptions, even crisis instability cannot produce nuclear war if statesmen are rational, see Robert Powell, "Reconsidering the Reciprocal Fear of Surprise Attack," (unpublished paper, Harvard University, 1987), and "Crisis Stability in the Nuclear Age," *American Political Science Review*, 83 (March 1989). Colin Gray reaches the same conclusion by a somewhat different path: "ICBMs

not required for the use of lower levels of violence, even including the limited use of nuclear weapons. Indeed these beliefs would make such managed exercises of force self-defeating. But as long as total war would be more disastrous than even the loss of a limited war or a crushing political defeat, statesmen would initiate a full-scale attack only if they thought that the other side was about to do so. If war is seen as inevitable, neither surrender nor deterrence is possible. The latter implies not only the threat to retaliate if the other attacks but also the promise not to attack if the other is similarly restrained.[2] By definition, a state that has concluded that war is certain will not believe such promises. Peace cannot be bought, even at the cost of enormous concessions, including surrender.[3]

A decision maker with even a modicum of sanity will prefer even a very unsatisfactory peace to war, but this choice might not be available. In a crisis of unprecedented severity, one may come to believe that the choice is between war right now and war in the immediate future, between a war one's own state starts and a war the other side initiates. If the former is seen as preferable to the latter, war can result even though both sides want to avoid it. This preference is also likely to influence the perceived likelihood of war; the state will expect the other to attack—and war to be inevitable—only if it thinks that the other sees such an advantage in striking first. This problem of crisis instability is in large part a psychological one, and because the psychological aspects have not been sufficiently appreciated, I focus on them in this chapter and say relatively little about other facets of the problem, although a more definitive treatment would need to be better rounded.

In this discussion I assume that central decision makers remain in control of their strategic nuclear forces. Of course this may not be true. In a limited nuclear war, the central authorities could be killed or the communication channels that link them to their forces could be severed. Furthermore, the fear of these eventualities may lead decision makers to delegate authority for nuclear use to field commanders. (Of course the belief that the state had carried out such delegation could deter the adversary from attacking by leading the latter to see that it could not

---

and Deterrence: The Controversy over Prompt Launch," *Journal of Strategic Studies*, 10 (September 1987), 285–309. Also see Barry O'Neill, "Crisis Instability with Space-Based Antimissile Systems," *Journal of Conflict Resolution*, 31 (December 1987), 631–72.

2. Thomas Schelling, *Strategy of Conflict* (Cambridge: Harvard University Press, 1960), p. 120.

3. Robert Powell demonstrates the extent to which the ability to terminate the crisis by concession controls crisis instability. See Powell, "Reconsidering the Reciprocal Fear of Surprise Attack" and "Crisis Stability in the Nuclear Age."

carry out a successful first strike.) Delegating would be dangerous because it would increase the number of people who could initiate massive nuclear strikes and these people would feel incentives and pressures different from those felt by the top civilian leadership. Nevertheless, the general dynamics I discuss could apply to local commanders as well as to the president and first secretary, although of course many of the details would be different.[4]

CRISIS INSTABILITY

More than twenty-five years ago, Albert Wohlstetter argued that the balance of terror was delicate (i.e., that a first strike could have major advantages). Building on this reasoning, Thomas Schelling explained that one of the greatest dangers of war was "the reciprocal fear of surprise attack."[5] Since each side fears being taken by surprise, each must remain on the alert, which means not only carefully monitoring the other side's military activities (although, as I will note later, even this seemingly harmless stance can be troublesome) but also preparing one's forces to act. These actions, however, can lead the other side to conclude that the state may be about to attack. The other side would then move to an increased state of readiness, thus confirming the state's suspicions that an attack was likely and causing it to move to an even higher level of alert. The result could be an awful self-fulfilling prophecy in which the actions each side takes out of the fear that it may be the victim of surprise fuel the fears of the other side, producing a war neither side sought.

It did not take outside experts to detect this danger. The historical lessons statesmen drew from 1914 and the memories of the surprise attacks of 1941 were reinforced by the belief that nuclear weapons made

4. For further discussions, see Richard Ned Lebow, *Nuclear Crisis Management: A Dangerous Illusion* (Ithaca: Cornell University Press, 1987), and Ashton Carter, John Steinbruner, and Charles Zraket, eds., *Managing Nuclear Operations* (Washington, D.C.: Brookings Institution, 1987).

5. Schelling, *Strategy of Conflict*, chap. 9, and *Arms and Influence* (New Haven: Yale University Press, 1966), chap. 6, "The Dynamics of Mutual Alarm." This concern grew out of the famous RAND study of how the Strategic Air Command's bombers should be deployed. For a sanitized version of the study, see Albert Wohlstetter, "The Delicate Balance of Terror," *Foreign Affairs*, 37 (January 1959), 211–34; a summary of the original study is now available: E. S. Quade, "The Selection and Use of Strategic Air Bases: A Case History," in E. S. Quade, ed., *Analysis for Military Decisions* (Chicago: Rand McNally, 1966), pp. 24–63; the study itself is now printed: A. J. Wohlstetter, F. S. Hoffman, R. J. Lutz, and H. S. Rowen, "Selection and Use of Strategic Air Bases," in Marc Trachtenberg, ed., *The Development of American Strategic Thought: Writings on Strategy, 1952–1960*, vol. 1 (New York: Garland, 1988), pp. 163–589.

such attacks even more devastating. Thus in November 1945 *Time* included as one of its twelve propositions about nuclear weapons: "Atomic weapons increase the incentive to aggression by multiplying the advantage of surprise."[6] When it looked ahead to the era when the Soviets would have a large nuclear force, NSC-68 reached the same conclusion: incentives to strike first, not stability, were foreseen, a judgment shared by the analyses of the incoming Eisenhower administration.[7] Indeed the desire to reduce these incentives led to many of Eisenhower's arms policies, from weapons development (Minuteman and Polaris), to still-born proposals (Open Skies), to important beginnings (the international conference on reducing the danger of surprise attack). Throughout the nuclear era, central concerns of American strategy have been the danger of being taken by surprise and, as I discuss below, the advantages to be gained by preemption.

The state's behavior is often closely linked to its foreign policy goals and to its analysis of those of the other side. There are no such links, however, in a situation of crisis instability. If the state believed that staying at peace was not possible, it could attack even though it preferred the status quo to starting a war and believed that the adversary was similarly defensive.[8] This is an extreme and particularly dangerous example of the security dilemma that characterizes so much of international politics. The term "security dilemma" is often used loosely to refer to the difficulties states have in gaining security. But more useful is the precise definition of the term: the means by which states try to make themselves more secure often have the undesired and unintended consequence of making others less secure.[9] Thus mutual security, even if desired by

6. *Time*, November 12, 1945, p. 28. The other eleven points were amazingly prescient.

7. NSC-68 in John Gaddis and Thomas Etzold, eds., *Containment: Documents on American Policy and Strategy, 1945–1950* (New York: Columbia University Press, 1978), p. 432; Department of State, *Foreign Relations of the United States, 1952–1954*, vol. 2, *National Security Policy* (Washington, D.C: Government Printing Office, 1984), pt. 1, p. 62 (hereafter cited as *FRUS*).

8. The analogy here is to Rousseau's *Stag Hunt*. See Kenneth Waltz, *Man, the State and War* (New York: Columbia University Press, 1954), pp. 167–71, 183–84 and Robert Jervis, "Cooperation under the Security Dilemma," *World Politics*, 30 (January 1978), 167–70.

9. The idea is as old as Thucydides. In the modern era, it was first discussed by Herbert Butterfield, *History and Human Relations* (London: Collins, 1951), pp. 19–20; John Herz, "Idealist Internationalism and the Security Dilemma," *World Politics* 2 (January 1950), 157–80; and Arnold Wolfers, *Discord and Collaboration* (Baltimore: Johns Hopkins University Press, 1962), p. 84. I have developed the implications and resulting problems in *Perception and Misperception in International Politics* (Princeton: Princeton University Press, 1976), chap. 3, and "Cooperation under the Security Dilemma."

both sides, may be beyond reach. The preparation (or "generation") of a state's forces to increase its security would not only increase the number of weapons that would survive an attack but would also at least marginally increase the number that would be available for a first strike.[10] Actions that had only the former, but not the latter, effect, would be safer, such as sending to sea submarines that were in port or dispersing land-mobile missiles.

But even these seemingly innocuous measures would entail dangers to the other side. First, any measure that would increase the number of weapons that could survive the adversary's first strike would also increase the number that would survive the adversary's counterforce response to the state's first strike. Second, the other side might see protective moves as indicating that the state's leaders had decided to go to war or would be unable to maintain political control of their forces. Third, because striking first is more effective against an adversary who has not yet put its forces on alert, the other side might attack in anticipation of the state's forces being generated. In a situation that was becoming tense, the knowledge that the advantages of a first strike would shortly be diminished could create crisis instability. Secretary of Defense McNamara recognized this dynamic in his Draft Presidential Memoranda on tactical nuclear weapons in the late 1960s, noting that in a crisis "the temptation would be high . . . to attack the enemy's nuclear delivery systems before they could be used or to destroy his massed ground forces before they could disperse."[11] Thus stability would be increased by forces that were always invulnerable or by policies that generated them before the crisis became severe.

Disadvantages of Crisis Stability

Three points about crisis stability should be noted. First, in a crisis each side will have two general objectives. Not only will it want to avoid a major war, it will also want to avoid a political defeat, if not gain a victory. The Chinese character for "crisis" is made up of two elements, one signifying danger, the other opportunity. Even if the former element is now so great that few statesmen are likely to look forward to crises with glee, the incentives at least to maintain one's

10. At least this is what the United States probably would do, as it has done in the past. The Soviet Union, however, has never put its nuclear forces on alert.

11. Quoted in Joshua Epstein, *Strategy and Force Planning* (Washington, D.C.: Brookings Institution, 1987), p. 19; also see p. 20.

position are strong. Thus states are driven by conflicting incentives when bargaining in crises, causing them to use conflicting tactics.[12] It would be simple for states to ensure crisis stability if they were willing to sacrifice their political goals.

Second, a high degree of crisis stability can conflict with other American security values, and, ironically, the belief that crisis stability is less than complete may itself be stabilizing by inhibiting provocations. This is one application of the stability-instability paradox.[13] While mutual second-strike capability creates stability at the level of all-out force, it also permits the adversary to threaten or use lower levels of violence with less fear that the state can respond with a a full-scale first strike, thus undercutting extended deterrence. Mutual security between the state and its adversary then carries disadvantages.

The problem is not new: as long as status-quo powers have alliance commitments or vital interests outside their boundaries, they need to be able to fight in response to attacks on others. For example, France was pledged to take the offensive against Germany in the 1930s if that country attacked France's East European allies. Before 1914, alliance commitments also were one reason why the great powers sought the ability not only to protect their own territory, but to go on the offensive.[14]

The limitations in the Washington Naval Treaty of 1921, which guaranteed the home territories of both Japan and the United States, thus created difficulties. "A forty-percent inferiority in capital ships and carriers rendered it unlikely that the Japanese could successfully invade the eastern Pacific. On the other hand, the absence of modern and large-scale facilities at Guam, Wake, the Philippines, and the Aleutians made the United States operations in the western Pacific extremely difficult, given the then state of naval technology."[15] Even had the

12. For a further discussion, see Glenn Snyder, " 'Prisoner's Dilemma' and 'Chicken' Models in International Politics," *International Studies Quarterly*, 15 (March 1971) 66–103.

13. In awareness of this problem, some have used the term "first-strike stability" for what most analysts call crisis stability and use the term "crisis stability" for a situation in which provocations as well as an all-out nuclear attack would seem disastrous. See David Williamson, Jr., Richard Wilcox, and Patrick Garrity, eds., *Opportunities for Crisis Control in a Nuclear Age* (Washington, D.C.: Center for Strategic and International Studies, October 1985), pp. 12–14. But while the dilemma is real, this terminology obscures more than it clarifies.

14. See Robert Jervis, "Cooperation under the Security Dilemma," pp. 183–86, and Scott Sagan, "1914 Revisited: Allies, Offense, and Instability," *International Security*, 11 (Fall 1986), 151–76.

15. Arthur Tiedemann, "Introduction: The London Naval Treaty, 1930," in James Morley, ed., *Japan Erupts: The London Naval Conference and the Manchurian Incident, 1928–1932* (New York: Columbia University Press, 1984), p. 5.

treaty been extended, it could not have facilitated the American protection of Asian countries. And it was this need, rather than a direct threat to the American homeland, that eventually drew the United States into war in the Pacific. Extreme stability, then, is an unmitigated blessing only in the rare instances in which the state can always stand on the military defensive.

Conversely, the fear of crisis instability can inhibit aggression and the creation of crises. Furthermore, this effect can be produced by the adversary's having a degree of first-strike capability. If the state's forces are so vulnerable that they might be destroyed if caught on the ground, the other side might see crises as too dangerous to provoke. Similarly, the inhibitions against the Russians' launching a conventional attack against Europe would be great if they believed that American decision makers would view such an attack as the opening stages of World War III (not an unreasonable inference). Alternatively, crisis instability can be produced by certain psychological dynamics (discussed later in this chapter) or by the actions of local military commanders who, no longer under the control of central decision makers, might escalate the conflict on their own. But no matter what the mechanism, the result is one of the nasty trade-offs common in the nuclear world: by making major provocations and limited wars more dangerous, crisis instability increases the probabilities both of complete Soviet-American peace and of all-out war.

A third and related point is that American war planning, in contrast to declaratory policy, has always embodied a significant element of striking first. In 1950, NSC-68 argued that "the military advantages of landing the first blow become increasingly important with modern weapons, and this is a fact which requires us to be on the alert in order to strike with our full weight as soon as we are attacked, and, if possible, before the Soviet blow is actually delivered."[16] Six years later, President Eisenhower wrote in his diary that "the only possible way of reducing . . . losses [in the event of war] would be for us to take the initiative sometime during the assumed month in which we had the warning of an attack and launch a surprise attack against the Soviets," although he also felt that because such an action would require both congressional approval and complete secrecy, "it would appear impossible

---

16. Reprinted in Gaddis and Etzold, *Containment*, p. 432. For a discussion of the related impulse toward preventive war among American decision makers, see Marc Trachtenberg, " 'A Wasting Asset'? American Strategy and the Shifting Nuclear Balance, 1949–1954," *International Security*, 13 (Winter 1988–89), 5–49.

that any such thing would occur."[17] Perhaps more serious was Curtis LeMay's report that, as head of SAC, he would launch the force if he received unambiguous warning of an impending Soviet attack. When he was informed that this was not national policy, he replied, "I don't care. It's my policy. That's what I'm going to do."[18] Even now, there are strong indications that the United States would strike first if it was certain that the Soviets were about to try to do so.

One reason for this stance is the American commitment to its allies. Other reasons are technical: the complications and uncertainties of fighting a nuclear war increase drastically if the other side gets the first blow in. Even the most sophisticated military planner—or especially the most sophisticated military planner—cannot know which of his forces will survive and how they can be controlled after the unprecedented shock of a nuclear attack.

Incentives to Strike First

Although a degree of crisis instability serves important functions, most worry has been about too much rather than too little of it. To reduce it, states primarily have sought to reduce the advantage the other side would gain if it attacked, taking measures not necessarily incompatible with trying to secure at least some first-strike advantage for themselves.[19] Bombers not ready for quick take-offs and vulnerable missiles that had to be fueled before they could be launched did not provide a secure second-strike force. To remedy these defects, the United States constructed effective warning systems and made the strategic systems as invulnerable as possible.

But until recently scholars and officials alike concentrated their attention on the weapon systems themselves, ignoring vulnerabilities of C^3 systems that would limit the ability of decision makers to decide that an attack was underway and to communicate the necessary orders

17. Quoted in Robert Ferrell, ed., *The Eisenhower Diaries* (New York: Norton, 1981), p. 312.

18. Quoted in Fred Kaplan, *The Wizards of Armageddon* (New York: Simon & Schuster, 1983), p. 134. Jerome Wiesner remembers LeMay's reply as quite different: "it's my job to make it possible for the president to change his policy" (quoted in Gregg Herken, "Early Takes on PBS's *Nuclear Age*," *Deadline*, 4 [January/February 1989], 4).

19. It is less clear whether the superpowers have sought to reduce their own gains from striking first. It seems unlikely that the Soviets have, and while many American theorists have seen advantages in mutual invulnerability and many American policy makers have claimed that the United States has foregone opportunities to increase its ability to strike first, the public record is not sufficiently full to permit a confident judgment on this point.

to the forces.[20] As long as these systems are much harder to protect than the weapons themselves and might not survive an attack, there is a trade-off between ensuring that the forces will not be used without authorization (negative control) and ensuring that the weapons can be fired if need be (positive control).[21] Taking the American side for the sake of convenience, to reduce the danger of accidents, the president needs to be sure that the weapons will not be fired unless he so orders. But this means that were he and his successors to be killed or cut off from SAC, the American forces would be impotent even if they remained undamaged. This situation obviously gives the Soviets strong incentives to launch a "decapitation" attack—that is, one aimed at Washington and the other few locations where designated leaders might be. The magnitude of this problem is not as great as some have implied, as I argue later, but nevertheless, the vulnerability of leadership and communications facilities could provide reasons to strike first.

Here, and in other arguments for the existence of incentives to strike first, it is assumed that the possibility of a first strike exists. This assumption might seem self-evident, and indeed true by definition, but it ignores two possibilities. First, the adversary might "launch on warning"—that is, respond to sensor indications that the state was attacking. Although the state would in some sense still have made a first strike, it would not gain many of its offensive advantages because many of its targets would no longer be there. Second, the adversary might have more advanced warning that an attack was coming and thus be able to preempt. First strike might then be an option for only one side. A nice example came out of the 1976 NATO exercises. Because of its ability

---

20. Desmond Ball, *Can Nuclear War Be Controlled?* Adelphi Paper no. 169 (London: International Institute for Strategic Studies, 1981); Congressional Budget Office, *Strategic Command, Control and Communications: Alternative Approaches for Modernization* (Washington, D.C.: Congress of the United States, 1981); Frank Klotz, "The U.S. President and the Control of Strategic Nuclear Weapons" (Ph.D. diss., Oxford University, 1980); John Steinbruner, "Launch under Attack," *Scientific American*, January 1984, pp. 37–47; Bruce Blair, *Strategic Command and Control* (Washington, D.C.: Brookings Institution, 1985); Carter, Steinbruner, and Zraket, *Managing Nuclear Operations*; Daniel Shuchman, "Nuclear Strategy and the Problem of Command and Control," *Survival*, 29 (July/August 1987), 336–59. A good discussion of NATO command systems can be found in Paul Bracken, *The Command and Control of Nuclear Forces* (New Haven: Yale University Press, 1983), chap. 5, and Desmond Ball, "Controlling Theatre Nuclear War," Working Paper no. 138 (Canberra: Australian National University, October 1987). In 1946 Bernard Brodie devoted a paragraph to the importance of secure C³: *The Absolute Weapon* (New York: Harcourt, Brace, 1946), p. 91.

21. See the discussion by John Steinbruner in "Choices and Trade-offs," in Carter, Steinbruner, and Zraket, *Managing Nuclear Operations*, pp. 539–41.

to intercept NATO communications, the Soviets at one point knew that NATO was about to employ nuclear weapons. And because their command and communications structure was more compact than that of NATO, they "announced two hours before . . . our troops had gotten approval that NATO was going nuclear."[22] In such a situation, NATO might not be able to use nuclear weapons first even if it wanted to.

Extent of Offensive Advantages Pressures to strike first may come from two sources. First, the state may fear that if it does not strike first, it will not be able to strike at all, that its forces may be so vulnerable that they could be destroyed or immobilized by the other's attack. Here, striking first would not yield positive benefits. Indeed if striking would not reduce the damage to the state or increase its ability to terminate the war on favorable conditions, it is not clear why the state would attack. But the desire to ensure that the adversary will not automatically dominate the postwar world can be strong and the threat to attack rather than be rendered helpless can deter the adversary from creating a crisis, although of course it can also lead to an undesired war once a crisis comes into sight.

The second kind of incentive to strike first is the more familiar hope of limiting or even preventing the other side's retaliation. Just as the state's strategic vulnerability produces the first incentive to attack, vulnerability of the adversary's forces creates the second. Of course both kinds of incentives can be present simultaneously—in extreme cases both sides could have first-strike capability—and if one side has one kind of incentive, the other side has the other kind. But defensive incentives may be irrationally magnified by moods of despair, and offensive incentives by moods of great optimism.

When states believe that they are better off receiving than giving the first blow, then even the belief that war is inevitable will not lead to war. When they believe that offense would be advantageous, the details matter more. Similarly, if all-out war is thought to be completely certain, then the country should attack even if it brings only a slight advantage.[23] But if the perceived probability of war is anything less

22. Quoted in Ball, "Controlling Theatre Nuclear War," p. 25.
23. Of course, this perceived advantage can be the summation of the utilities expected under a variety of conditions. That is, it is unlikely that the statesman would be certain what the effect of his first strike would be. Although a great deal of analysis has been devoted to trying to determine such factors as the reliability and accuracy of missiles, the vulnerability of silos, and the danger of "fratricide" (the explosion from one incoming warhead destroying others), the technical uncertainties are still very great. Political uncertainties remain as well, primarily whether either side would fire its missiles before

ne, then a rational decision involves judging the probability of he extent to which striking first is better than striking second, he value of remaining at peace.

A completely rational assessment renders the problem of crisis stability relatively manageable because under most reasonable assumptions the advantages to striking first are minimal at best.[24] Each side has so many nuclear weapons, and the number of targets that need to be destroyed in order to devastate the country is so small, that even an extremely successful first strike will not greatly reduce the damage that the country will suffer. Furthermore, attacks on vulnerable forces are dangerous—more dangerous than attacks on invulnerable ones—because of the chance that the defender will fire immediately rather than allow its forces to be destroyed. Of course there are weighty arguments against establishing such a launch-on-warning system, and it is not clear whether either side has adopted this policy. Still, the attacker could never be confident that the other's forces were *not* so configured.

Earlier we noted the current concern with the vulnerability, not of weapons, but of leadership and C^3. A successful decapitation attack, it can be argued, could prevent retaliation. But this problem should not be exaggerated. The very fact that the danger is known indicates that statesmen will take steps to try to ameliorate it. Most obviously, both sides have moved to protect both C^3 and leadership, although there are severe limits, partly political ones, to what the United States can do in the latter regard. As an alternative or supplement to protection, the president could "predelegate" the authority to fire the force to military leaders. The dangers here are obvious and even those who resent the caricatures in *Dr. Strangelove* prefer to minimize the number of people who could start World War III. Furthermore, predelegation would increase the chance that the other side would believe that war was inevitable if a sharp crisis arose, even as it simultaneously decreased the advantage the other would see in striking first.

One compromise would have the president maintain complete (neg-

---

those of the other side landed. Thus it is quite possible that careful analysis would render the mixed judgment that while striking first would yield advantages if the systems and the adversary behaved in certain ways, under other assumptions striking second would be advantageous.

24. For similar discussions, see Richard Betts, "Surprise Attack and Preemption," in Graham Allison, Albert Carnesale, and Joseph Nye, Jr., eds., *Hawks, Doves, and Owls* (New York: Norton, 1985), pp. 54–79; Robert Jervis, *The Illogic of American Nuclear Strategy* (Ithaca: Cornell University Press, 1985), pp. 128–29; Lebow, *Nuclear Crisis Management*. This might not be true in a limited counterforce war, as I discuss below.

ative) control of the forces in normal times, since the danger of a "bolt from the blue" is vanishingly small. But in a severe crisis, he could predelegate, thus removing the Soviets' incentives for a decapitation strike. Such a compromise is sensible and may well be American policy, but if the Soviets believed this to be the case, the early stages of the crisis would be extremely dangerous. If attacking before authorization has been delegated could provide at least a chance that the United States could not retaliate, whereas any war that occurred after delegation would be disastrous, then striking early would make a small but unfortunate amount of sense. This would be especially true if the Soviets believed that it would be difficult to maintain the peace after authority to fire the weapons had been widely dispersed, thus giving the Soviets defensive as well as offensive reasons to strike. Furthermore, the United States, knowing of those dangers, would be faced with the dilemma of either predelegating authority very early, before the Soviets realized that the situation was becoming serious (and then demonstrating that this had been done), or convincing the Soviets that it was not about to predelegate.

The other obvious approach, which also may be one the United States has adopted, would be informal and ambiguous predelegation. The submarines have the ability, if not the authorization, to fire their missiles without word from Washington; the SAC flying command post has the codes to unlock the ICBM warheads and bombs and send them to their targets.[25] Thus even a successful decapitation strike would not physically prevent nuclear weapons from being fired. What the commanders' orders are in the event that communications with Washington cease is secret, but the crucial factor is that the Soviets could not be sure that the commanders would not retaliate.

As a consequence, the first-strike incentives created by C^3 vulnerability are sharply limited. Although the problem remains serious and further efforts to cope with it are warranted, the destruction of the adversary's leadership or communications facilities probably would not prevent re-

---

25. That the SAC flying command post has the nuclear codes was revealed by Raymond Tate, formerly a deputy assistant secretary of the navy and deputy director of the National Security Agency, in "Worldwide C^3I and Telecommunications" (Incidental Paper for the Seminar on Command, Control, Communications, and Intelligence, Program on Information Resources Policy, Harvard University, 1980), p. 43. I am grateful to Desmond Ball for telling me of this source. Also see Curtis LeMay's discussion of acting without formal authorization in case "we woke up some morning and there wasn't any Washington or something" (Richard Kohn and Joseph Harahan, eds., "U.S. Strategic Air Power, 1948–1962: Excerpts from an Interview with Generals Curtis E. LeMay, Leon W. Johnson, David A. Burchinal, and Jack L. Catton," *International Security*, 12 [Spring 1988], 83–86).

taliation. Indeed, it might ensure that the response would be unrestrained. There is much validity to the question posed by Jacob Viner a few months after Hiroshima: "What difference will it then make whether it was country A which had its cities destroyed at 9 A.M. and country B which had its cities destroyed at 12 A.M. or the other way round?"[26]

As long as the advantage of striking first is slight, holding back makes sense even if the perceived probability of war is high but still less than one. Because decision makers could not be absolutely certain that war was about to start, preemption, although still a necessary link in any chain leading to total war, is extremely unlikely unless complicating psychological factors to which we will now turn play a large role.[27]

PSYCHOLOGY AND CRISIS STABILITY

If the danger of crisis stability has been exaggerated in some respects, it simultaneously has been underestimated because four kinds of psychological factors have been ignored. First, many general psychological biases, compounded by the stress of a crisis, interfere with the quality of decision making. Second, the way people process information is

26. Jacob Viner, "Implications of the Atomic Bomb for International Relations," *Proceedings of the American Philosophical Society*, 90 (January 1946), 54.

27. American leaders, especially in the Truman and Eisenhower administrations, often spoke of the need to attack if and when it became certain that the Soviets were about to start a war. But, perhaps because key documents remain classified, it is not clear what reliable warnings they expected. In part, they relied on the fact that before the Soviets struck they would have to stage their bombers to forward bases, but if such moves were necessary for an attack, they were not sufficient for it. See, for example, the discussions in the documents reprinted in Gaddis and Etzold, *Containment*, pp. 285–342; David Rosenberg, "The Origins of Overkill: Nuclear Weapons and American Strategy, 1945–1960," *International Security*, 7 (Summer 1983), 17–18, 25–26, 34–35, 63–64; Trachtenberg, "'A Wasting Asset'?"; NSC-5515, March 21, 1955, "Study of Possible Hostile Soviet Actions," provides a list of "specific Soviet actions [that] should be judged . . . as clear evidence that a Soviet attack upon the continental U.S. is certain [or] imminent." Included are "penetration of the continental air control and warning system by Soviet aircraft in a flight pattern indicating attack upon the continental U.S.," "concentration of Soviet submarines in a position and in sufficient numbers to permit effective attacks on major U.S. ports," and, particularly interesting for extended deterrence, "Soviet attack against the countries or territories covered by the NATO mutual defense guarantees." (I am grateful to Scott Sagan for referring me to this document, which is available as Declassified Documents Reference System, no. 002158 [Carrolton Press, 1986], the quotations are from p. 4.) Stansfield Turner's views are very different: "I cannot imagine a Director of Central Intelligence ever having anything approaching 100 percent confidence in his prediction that the Russians were truly going to attack" ("Winnowing Our Warheads," *New York Times Magazine*, March 27, 1988, p. 69). LeMay was not helpful when Herken pressed him on what would constitute unambiguous warning: academics should "not get their nuts in an uproar over that." Quoted in Herken, "Early Takes on PBS's *Nuclear Age*," p. 4.

likely to lead them to overestimate the likelihood that the other side is about to attack during a crisis. Third, related processes can lead them to fail to see the extent to which their actions are convincing the adversary that war is inevitable. Fourth, psychological factors can lead decision makers to overestimate the advantages of striking first. On the other hand, psychology can also produce restraint. These topics will be considered in turn.

General Psychological Biases

Research indicates a curvilinear relationship between stress and the quality of decision making.[28] People do not use their full resources when the matters they are dealing with are inconsequential and do best when they are under some pressure. But past a certain point of stress several factors conspire to decrease people's ability to think clearly, and in the event of a possible nuclear war, decision makers would most assuredly pass that point. First, it is likely that information would be abundant but ambiguous. In the modern age, sensors and bureaucracies produce much more news than recipients can evaluate and assimilate. Thus during the Iranian hostage crisis, the NSC staff member in charge of Iran found himself confronted with over 1,000 pages of reports a day.[29] Second, decisions would have to be reached quickly, often without permitting the solicitation of a wide range of opinions or the discussion of more than a few alternatives. Third, people would have to work round the clock, thus functioning without adequate rest or energy. Fourth, the awareness that millions of people could die as a result of the actions being ordered would produce incredible strain. In such circumstances, it is not surprising that research indicates that some decision makers would literally collapse. Prime Minister Eden did so during the Suez crisis, as did Chief of Staff Rabin during the Six Days' War. Robert Kennedy and Theodore Sorensen

28. George, "Problems of Crisis Management and Crisis Avoidance in U.S.–Soviet Relations," pp. 15–16. For a fuller discussion, see Ole Holsti and Alexander George, "The Effects of Stress on the Performance of Foreign Policy-Makers," in Cornelius Cotter, ed., *Political Science Annual*, vol. 6, 1975 (Indianapolis: Bobbs-Merrill, 1975), pp. 255–319; Ole Holsti, "Theories of Crisis Decision Making," in Paul Gordon Lauren, *Diplomacy* (New York: Free Press, 1979), pp. 99–136; Alexander George, "The Impact of Crisis-Induced Stress on Decision Making," in Frederic Solomon and Richard Marston, eds., *The Medical Implications of Nuclear War* (Washington, D.C.: National Academy Press, 1986), pp. 529–52; Holsti, "Crisis Decision-Making," in Philip Tetlock et al., eds., *Behavior, Society, and Nuclear War*, vol. 1 (New York: Oxford University Press, forthcoming). The psychological literature is summarized in Richard Lazarus, *Psychological Stress and the Coping Process* (New York: McGraw-Hill, 1966).

29. Gary Sick, *All Fall Down* (New York: Random House, 1985), p. 280.

ιave hinted at these problems during the Cuban missile crisis and one nigh official told Alexander George "that two important members of the President's advisory group ... had been unable to cope with the stress, becoming quite passive and unable to fulfill their responsibilities."[30]

These sources of stress do not always operate simultaneously. For example, in some situations crucial values are at stake but there is no need for haste, in others an immediate decision is necessary but the consequences of error are manageable.[31] In a nuclear crisis, however, all these elements would be present. The likely effects have been well summarized by George:

1. Impaired attention and perception
   a. Important aspects of crisis situation may escape scrutiny
   b. Conflicting values and interests at stake may be overlooked
   c. Range of perceived alternatives is likely to narrow but not necessarily to the best option
   d. Search for relevant options tends to be dominated by past experience; tendency to fall back on familiar solutions that have worked in the past, whether or not they are appropriate to present situation

2. Increased cognitive rigidity
   a. Impaired ability to improvise; reduced creativity
   b. Reduced receptivity to information that challenges existing beliefs
   c. Increased stereotypic thinking
   d. Reduced tolerance for ambiguity leading to cut off of information search and premature decision

3. Shortened and narrow perspective
   a. Less attention to longer-range considerations and consequences of action
   b. Less attention to side-effects of options

30. Robert Kennedy, *Thirteen Days* (New York: Norton, 1969), p. 22 (a blunter version is reported in Arthur Schlesinger, Jr., *Robert F. Kennedy and His Times* [Boston: Houghton Mifflin, 1978], p. 507: Rusk, Kennedy thought, "had a virtually complete breakdown mentally and physically," a view that is not confirmed by the transcripts of the NSC meetings at the end of the crisis [McGeorge Bundy, transcriber, and James Blight, ed., "October 27, 1962: Transcripts of the Meetings of the ExComm," *International Security*, 12 (Winter 1987–88), 30–92]); Theodore Sorensen, *Decision-Making in the White House* (New York: Columbia University Press, 1964), p. 76; George, "Impact of Crisis-Induced Stress," p. 541.

31. See Charles Hermann, "International Crisis as a Situational Variable," in James Rosenau, ed., *International Politics and Foreign Policy*, rev. ed. (New York: Free Press, 1969), pp. 409–21, for an extended treatment of a typology of situations created by the variables of surprise, time available for decisions, and the importance of the values at stake.

4. Shifting the burden to the opponent
   a. Belief that one's own options are quite limited
   b. Belief that opponent has it within his power to prevent an impending disaster[32]

Furthermore, crises are likely to exacerbate several psychological processes that, even under more benign circumstances, reduce the quality of decision making. Three factors are of particular importance to crisis stability: the tendency to avoid facing hard value trade-offs, the difficulties in correctly understanding the messages others are trying to convey, and the paucity of empathy with which statesmen view adversaries.

Earlier I noted that there are two imperatives in a crisis: to avoid war and to avoid political defeat, if not gain victory. To stand firm serves the latter value, but, if the other side also refuses to back down, may lead to war. Thus it is crucial that statesmen carefully judge their adversaries and decide whether some chance of peace must be sacrificed in order to increase the probability of a favorable political outcome or whether political costs must be accepted in order to reduce the danger of war. But people often resist facing painful choices.[33] If they come to believe that standing firm is necessary to avoid defeat, they are likely to conclude that the policy can succeed. That is, instead of weighing the risks in an unbiased manner they are likely to come to believe that their policy will maximize the chances of preserving peace as well as of avoiding defeat.[34]

In a nuclear crisis this perceptual tendency would make it even harder for decision makers to manage the tension between the competitive tactics of crisis bargaining and the more cooperative approach of crisis management. The danger with stressing the former is undesired war; with the latter the danger is excessive concessions that not only are inherently costly but also may give the impression of weakness and therefore invite further predations. It is rarely easy to determine the proper balance, and the chance for error is great; the likelihood of statesmen convincing themselves that the tactics they adopt will simultaneously reduce both dangers makes that chance even greater.

32. George, "Impact of Crisis-Induced Stress," p. 542.
33. See Jervis, *Perception and Misperception in International Politics*, pp. 128–42, and the literature cited there.
34. For a further discussion, see Jack Snyder, "Rationality at the Brink," *World Politics*, 30 (April 1978), 345–65. Although I believe Snyder's conclusions are valid, his discussion does not fully come to grips with the possibility that some of the links among the beliefs he is examining can be explained by logic.

What would actually be reduced would be their ability to comprehend and cope with the crisis.

The propensity for people to assimilate incoming information to their preexisting beliefs also affects behavior in a crisis because expectations about how the adversary will act change slowly and only in response to unambiguous information. As Glenn Snyder and Paul Diesing have documented, incorrect beliefs are as likely to be compounded as corrected during the course of a confrontation.[35] Even though each side carefully scans the behavior of the other, the perceiver's predispositions strongly influence the inferences that are drawn.

As a result, signals are often interpreted very differently from the ways they were intended. States often try to send carefully crafted and subtle messages, but the noise in the system, the fear of deception, and the power of the perceiver's beliefs and images mean that what is received is likely to be very different. Complexity and balance are apt to get filtered out. It would be difficult for states to signal simultaneously that they are planning to stand firm on the issue at stake and also that they will keep their military forces restrained—that is, that they will not readily retreat but neither will they strike first, at least not yet.[36]

A final general complicating psychological factor is the difficulty statesmen have in empathizing with the other side.[37] Especially when relations are hostile, people rarely attempt to put themselves in the other's shoes and try to see how the situation could appear from another vantage point. Of course doing this with the assumption that the other side has the same values and beliefs as you can lead to terrible errors: Chamberlain and his colleagues erred in seeing Hitler as like themselves. But more often, statesmen see other states as very different from their's. As a cause and an effect of this they tend to attribute others' undesired behavior to their hostile predispositions rather than

35. Glenn Snyder and Paul Diesing, *Conflict among Nations* (Princeton: Princeton University Press, 1977), pp. 389–405.

36. For a good analysis of the cognitive and organizational impediments to the sending and receiving of complex, balanced, and subtle signals, see Wallace Theis, *When Governments Collide* (Berkeley: University of California Press, 1980).

37. This was not true, however, for the Israelis in 1973. Because they viewed the previous war as an avoidable war, they focused on the danger of the reciprocal fear of surprise attack and so were very restrained. See Janice Stein, "Calculation, Miscalculation, and Conventional Deterrence II: The View from Jerusalem," in Robert Jervis, Richard Ned Lebow, and Janice Stein, eds., *Psychology and Deterrence* (Baltimore: Johns Hopkins University Press, 1985), pp. 60–88. Richard Betts argues that similar fears could militate against NATO's mobilizing (*Surprise Attack* [Washington, D.C.: Brookings Institution, 1982]).

to situational factors and, when they are planning a forceful response, fail to ask how they would act if they were confronted by such a stance. In a crisis, the result can be that decision makers both too quickly infer that the other side's preparations indicate that it is about to go war and too slowly consider that their actions may produce this impression on the other.

WAR AS INEVITABLE: PSYCHOLOGICAL FACTORS

As noted earlier, crisis instability is driven by the twin beliefs that war is inevitable and that striking first would yield some advantage. To begin with the former, the ways people process information and draw inferences could lead them to overestimate the likelihood that the other side was about to strike.

During a crisis, the heightened fear of attack leads people to gather more evidence and examine it more closely than they do in calm times. Although this makes good sense, it also creates problems, especially because in any nuclear crisis each superpower would see a great deal of unfamiliar military activity. The United States has only gone on nuclear alert twice in the past twenty five years (1962 and 1973); the Soviet Union has never done so. Making sense of events that are seen for the first time is difficult in the best of circumstances. But in a crisis, the unusual is likely to seem threatening. Of course conveying such a threat is one reason why a state would go on alert, but the inference may be, not that the state will attack if the conflict cannot be resolved, but that it is about to attack no matter what happens.

Furthermore, the conclusion that the adversary is engaging in unprecedented preparations for war may be a product of the increased perceptual sensitivity that accompanies a crisis. Even if the other's behavior has not in fact changed, looking at it especially closely will usually lead the person to see things not previously noticed. For example, in a crisis, intelligence officers and decision makers may detect details of troop movements that, although routine, will not be recognized as such because they had never been examined so carefully. The activities will then be seen as new and, given the context provided by the alert, as threatening.

Ignoring Negative Evidence

Statesmen and analysts, like people in their everyday lives, usually fail to treat their expectations as hypotheses. The "scientific method" implies that we should ask ourselves, "If the proposition that the other is going to attack is correct, what evidence should I be able to detect?" The investigator should note not only the behaviors that are consistent with the proposition, but those that are inconsistent, including actions that should have occurred were the hypothesis correct, but that in actuality were not taken. As we know from Sherlock Holmes, dogs that do not bark can provide crucial evidence. But as we also know from the story, most people are slow to realize this. Things that have not happened do not call attention to themselves and are easy to overlook.[38]

Most of the evidence that the adversary is going to attack will consist of dramatic positive instances—for example, putting forces on a wartime footing. But things the other is not doing that it would do were it about to strike are nonevents and therefore are likely to receive less attention. For example, during the Cuban missile crisis, little attention was paid to the fact that the Soviets had not put their nuclear forces on alert. Even in deliberations that were noteworthy for their thorough examination of diverse aspects of the situation, nonevents were slighted.

The intelligence community has attempted to correct for this bias by its system of "indications and warning," which is designed to keep track of what the other is—and is not—doing with its forces. But it is not clear that this degree of systematization, useful as it is, can entirely overcome the natural tendency to miss evidence whose significance lies in being absent. The result could easily be that the evidence that the other side is ready to strike would seem more overwhelming than it should.

Cognitive Predispositions

The effects discussed so far are magnified by the propensity of people to assimilate new information to their preexisting beliefs.[39] During

38. I have analyzed some of the implications of this in "The Drunkard's Search" in Shanto Iyengar and William McGuire, eds., *Current Approaches to Political Psychology* (Urbana: University of Illinois Press, forthcoming).

39. The path-breaking studies of the impact on cognitive predispositions in international politics are Ole Holsti, "Cognitive Dynamics and Images of the Enemy: Dulles and Russia," in David Finlay, Ole Holsti, and Richard Fagan, *Enemies in Politics* (Chicago: Rand McNally, 1967), pp. 25–96, and Roberta Wohlstetter, *Pearl Harbor: Warning and Decision* (Stanford: Stanford University Press, 1962). For a summary of the psychological literature, a discussion of the extent to which this process is irrational, and the examination of many examples from international politics, see Jervis, *Perception and Misperception in International Politics*, chap. 4.

times of calm, ambiguous information is not seen as alarming; its interpretation is shaped by the expectation of continued peace. But because in a crisis statesmen are predisposed to see the other side as about to attack, the identical evidence is seen as much more menacing. This effect is compounded because people are unaware of it. They usually believe that their inferences are driven exclusively by the evidence before them rather than by the beliefs and expectations they already hold. As a result, people grow increasingly confident as they are presented with news that is in fact highly ambiguous because they incorrectly believe that each new bit of information provides independent confirmation of their views.[40] Thus the expectation that the other is likely to strike could become solidified by the receipt of a stream of information that, while not totally discrepant with this belief, does not point only in this direction.

Perceptions of Coordination, Planning, and Centralization

A state tends to see the behavior of others as more planned, coordinated, and centralized than it is. Actions that are accidental or the product of different parts of the bureaucracy following their own policies are likely to be perceived as part of a coherent, and often devious, plan.[41] In a nuclear crisis, the propensity to see all of the other side's behavior as part of a plan would be especially likely to yield incorrect and dangerous conclusions. Routine actions would be viewed with suspicion: during the Cuban missile crisis President Kennedy was right to worry that the Soviets did not believe that the U–2 that strayed over Siberia was a weather plane that had lost its way. Furthermore, as each side went on alert, military units would not only carry out the prescribed instructions, but would act on their own discretion. Thus it now appears that the decision to shoot down the U–2 over Cuba was made by a local Soviet SAM commander.[42] But it is not surprising that

---

40. For further discussion, see Jervis, *Perception and Misperception in International Politics*, pp. 181–87. Experimental confirmation is provided in Charles Lord, Lee Ross, and Mark Lepper, "Biased Assimilation and Attitude Polarization: The Effects of Prior Theories on Subsequently Considered Evidence," *Journal of Personality and Social Psychology*, 37 (1979), 2098–2109.

41. For further discussion and evidence, see Jervis, *Perception and Misperception in International Politics*, chap. 8.

42. Richard Bernstein, "Meeting Sheds New Light on Cuban Missile Crisis," *New York Times*, October 14, 1987. Alexander George noted this possibility years ago: Alexander George, David Hall, and Richard Simons, *The Limits of Coercive Diplomacy* (Boston: Little, Brown, 1971), p. 124.

this possibility did not occur to Kennedy and his advisers, who reasoned that "the Soviets must have . . . decided on a showdown."[43]

Each superpower is also likely to view the acts of small states on the other side as being controlled by the main adversary. During the Cuban missile crisis the United States did not think of Castro as an independent actor, and in 1973 the Soviets probably overestimated the American control over Israel and may have attributed the encirclement of the Egyptian army to United States bad faith. Since future Soviet-American crises would almost certainly grow out of conflicts among clients in the Third World, the propensity to underestimate the autonomy of the smaller states is especially troublesome. Clients' bellicosity would lead the other superpower to conclude that its adversary had decided on a showdown.

Resistance to Seeing Trade-offs

There are logical links between the belief that striking first yields significant advantages and the perception that war is inevitable because the greater the advantage to the state of striking first, the more likely it is to attack. Similarly, if the state thinks the adversary has concluded that there are significant advantages to striking first, then it will expect the adversary to attack in a crisis. But some of the links between the two elements are psychological. As we noted earlier, people resist seeing trade-offs among deeply held values. A statesman who is convinced that striking first is better than striking second (but still is much worse than maintaining the peace) will come under increasing psychological pressure as a confrontation develops. To strike first would be to sacrifice the chance of peace; to hold back would be to run the risk of the worst possible outcome. In order to escape from this painful choice, the statesman may distort some of the information and make his decision seem less costly. This can help lead to peace if he reduces his estimate of the likelihood of war, thereby justifying his inclination to hold back. But if the advantages of striking first (and the costs of allowing the adversary to do so) are uppermost in his mind, he may come to exaggerate the probability of war in order to bolster the decision to attack.

It is difficult to determine which of these distortions is likelier or, more important, what conditions are likely to trigger one or the other. Preliminary research indicates that the controlling value usually is the

43. Roger Hilsman, *To Move a Nation* (Garden City, N.Y.: Doubleday, 1967) p. 220. Also see Blight and Bundy, "October 27, 1962: Transcripts," pp. 71, 80.

one that first becomes firmly planted in the mind of the decision maker.[44] Thus crisis stability may be enhanced by the fact that most of the time decision makers pay little attention to the possible advantages of striking first and are always deeply aware of the need to preserve the peace. With the need to avoid war so salient, they may resist seeing new information as indicating that this goal cannot be reached.

Circular Nature of Beliefs

One important, if vague, factor that would probably influence whether war would be seen as inevitable during a crisis is the general sense of optimism or pessimism that prevailed in the period of time just before it. Gloom produced by beliefs that the tide of events was running against the country has been important in the past, most clearly in 1914. But because of the great stability of the nuclear balance, what may be more important now are feelings about whether war can be avoided indefinitely. This is not a question with an objective answer and so is susceptible to swings in national—and international—mood. If people become convinced that nuclear weapons cannot be held at bay forever, then the chances are greater that a severe crisis will lead to war. Although optimism cannot cure all ills, the belief that nuclear deterrence has made our world quite safe and the expectation that this security can be maintained may themselves noticeably contribute to crisis stability.

Finally, we should remember the self-fulfilling nature of beliefs about the inevitability of war. Given a perceived advantage to striking first, war will become more likely as one or both sides think that the other believes that war is likely. This estimate of the likelihood of war, in turn, depends on the state's judgment of the other side's estimate of how likely it is that the state will strike first. It is unclear how such estimates of estimates of estimates are formed; indeed, we cannot be

44. See Robert Jervis, "Motivated Biases—The Functions of Beliefs" (unpublished manuscript). It also seems that particular contexts can evoke the dominance of one or the other of two conflicting values. This appears to explain how in the course of a relatively brief meeting Eisenhower could give flatly contradictory answers to the question of whether a nuclear war could be won. The question first came up during a discussion of stockpiling, which he felt was necessary, arguing that nuclear war might depend on such preparations. When the meeting turned to a consideration of a report on the effects of nuclear weapons, he argued that marginal effects did not matter because the destruction would be so great that no one could win and we might "ultimately go back to bows and arrows" (Discussion at the 272d Meeting of the National Security Council, January 12, 1956, Ann Whitman File, NSC Series, box 7, pp. 3, 18), Eisenhower Library, Abilene, Kans.

sure how far along the road to infinite regress statesmen's thinking would travel. But the problem is an odd and peculiarly psychological one.

LEADING THE ADVERSARY TO THINK WAR
IS INEVITABLE: PSYCHOLOGICAL FACTORS

Because crisis instability is driven by the interaction between the two sides, it is important to ask how the state might inadvertently lead its adversary to believe that war is inevitable. Decision makers may be unable or unwilling to see the implications of their acts. Statesmen often have less control than they realize; what their state does is not always the same as what they have ordered. Furthermore, their understanding of their own behavior is often flawed. Just as others view the state's actions through distorted lenses, statesmen are not disinterested observers of what they do. Even if they were, they would need to take account of the particular perspective of the other side, which would vary with the information the other has, its cognitive predispositions, and its distorting needs. Given the difficulty of the task, it is not surprising that states often fail to understand how others will interpret their behavior and that, partly for this reason, their acts often produce unanticipated and undesired effects.

Not Knowing Your Own Actions

Earlier we discussed the danger that one side would see actions taken by local military commanders as evidence of a coherent plan to start the war. The other side of this coin may be even more important. As John Steinbruner, Scott Sagan, and others have stressed, in an alert neither the American nor the Soviet top leadership is likely to know what their own forces are doing.[45] Alert procedures, like the military organizations that produce them, are so large and complex that the details are beyond the comprehension and memory of any individual. It is unlikely that even well-informed generals and admirals, let alone the civilian decision makers, know exactly what the orders call for.

45. John Steinbruner, "An Assessment of Nuclear Crises," in Franklyn Griffiths and John Polanyi, eds., *The Dangers of Nuclear War* (Toronto: University of Toronto Press, 1979); Steinbruner, "Choices and Trade-offs," in Carter, Steinbruner, and Zraket, eds., *Managing Nuclear Operations*; Scott Sagan, "Nuclear Alerts and Crisis Management," *International Security*, 9 (Spring 1985), 99–139. Also see Desmond Ball, "Nuclear War at Sea," *International Security*, 10 (Winter 1985–86), 3–31.

Thus when they recall the 1962 and 1973 alerts, key officials, even those who were close to the military activity, acknowledge that they knew only the general outlines of what their forces would do.[46] Also vital and complex are the "rules of engagement," which describe how forces are to behave when a military clash is believed imminent or has begun. The generals in Washington and Moscow may have written these rules, but once local commanders have been given significant discretion, those at home cannot be certain about what their forces are doing. Civilian leaders, of course, will know much less because there are no incentives for them to learn the details during times of calm and no time for them to do so during a crisis.[47]

As a result, it is quite likely that actions carried out in the name of the state during a nuclear crisis would be more provocative than those intended by the top leadership and that the leaders would be unaware of what had happened.[48] This may have been the case, for example, during the Cuban missile crisis, when Kennedy and his advisers apparently did not know of many of the navy's aggressive tactics.[49] Thus when McNamara recently learned that the decision to shoot down the U-2 over Cuba had been made not in Moscow but by the military on the spot, he said:

This sort of thing happened to me many times. I'll just give you one example. I remember one time that the air force wanted to bomb Hanoi harbor, but we didn't because there was a Soviet ship in port there, and we didn't want to run the risk of hitting it and causing an incident with the Soviets. All of a sudden one Sunday, the Soviets said that we'd hit their ship, and they were very upset about it. I was told by our people that the Soviets were lying; we hadn't hit their ship, because we'd never sent the mission to bomb the harbor. We even looked over the films from the mission, and sure enough, they hadn't even come close to hitting the ship. Well, it turned out that I discovered by accident some

46. Sagan, "Nuclear Alerts"; interviews with military officers, 1983–85.

47. Thus Alexander George stresses the need for Soviet and American leaders to understand the problems and ensure that military policy and actions will support the political goals of crisis management ("Crisis Management: The Interaction of Political and Military Considerations," pp. 223–34, and "Problems of Crisis Management and Crisis Avoidance in U.S.–Soviet Relations").

48. For similar cases in the prenuclear era, see Jervis, *Perception and Misperception in International Politics*, pp. 329–38.

49. The details of the navy's activities and, more important in this context, the extent to which the top decision makers were aware of them, still remain unclear. See Sagan, "Nuclear Alerts," p. 113. I am grateful to Alexander George for discussions on this point.

two months later when I was in Thailand, where our planes were based which were used for those raids, that the ship *had* been hit. But the pilot who'd hit it wouldn't confess, and he'd conspired with the other crewmen to destroy the film of the mission and substitute another flight's film when the inquiry came down![50]

Furthermore, because decision makers tend to assume that their forces are highly restrained, they would see any local clashes as stemming from the aggressive actions of their adversary—actions that they would attribute to orders from the other's central authorities. Of course this inference could lead statesmen to conclude that immediate concessions were necessary, but it could also lead them to order what they incorrectly believe to be matching escalation, which could increase the level of violence and be perceived by the adversary as showing that a wider war could not be avoided.

Ignoring the Security Dilemma

We have noted the tendency for decision makers to assume that if the adversary's actions menaced them, this was its goal. Equally important is that even when decision makers know what actions their state is undertaking, they often underestimate the extent to which this menaces others.[51] Thus in the fall of 1950 the United States did not think that moving its troops to the Yalu would threaten China's security, and in the review of American foreign policy early in the Eisenhower administration some officials said that their desired policy of building up military strength on the borders of Eastern Europe and "hamper[ing] consolidation of Soviet control over [the] satellites" would "pose no threat" to the USSR.[52] Similarly, in a nuclear crisis

50. Proceedings of the Cambridge Conference on the Cuban Missile Crisis, Cambridge, Mass., October 11–12, 1987, pp. 106–7.

51. For further discussion, see Jervis, "Realism, Game Theory, and Cooperation," *World Politics*, 40 (April 1988), 336–40. Of course the most important factors here are not entirely psychological. Given current and foreseeable technology, it is extremely difficult for states to take measures that decrease the vulnerability of their forces without simultaneously increasing their ability, if not to strike first, then at least to undertake provocative actions. Indeed, if the state is not willing to back down, it must take actions that convince the other of the need to retreat, or at least to seek a compromise. But the objective problems are compounded by the tendency for decision makers to believe that the other side knows that they are reasonable and not to feel unduly threatened by the measures they are taking in their own self-defense. Also see Robert Osgood, *Limited War* (Chicago: University of Chicago Press, 1957), pp. 240–41.

52. *FRUS, 1950–1952*, vol. 2, *National Security Affairs*, pt. 1, p. 425.

statesmen who were preoccupied with their own fears could easily forget that the adversary's fears would be increased by the state's measures that were motivated by the desire to ensure that its forces would survive an attack. For example, the Soviets might evacuate their cities as a precaution in the belief that the Americans would know full well that this move was purely defensive. The Americans, in fact, would almost surely be alarmed as they saw one set of hostages disappear. On both sides, decisions to put forces on alert might be taken on the basis of contemplating only how the move might directly affect the state's security. To the extent that the other side was considered at all, the only question likely to receive attention would be whether the adversary would be deterred.

The problems would be even greater in a limited war. An unusual degree of empathy would be required for each side to see the extent to which its military actions threatened the other. The rules that seem fair to it would not automatically appear so to the adversary; the actions each was taking in accord with its vision of a limited conflict could easily cut deeply into the other's security requirements. The American plans for naval activities during a limited war, for example, do not seem to have been calculated with an eye toward how the Soviets might respond. To attack Soviet naval bases and missile-carrying submarines might trigger a much wider war.[53] Dynamics of this kind operated powerfully in one well documented simulation. Each side consistently failed to see that the moves it intended as reassuring would not be so perceived by the adversary and that actions taken for self-defense would be seen as deeply threatening.[54]

Even measures that did not directly menace the other could lead it to infer that the war could no longer be avoided. This might be the effect, for example, of an American decision to send the vice-president aloft in the presidential flying command post. Although this would not increase the American ability to launch a first strike, the Russians might read it as indicating that the United States believed that war was almost certain. Sensing the other's fears requires a knowledge of how the other sees the world and an appreciation of the fact that one's restraint may not be apparent to the other side. But empathy is likely

---

53. John Mearshimer, "A Strategic Misstep: The Maritime Strategy and Deterrence in Europe," *International Security*, 11 (Fall 1986), 3–57. For a rebuttal, see Linton Brooks, "Naval Power and National Security: The Case for the Maritime Strategy," ibid., pp. 58–88.

54. Alexander George, David Bernstein, Gregory Parnell, and J. Philip Rogers, *Inadvertent War in Europe: Crisis Simulation* (Stanford: Stanford University Center for International Security and Arms Control, 1985), pp. 24–26, 38–39, 47, 51.

to be in especially short supply when tensions and hostility are at their highest.

The same processes can lead the state to underestimate the extent to which it is painting the other into a corner and foreclosing all the other's diplomatic options. Under these circumstances, the other may attack even though it knows that the prospects for victory are slight. In the 1962 and 1973 crises, the United States provided "golden bridges" over which the other could retreat. In the former, Kennedy did not seek to overthrow Castro, privately promised that the United States would soon withdraw its missiles from Turkey, indicated that he would not take a Soviet retreat as evidence of a general lack of resolve, and instructed the members of his administration not to humiliate the Soviets. In 1973, as the United States put its nuclear forces on alert, it simultaneously maintained its pressures on the Israelis to comply with the cease-fire agreement, which was the explicit objective of the Soviet policy.[55] But we cannot be confident that statesmen will exhibit the same sensitivity in the future. It is tempting to push the adversary hard when the state has an advantage and difficult for it to sense the desperation that could lead the other side to feel that war is either unavoidable or worth risking in order to reverse the verdict of the previous bargaining.

Tendency to Neglect the Necessity for Promises

In a crisis, leaders usually see their main task as convincing the other side that their resolve is high and slight the need also to reassure the other that they will accept a reasonable solution rather than go to war. Combining threats and promises is a tricky enough task in the best of circumstances; it is rendered even more difficult because both academics and decision makers have paid little attention to the latter.[56] The

55. Unfortunately, American statesmen seem to have forgotten the role they played by pressuring Israel to spare the Egyptian army and have attributed the Soviet restraint to the nuclear alert. This is brought out nicely in the way the 1973 analogy was used by former high government officials when they played the simulations reported in Andrew Goldberg, Debra van Opstal, Michael Brown, and James Barkley, *Leaders and Crisis: The CSIS Crisis Simulations*, Significant Issues Series, vol. 9, no. 5 (Washington, D.C.: Center for Strategic and International Studies, 1987).

56. The importance of rewards is argued in David Baldwin, "The Power of Positive Sanctions," *World Politics*, 24 (October 1971), 19–38. The need to combine threats and rewards is discussed in George, Hall, and Simons, *Limits of Coercive Diplomacy*, pp. 100–3; Snyder and Diesing, *Conflict among Nations*, pp. 489–93; Jervis, *Perception and Misperception in International Politics*, pp. 111–13; Jervis, "Deterrence Theory Revisited," *World*

frequently discussed problem of maintaining credibility refers to threats; there is no such literature on promises. The implication is that aggressors might doubt that the defender would use force, but—and partly because—it has no doubts about the latter's desire and ability to remain at peace.[57] To some extent, this is a generalization from a particular pair of actors. Hitler probably would not have worried about a British first strike even in a situation of extreme crisis instability. But whether the same could be said about the Soviet analysis of the United States is doubtful.

Self-knowledge and self-image are important here: statesmen who know they are not going to strike cannot imagine how anyone would think differently. Of course even if they were aware of the need to reassure the other side, statesmen might not be able to do so. Authority to fire nuclear weapons could have been delegated to local command- ers, harsh bargaining tactics that interfere with reassurance may seem required, or the adversary simply might not be willing to see that the state wanted to keep the peace. Nevertheless, the problem will be even more severe if decision makers do not even know that it exists.

This problem has not been totally ignored. In his original discussion of the reciprocal fear of surprise attack, Schelling noted the value of "positive inspection."[58] During a crisis, a state that wanted to show its adversary that it was not about to attack could invite the other to observe its military facilities to determine that this was not the case. One historical precedent was the tour taken by the British military attaché in Germany in May 1938, which revealed that, contrary to the reports from Czechoslovakia, the German army was not about to march. The delayed effects of this incident were unfortunate—the Brit- ish mistrust of the Czechs increased, and Hitler, feeling humiliated, became more committed to smashing his enemies. But this example does not detract from the virtues of the technique. Although missiles do not lend themselves to such inspection, a state that went on a full military alert could not disguise this from the adversary, and so the absence of such an alert is also relatively easy to detect. Verbal reas- surances can also be used, as they were by Khrushchev in 1962 when he stressed that he and not Castro controlled the missiles. His elabo-

Politics, 31 (January 1979), 304–5; Richard Ned Lebow, "The Deterrence Deadlock: Is there a Way Out?" in Jervis, Lebow, and Stein, *Psychology and Deterrence*; and Janice Stein, "Deterrence and Reassurance," in Philip Tetlock et al., *Behavior, Society, and Nuclear War*, vol. 2 (New York: Oxford University Press, forthcoming).

57. Of course the other's fear of a first strike brings pressure on him to terminate the crisis quickly and so reassurance should not be unconditional.

58. Schelling, *Strategy of Conflict*, p. 250.

ration was interesting: "You can regard us with distrust, but, in any case, you can be calm in this regard, that we are of sound mind and understand perfectly well that if we attack you, you will respond the same way. . . . This indictates that we are normal people, that we correctly understand and correctly evaluate the situation."[59]

While this example shows the decision maker's awareness of the need for reassurance, the problem was not great in 1962 because Khrushchev was preparing to concede and did not desire to flex his muscles. The real dilemma would arise if a state wanted to generate its forces, both to demonstrate resolve and to safeguard its second strike capability, but also needed to show that it sought to maintain the peace. The proposals and agreements on "confidence building measures" designed to prevent unwarranted fears caused by military maneuvers in Europe similarly will be most effective in the least demanding situation and least helpful when they come under greater pressures.[60] That is, they can help demonstrate peaceful intentions as long as the state does not undertake extraordinary measures, but it is not clear how well they could work when and if the state mobilized its forces both for self-protection and to bring pressure to bear.

PSYCHOLOGICAL FACTORS CONTRIBUTING TO WANTING TO STRIKE FIRST

Even if war is believed to be inevitable, crisis instability will arise only if one or both sides believe that it is better to strike first than to permit the other side to do so. Earlier I noted the real vulnerabilities of weapons systems and, even more, of C³, and I also argued that these should not be exaggerated. Here I want to discuss how decision makers might overestimate the advantages of striking first, thereby increasing if not creating crisis instability.

Strategic Doctrines

What would be seen as an advantage depends in part on one's beliefs about how the war would be fought. Because an attacker is

59. "Premier Khrushchev's Message," in Arthur Schlesinger, Jr., ed., *The Dynamics of World Power: A Documentary History of United States Foreign Policy, 1945–1973*, vol 2, *Eastern Europe and the Soviet Union*, ed. Walter LaFeber (New York: Chelsea House, 1973), p. 700. Also see Sagan, "Nuclear Alerts," p. 111.

60. In order to reduce dangerous misinterpretations, the United States has taken Soviet fears into account in its conduct on routine airborne intelligence operations. See Seymour Hersh, *"The Target Is Destroyed"* (New York: Random House, 1986), pp. 38–43.

unlikely to believe that striking first could greatly reduce damage to his society if the other should fully retaliate against it, crisis stability is high if the states think that attacks will be directed primarily against the others' values. It is especially high if those values are relatively easy to destroy, as cities are. But the case is more complex when one side believes that while its values are easy to destroy—and thus cannot be protected by even a relatively successful first strike—the other's are not. The idea embodied in current American doctrine that the Soviets value, not their civil society, but the Communist control of their country, creates some incentives to strike first because the targets the United States would need to destroy are very numerous (e.g., party and KGB headquarters throughout the country). American forces that had been depleted by a prior attack might not be sufficient for this task.

The greatest problems, however, arise when the states hold counterforce doctrines. In such a contest, there would be strong incentives to strike first because gaining an advantage in surviving warheads—and particularly warheads that could destroy hardened military targets—would be important and aided by attacking. Not only are American ICBMS vulnerable,[61] but SLBMS, which cannot be attacked successfully, are less useful against military targets. Furthermore, fighting a counterforce war would require not only warheads but up-to-date intelligence on the status and location of the other's forces, exquisite timing, and the matching of one's own remaining forces with the highest priority targets that had not yet been destroyed. Thus the side whose C^3I continued to function relatively well would have an enormous military advantage. Attacks against these facilities would be almost certain to degrade them badly. In a counterforce conflict, then, a first strike, directed largely at C^3I, would be likely to yield great dividends. As a result, counterforce doctrines increase crisis instability. The problem would be exacerbated if the state believed that the other also had such a doctrine. This belief would lead it to suspect that the other would attack even if war was far from certain, thus making it even more likely that the state itself would attack, and so on through the familiar steps of infinite regress.

Of course it can be argued that providing incentives to strike first is one of the virtues of counterforce. By creating a degree of crisis insta-

---

61. Whether the Soviet missiles are similarly vulnerable to an American attack is a matter of some debate. Crucial are the classified technical details of the accuracy of American warheads and the hardness of Soviet silos. But even with classified information, both these factors can only be estimated.

bility, it mitigates the stability-instability paradox and deters the Russians from creating dangerous situations. Whether an advantage or not, it seems clear that the preemptive strain in American military planning is caused in large part by the belief that extended deterrence requires the United States to be prepared to respond to a Soviet conventional attack on Western Europe not only with nuclear weapons but with a militarily effective counterforce thrust. Thus the advantages of striking first are not entirely a matter of vulnerabilities and hardware but crucially depend on statesmen's beliefs about how a war would be fought. Under most circumstances, counterforce and great crisis stability are incompatible.

Military Biases in Favor of the Offensive

Military organizations tend to prefer taking the offensive to standing ready to receive the first blow, in part because they are attracted to the notion of counterforce and seek to maintain control of the war.[62] It is rare to find military officers arguing for a defensive posture even when technology permits the state to reach its political goals by making attack unrewarding rather than by being able to push into the adversary's territory. In the nuclear era, this bias is compounded by the understandable resistance of both the American and Soviet military to the notion that their purpose is to prepare to incinerate millions of civilians rather than to fight the other's military. Furthermore, military leaders on both sides are fully aware that a counterforce war is easier to wage with a first than with a second strike, even if the former cannot promise to disarm the adversary. They also know that taking the initiative is one way of reducing the uncertainty that accompanies any battle. I do not mean to imply that military leaders are belligerent, expansionistic, or ignorant of the costs of a war. But the mission of being ready to fight if need be and the awareness of the overwhelming difficulties of fighting a war with a force that has been badly damaged by an enemy first strike predisposes them to conclude that if there is going to be a war, the chances of a favorable outcome are greatly increased if they can strike first. How strong the military's voice would be during a crisis cannot be determined, but the potential for such influence, linked to the belief in the advantages of striking first, is significant.

62. This paragraph draws heavily on Barry Posen, *The Sources of Military Doctrine: Britain, France, and Germany between the Two Wars* (Ithaca: Cornell University Press, 1984).

Minimizing the Costs of Striking First

In a previous section I noted that states might inadvertently provoke others by foreclosing acceptable alternatives to war. Under these circumstances, a decision to go to war could be rational. What is of concern here is that a decision for war is possible even if rationality dictates staying at peace. A decision maker who believes that the alternative to fighting is the sacrifice of core values may avoid the painful value trade-off that confronts him by underestimating the costs of war and overestimating the chances of victory. This is part of the explanation for the behavior of Japan in 1941, Pakistan in 1965, and Egypt in 1973.[63] In these cases states attacked much stronger adversaries. Seeing the prospects for diplomacy as bleak, they came to believe that attacking might reach their goals. Although the nature of the cases precludes proof either of whether the estimates of probabilities were incorrect or of whether the errors can be traced to the process outlined here, it seems likely that the repelling characteristics of remaining at peace led decision-makers to underestimate the unattractiveness of going to war.[64]

In a Soviet-American crisis, a statesman who felt that his country's position was deteriorating badly would feel psychological pressure to believe that a first strike offered a way out of the dilemma. Furthermore, if he believed that concessions would only provide a short respite, he might conclude that if his country were not to surrender, it would have to fight sooner or later. This set of beliefs would not be as likely to lead to war as it was in the past because the costs of any conceivable first strike are so high, but the horror of decline and the fear of future demands that could not be resisted could still produce a degree of unjustified optimism about the military alternative.[65]

63. The theoretical argument here is based on the concept of "defensive avoidance," developed in Irving Janis and Leon Mann, *Decision Making* (New York: Free Press, 1977). For a discussion of previous wars that can be aptly explained by these processes, see Lebow, *Between Peace and War*; Jervis, Lebow, and Stein, *Psychology and Deterrence*; Jervis, "Deterrence and Perception," *International Security*, 7 (Winter, 1982–83), 29–30; Sumit Ganguly, "Deterrence Failure Revisited: The Indo-Pakistani Conflict of 1965" (manuscript, Hunter College, 1987).

64. For a discussion of the methodological issues, see Jervis, "War and Misperception," *Journal of Interdisciplinary History*, 18 (Spring 1988), 679–81. For claims that the Japanese errors cannot be traced to these processes, see Scott Sagan, "The Origins of the Pacific War," *Journal of Interdisciplinary History*, 18 (Spring 1988), 914–22. Also see John Orme, "Deterrence Failures: A Second Look," *International Security*, 11 (Spring, 1987), 96–124.

65. For a discussion of earlier crises in these terms, see Snyder, "Rationality at the Brink."

Emotions, Fatalism, and Taking the Initiative

The previous discussion implies the existence of a high degree of calculation, albeit much of it misguided. But a decision maker who believed that war was inevitable might not carefully calculate whether striking first was advantageous. As the strain of waiting mounted, the common instinct that it is better to take the initiative than to remain passive could push him toward a decision to launch. When faced with the question: "Do you prefer entering the conflict with undamaged forces or waiting and retaliating with what remains at your disposal after having been struck?" most leaders would be hard put to answer the latter, especially in light of the vulnerability of C^3 systems. Even more than the previous arguments, this one must be almost completely speculative because we lack both strong theories and, fortunately, experience. Enormous pressures affect different people in different ways: reactions range from passivity to hyperactivity. But we cannot dismiss the danger that a first strike would be produced not out of the specific mechanisms and processes discussed in the rest of this chapter but out of the instinctive impulse to act and move before the other side did. We often dismiss the role of emotions in national decisions, perhaps in part because we think they make the world less predictable and manageable. But such dismissal does not mean they are unimportant. Indeed any decision to retaliate after a full first strike would have to be based largely on the desire for revenge, and most analysts and decision makers have no trouble seeing that such a response is likely. We should, then, not assume that only rational impulses will be operating in other situations.

Risk Acceptance for Losses

It is a commonplace that no sane decision maker would wager the fate of his country on one cosmic throw of the dice. This confidence is based on more than blind optimism: under most circumstances people are averse to taking risks.[66] As numerous experiments have shown, most of us would choose a certainty of winning $10 over a 20 percent

---

66. This discussion is drawn from Daniel Kahneman and Amos Tversky, "Prospect Theory: An Analysis of Decision under Risk," *Econometrica*, 47 (March 1979), 263–91; Tversky and Kahneman, "The Framing of Decisions and the Psychology of Choice," *Science*, January 30, 1981, pp. 453–58; Kahneman and Tversky, "Choices, Values, and Frames," *American Psychologist*, 39 (April 1984), 341–50; Tversky and Kahneman, "Rational Choice and the Framing of Decisions," *Journal of Business*, 59 (October 1986), S251–78.

chance of winning $55. This caution contributes to crisis stability be-
cause it inhibits people from pushing hard to make gains. Thus President Kennedy was not inclined to try to use the leverage generated
by the Cuban missile crisis to remove Castro from power. But what
could prove to be disturbing is that people seem to accept risks in order
to avoid losses. If the choice is between a 100 percent chance of losing
$10 and a 20 percent chance of losing $55, many will gamble and opt
for the latter. In other words, to increase the chance of avoiding any
loss at all, people are willing to accept the danger of an even greater
sacrifice. Such behavior is consistent with the tendency for people to
be influenced by sunk costs, which rationally should be disregarded,
and to continue pursuing losing ventures in the hope of regaining all
when they would be better off cutting their losses.

The explanation is threefold. First is the "certainty effect"—the tendency for people to weight more heavily outcomes that are more certain. Because high probability outcomes exert more influence than they
would if people used pure probability-utility calculus, gains that are
near certain are attractive even if they are quite small and losses that
are quite certain will be avoided even if they are relatively slight. Second, the law of diminishing returns operates. The gain (or loss) of $80
is not felt to be four times as good (or as bad) as the gain (or loss) of
$20. Furthermore, the pain inflicted by a given loss is greater than the
positive value of an equal gain. That this is so helps explain why even
relatively small losses are so painful that the person will accept significant risks of a greater sacrifice in order to win a chance of avoiding
all losses.[67]

While the law of diminishing returns is not evidence of people's
irrationality, its operation in this way is odd because outcomes are
being judged not in absolute terms but by reference to the status quo.
This characteristic, which constitutes a third explanation for the phenomenon, makes psychological sense because we judge results by how
they move us from where we are. But it is not logical because what
really matters is our total value position. That is, if we had no money
at all, the law of diminishing returns should make $80 less than four
times as valuable as $20, but this effect should not occur if we already
have $20,000. Similarly, for people with even an academic salary, it is
hard to construct a rational explanation for why losing $10 should feel
significantly more annoying than the finding of the same amount of
money on the street would be gratifying. The shape of the utility curve

67. The effect here can be similar to cognitive dissonance as people come to value an
objective in proportion to the resources they have expended to try to gain it.

should be quite smooth in the region of such small changes in the person's possessions, but it is not, because what the person has is taken as the zero-point.

That losses hurt more than gains gratify is explained in everyday life partly by the fact that we adjust to the status quo we live with. Of course gains are pleasant, but one has gotten by without them. By the same token, because we are accustomed to our life as it has been, a lowering of that standard is particularly painful. Whether we want to call this kind of adjustment to one's current position irrational may be largely definitional. But it is hard to avoid this term when people are willing to pay a high price to keep a fairly small value they have just been given, as has been shown to be the case in classroom experiments.[68]

As in so many areas, politics pulls in the same direction as psychology. Public opinion is likely to be intolerant of defeats; the leader who accepts one will probably be punished. Indeed, persisting in a losing cause in the hope of reversing the course of events may be a gamble that is bad for the national interest but justified in terms of the politician's personal power because the political consequences of a major defeat may not be much worse than those of a limited reverse. Furthermore, while statesmen rarely expect international gains to produce more of the same, they often fear that defeats will compound (i.e., they fear the domino effect). Thus to accept what appears to be a limited defeat actually may be to incur much higher costs.

The implications of this psychology of choice for crisis stability are several. First, because the status quo forms people's reference point, they are willing to take unusual risks to recoup recent losses. Although a setback may be quite minor when compared with the person's total value holdings, he will see it in terms of where he was shortly before and so may take the gamble of an even greater loss in order to gain a chance of reestablishing his position. In a crisis, then, a decision maker might risk costly escalation or even world war if it held out the possibility of reversing a defeat. Where fully rational analysis would lead a person to cut his losses, the psychological unacceptability of anything less than the status quo could lead him to persevere.

In such attempts to maintain the status quo, decision makers will fail to give adequate weight to the losses they will have to bear if the policy continues to fail, and limited engagements will be hard to terminate (as in Vietnam, perhaps). Thus in February 1918, Gen. Erich

---

68. See Jack L. Knetsch, Richard H. Thaler, and Daniel Kahneman, "Experimental Tests of the Endowment Effect and the Coase Theorem" (unpublished paper, rev., 1988).

Ludendorff strongly resisted the notion of a peace treaty that would involve surrender of the lands occupied since 1914, arguing that "then Germany has lost the war." As one scholar notes; "What curious inability to distinguish between the loss of some territories and the loss of the nation!"[69] This stance is less curious psychologically than logically, but that does not make it less disturbing. Similar judgments in a nuclear crisis could lead states to take risks that otherwise would be inexplicable.

The danger would be especially great if both sides believed they were losing; and this could easily happen, because antagonists often have different perspectives and use different baselines. The Middle East crisis of 1973 may be an example of such a situation, with the Americans feeling that they could not allow Israel to lose and the Soviets feeling that at least a limited Arab victory was necessary to regain their influence. Indeed, if the Soviets consider the status quo to be constant movement in their favor, they might be prone to take high risks when the United States thinks it is maintaining the status quo.

The fact that both sides can simultaneously be impelled by loss aversion can render dangerous the strategy of the fait accompli.[70] Alexander George and Richard Smoke note that deterrence can be circumvented if an expansionist can alter the status quo before the defender has time to react. But unless the latter quickly adjusts to the new situation, it may be willing to run unusually high risks to regain its previous position. The other side, expecting the first to be rational, will in turn be surprised by its continued resistance. Because each side will see itself as defending the status quo, it will have strong incentives to stand firm and—believing the adversary sees the situation as the state does—will expect the other side to retreat. Each will be driven by a strong resistance to accepting what it sees as an unfavorable change.

A second consequence of loss aversion is that if the decision maker thinks that war—and therefore enormous loss—is almost certain if he does not strike and that attacking provides a small chance of escaping unscathed, he may decide to strike even if the standard probability-utility calculus calls for restraint. Similar dynamics could operate in less severe crises, such as those set off by a hostile coup in an important Third World country or the limited use of force by the adversary in a

69. Fred Iklé, *Every War Must End* (New York: Columbia University Press, 1971), p. 82.

70. See Alexander George and Richard Smoke, *Deterrence in American Foreign Policy* (New York: Columbia University Press, 1974), pp. 536–40.

disputed area. With his attention riveted on the deterioration that will occur unless he is able to reverse the situation, the decision maker might take actions that entail an irrationally high chance of major escalation.

Third, the response can be influenced by how the decision is framed. While the powerful aversion to losses could lead the decision maker to strike when the alternatives are posed as they were in the previous paragraphs, it could lead him to hold back if he thought that he might be able to keep the peace by so doing and that striking first would lead to certain retaliation. As long as there is any hope of avoiding total war, decision makers are likely to recoil from the thought of starting it.[71] Even Gen. Curtis LeMay's successor as head of SAC, Gen. Thomas Power, argued against preemption "so long as there is the slightest hope that we can prevent a Soviet attack through diplomatic means or a strong posture of deterrence."[72]

Similarly, if the decision maker takes as his baseline not the existing situation of no casualties but the losses that would be suffered in a war, his choice between the same alternatives might be different. In the latter case he would choose a course of action that he believed would certainly save some lives rather than another that might save more but might not save any. The obvious danger is that a first strike that would significantly reduce the other side's strategic forces would meet the former criterion while restraint could not provide the certainty of saving any lives and so would not seem as attractive as standard utility maximization theory implies.

Some evidence, although not strong, indicates that people are more willing to accept disadvantages that are seen as costs (as in insurance premiums) rather than losses.[73] If the phenomenon is real it could lead decision makers to take higher risks when they are seen as the cost of conducting foreign policy than when they are conceptualized as a sacrifice in the status quo. It seems unlikely that a first strike could ever be seen in the former terms, but a strategy that increases the chance of war could be.

Crisis stability may be endangered less by the objective incentives to strike first than by the way people are likely to think during a crisis. If an all-out war will lead to the destruction of both side's societies,

71. For a good discussion, see Richard Ned Lebow, "Windows of Opportunity: Do States Jump through Them?" *International Security*, 9 (Summer 1984), 147–86.

72. Thomas Power with Albert Arnhym, *Design for Survival* (New York: Coward-McCann, 1964), pp. 80–81.

73. Kahneman and Tversky, "Choices, Values, and Frames," p. 349.

then it does not matter who goes first. Attacking, especially against C³ systems, has more advantages in a counterforce war, but even here the expected devastation is likely to be so great that only if it were believed that war was highly probable would striking first be rational. This is not to deny that vulnerabilities are troublesome, even if their importance has been exaggerated. But more important is the danger that people will exaggerate the probability of war and the advantages of striking first and act in ways that are more provocative than they intend. The result could be a war even though rationality would dictate staying at peace.

A world with complete crisis stability would not, of course, be without its dangers. The knowledge that crises can lead to inadvertent war gives decision makers good reason to avoid sharp confrontations; fear of crisis instability may help keep the peace. A world in which statesmen believed that crises could be safely manipulated could be more dangerous than the one we now live in. If those beliefs were right, the limited use of violence might be more frequent; if they were wrong, the results would be even worse. A Soviet Union that was strongly motivated to try to change the status quo could see crises as a usable tool; an America that felt confident that no one could move from the brink of war to war itself might seek confrontations rather than accept limited diplomatic setbacks.

Nevertheless, on balance a reduction in crisis instability would probably make the world safer. Neither side seems prone to seek risky situations; the greatest danger of world war is the escalation of a conflict that neither of them sought. The beliefs that war was not inevitable, that even in a crisis neither side would jump to the conclusion that the other was about to strike, and that everyone knew that striking first was foolish, would be stabilizing. Indeed, as we will discuss in the next chapter, the most important contribution of arms control may be to increase statemen's confidence that the adversary does not want war and that they can manage their common problems peacefully. Failures of rational decision making can lead to wars, and an appreciation of human errors can help correct them and keep the peace. Were statesmen to find themselves in a crisis, the chances of a peaceful solution would be increased if they understood the psychological factors that could lead them to strike.

[6]

The Symbolic Nature of Nuclear Politics

PSYCHOLOGICAL EFFECTS

Shortly after the first Soviet atomic bomb test, a CIA report stated, "The capacity to produce atomic weapons bolsters Soviet prestige and greatly increases Soviet capabilities for exerting psychological pressure on Western Europe." In the opinion of the chairman of the Joint Chiefs of Staff, Omar Bradley, developing the hydrogen bomb "would have psychological value" in bolstering the American deterrent posture. David E. Lilienthal, the chairman of the Atomic Energy Commission, feared that "to proceed forthwith" to develop the H-bomb would be "to miss an opportunity to reexamine and realign policy and promote something better than a headlong rush to a war of mass destruction weapons." George Kennan believed that "the peculiar psychological overtones by which [nuclear] weapons will always be accompanied will tend to give them a certain top-heaviness, as instruments of our national policy, and that this top-heaviness, in turn, will inevitably impart a certain eccentricity to our military planning, where there should be equilibrium." In their "Estimate of the World Situation through 1955," the authors of National Intelligence Estimate–99 reported, "As [the] Soviet [nuclear] capability increases, Western superiority in numbers of nuclear weapons will be relatively less significant so far as the psychological factor is concerned." James Schlesinger, the former secretary of defense, said, "What you declare in advance [about the way you would fight a war] is designed to affect the psychology of the other side." In 1957, President Eisenhower stated his belief that ballistic missiles are not "much [as] military weapons," but that they have "great psychological importance." And in 1964, the Indian ambassador to the

United States, B. K. Nehru, reported that "there were strong pressures in India to have the government explode a nuclear device so as to offset the genuine psychological advantages which the Chinese had obtained . . . by virtue of their explosion."[1]

Something is extremely odd here. Hard-headed statesmen are talking about the most destructive weapons the world has ever known. Yet they are using a strange vocabulary—they talk not of military victory or military defeat, not of armies vanquished and factories destroyed, but of psychological effects. This seems much too pallid; we are dealing with weapons of mass death and destruction, not with subtle instruments of persuasion. In what might seem to be the ultimate absurdity, in 1952 the top secret evaluation of the damage the United States would suffer in an atomic attack first presented the expected casualties of 10 million to 91 million and then concluded: "The potentially most serious consequence of the Soviet attack would be the psychological impact of a large-scale atomic attack. There would be morale and political problems of a magnitude which it is impossible to estimate, or even comprehend, on the basis of any presently available valid data."[2]

Although the processes remain elusive and the phraseologies are often imprecise, statesmen are trying to accommodate some profound paradoxes of nuclear weapons. But neither they nor scholars have fully explicated the dilemmas and understood the extent to which our conceptions of the role of nuclear weapons in world politics change the world—and, indeed, create it—as much as they mirror it. Many of our standard analytical tools do not serve us well here. The general framework of Realism, which underlies most American analyses of international politics, simply does not provide the concepts or orientations that are needed to understand situations in which psychological and

1. These quotations came from the following sources: CIA report (November 16, 1949), quoted in Thomas Lairson, "Hegemony, Credibility, and the Risk of War: American Strategy, 1947–1950" (unpublished manuscript), p. 45; Bradley, quoted in David Lilienthal, *The Journals of David Lilienthal*, vol. 2, *The Atomic Years, 1945–1950* (New York: Harper & Row, 1964), p. 581, also see p. 583; Lilienthal's own comments, *Journals of David Lilienthal*, 2:630; Kennan, quoted in *Foreign Relations of the United States, 1950*, vol. 1, *National Security Affairs; Foreign Economic Policy* (Washington, D.C.: Government Printing Office, 1977), p. 37 (hereafter cited as *FRUS*); NIE–99, *FRUS, 1952–1954*, vol. 2, *National Security Affairs* (Washington, D.C.: Government Printing Office, 1984), p. 552; Schlesinger, quoted in Gregg Herken, *Counsels of War* (New York: Knopf, 1985), p. 263; Eisenhower, memorandum, June 26, 1957, quoted in Stephen Ambrose, *Eisenhower the President* (New York: Simon & Schuster, 1984), p. 396; Nehru, quoted in Glenn Seaborg with Benjamin Loeb, *Stemming the Tide: Arms Control in the Johnson Years* (Lexington, Mass.: Lexington Books, 1987), p. 117.

2. Report of the Special Evaluation Subcommittee of the National Security Council, in *FRUS, 1952–1954*, vol. 2, p. 349. Henry Kissinger presented a similar analysis in *Nuclear Weapons and Foreign Policy* (New York: Harper & Row, 1957), pp. 111–14.

symbolic factors loom so large. I do not mean to imply that I can create a new, appropriate approach. But the statement at least provides a start to understanding the liability of our general social science tradition that analyzes reality apart from the beliefs that both we as scholars and the actors themselves hold.

When I say that an effect is a psychological one, I mean that it is in some sense problematic, that we cannot determine the reaction solely from the physical stimulus itself. Between the stimulus and the response intervene factors that are hard to predict, that may vary from individual to individual, and that can be influenced without influencing the stimulus itself. But exactly how do the psychological effects operate? Why are people modifying their behavior? One crucial question of current concern can be presented more sharply. Both decision makers and analysts often say that although nuclear weapons lack military utility, they have great political utility. But how is this possible? How can a military instrument that is useless for military missions influence behavior?[3]

Even in cases in which the military component seems primary, closer inspection may reveal that arms are less important for directly influencing the outcome of an armed struggle than they are as symbols. This, I think, is true of the controversy between the United States and the People's Republic of China (PRC) over American military sales to Taiwan. Although Taiwan would be better able to resist attack if it had modern weapons, such as the F–16s it sought, the PRC is deterred from invading not because it could not win but because conquest would cost it dearly in terms of world opinion and, more important, in her ties to the United States. Thus Taiwan wants the arms and the PRC opposes the sales because they are seen as conveying information about, and indeed constituting, the state of American relations with the two actors. For this reason, sales buoy the morale and the will of the government of Taiwan, allowing it more easily to resist blandishments and threats from the PRC. The arms sales, then, have a political significance that is far greater than their military impact. The same effect could be produced by the sale of diamonds if the participants would grant it the appropriate meaning.

Of course international politics is not unique in this regard. In other areas as well our beliefs can strongly shape reality. For example, at the height of the controversy over President Reagan's planned visit to the

---

3. Some scholars argue that the psychological effects are relatively minor and therefore that American nuclear policy has to be militarily effective. See Colin Gray, *Nuclear Strategy and National Style* (Lanham, Md.: Hamilton Press, 1986).

German cemetery, Elie Wiesel said, "If he visits Bitburg . . . it is the rehabilitation of the SS."[4] One meaning of Wiesel's statement is that Reagan's attitude is typical of that held by the population at large. Thus the fact that he was willing to visit the cemetery is an indication of the fact that many people no longer hold the SS responsible for mass murder. But if this is what he meant, there would have been no point in his trying to pressure Reagan to change his plans; such a victory would not have altered the underlying acceptance of the SS. So a second meaning seems appropriate—for Reagan to visit the cemetery would be to indicate to many people that the SS is now acceptable. But if we take Reagan at his word—and on this point there is no reason not to— this was neither his personal belief nor the message he was trying to convey. So only if people accept Wiesel's prophecy will it be correct. But unlike the self-fulfilling prophecy of the run on the bank, here the underlying reality has no objective status at all. That is, the bank ac- tually runs out of money after a certain point and this is a brute fact that, although created by people's behavior (which is based on their predictions concerning the bank's solvency), has a status apart from what we believe about it. This simply is not the case with whether the SS is rehabilitated or not.[5]

An example from social life brings up a different dynamic, but one that also could apply to international politics. When New York City schools reopened in January 1987 after a vacation that had seen serious racial vio- lence, the chancellor said that he had decided against putting extra guards in the schools because "we don't want to give the impression that our expectation is that students will act in an abnormal fashion. . . . If a student goes into a school . . . and sees a phalanx of police, that student is going to feel that something untoward is going to happen."[6] A sense of security is subjective; measures that objectively would seem to make a person—or perhaps a state—more secure can induce the opposite feel- ing. Indeed, the actor's behavior may be altered in a way that leads others to menace him, thus making his insecurity objectively correct.

Two questions should be raised at the start even though I cannot fully answer them. First, to use the language of the 1960s, are the analyses of national security developed by scholars and decision mak-

4. Bernard Weinraub, "Reagan Seeking to Take Focus Off Cemetery Visit," *New York Times*, April 28, 1985.

5. Thus when *Newsweek* ran a cover story on Richard Nixon featuring a smiling picture and entitled "He's Back: The Rehabilitation of Richard Nixon" (May 19, 1986) it could not help contributing to the phenomenon it was analyzing.

6. Quoted in Nick Ravo, "In the Wake of Racial Attack, Security Is Stiffened at Six Schools," *New York Times*, January 5, 1987.

ers part of the solution or part of the problem? Have these exercises actually made the world less safe? Have we called into existence problems that, had we defined them differently, would not have been troublesome? The well-known possibility that our perception of high Soviet hostility may be a self-fulfilling prophecy is not the sort of problem I have in mind. Rather I mean to raise the broader question of whether the ways in which we have been thinking about nuclear weapons have called up dragons that we then must go forth and slay. I will return to this topic below.

A second critical question is the extent to which any one state can exercise influence. That many of the claims that we must follow certain policies because they will be persuasive to the Soviets are disingenuous does not make them incorrect. Credibility is in the eye of the beholder and so our ability to work our way out of certain problems may be limited. Economists talk about price makers and price takers. The former are large and powerful enough to influence the market; the latter are not and so must treat prices as givens. Perhaps a similar distinction can be made between "reality makers" and "reality takers." Countries like the United States that are large, powerful, and speak out on most issues with enormous volume, if not with enormous clarity, can influence others' definitions of reality.

For example, Third World countries, our European allies, and probably to a significant extent the Soviets, judge strategic superiority and inferiority on the basis of the measures of assessment that the United States has propagated. Indeed, in most cases opinion in those countries is not based on indicators of the balance at all, but rather on what American leaders say about the balance. By claiming that the Soviet Union has a significant advantage, the United States can probably convince many other countries that it is so. Even the Soviets may be influenced. Although they may not derive their estimates of the strategic balance from American pronouncements, this is likely to be the evidence they use to draw inferences about the way American decision makers see the balance. These inferences are important, because whether the Soviets think they can afford to stand firm in a crisis is influenced by their beliefs about the American estimate of the state of the strategic balance. Thus by saying that the United States is behind in important respects, American leaders increase the chances that the Soviets would be willing to stand firm.[7] But it is much harder to say

7. For a further discussion of this dynamic and an application both to the current period and to the 1930s, see Jervis, "Deterrence and Perception," *International Security*, 7 (Winter, 1982–83), 3–30.

how much of a "reality maker" the United States could be when the view it was propagating was one that was contrary to the Soviets' interests or framework of beliefs. It should be noted, however, that the fact that the Soviets usually deny that indicators like the number of warheads explain and predict national behavior means that it is hard for them to gain a bargaining advantage by "superiority" of this kind.

Some Puzzles

The quotations with which I began this chapter are one indication that a straightforward analysis of power and influence is inappropriate in the nuclear context. Another indication is the existence of a series of puzzles that one can unravel only by understanding the psychological nature of the issues. One such puzzle concerns the lack of preoccupation by many of those most concerned about Soviet aggressiveness with the danger that the Soviet Union could quickly add an extremely large number of warheads to its inventory.[8] No one denies that the Soviets can field the SS-24 and SS-25 much more quickly than the United States can respond. But those who are most vociferous in their calls for vigilance against Soviet military superiority are not greatly alarmed by this prospect.

A second puzzle is the incoherence of many of the claims for the significance of nuclear superiority. I have discussed this at greater length elsewhere and just want to stress that the links between a nuclear arsenal that provides more than a second-strike capability and favorable political outcomes remain obscure and elusive.[9] Paul Nitze's argument of over thirty years ago is representative: "The atomic queens may never be brought into play: they may never actually take one of the opponent's pieces. But the position of the atomic queens may still have a decisive bearing on which side can safely advance a limited-war bishop or even a cold-war pawn."[10] But claims like this never explain how this political efficacy is generated. The failure of logic is further underlined by the results of Stephen Kull's fascinating interviews with those who stress the importance of superiority. In brief, he

8. Robert Gates and Lawrence Gershwin, "Soviet Strategic Force Developments," testimony before a joint session of the Subcommittee on Strategic and Theater Nuclear Forces of the Senate Armed Services Committee and the Defense Subcommittee of the Senate Committee on Appropiations, June 26, 1985.

9. Jervis, *The Illogic of American Nuclear Strategy* (Ithaca: Cornell University Press, 1984).

10. Paul Nitze, "Atoms, Strategy and Policy," *Foreign Affairs*, 34 (January 1956), p. 195.

[179]

finds that the proponents quickly abandon many of the central tenets of their beliefs and find it difficult to maintain a consistent argument.[11]

A third puzzle regards the highly inappropriate ways by which we measure the strategic balance. As I discuss later, many arguments revolve around the question of who is "ahead" on various measures of nuclear power. But this question literally makes no sense even if one takes seriously the notion of having to fight a nuclear war.

A fourth puzzle is the frequent claims that a state has to act in certain ways in order to convey a message even though the actions will not in fact improve the state's military position. To take just one example, the Gaither Committee of 1957 called for an extensive and expensive program of bomb shelters, in part to "symbolize to the nation the urgent threat, and demonstrate to the world our appraisal of the situation and our willingness to cope with it in strength." The program "would symbolize our will to survive, and our understanding of our responsibilities in a nuclear age."[12] But if the measures will not be efficacious, why should they convey the desired impression?

A final puzzle has to do with the belief held by most people—experts and members of the public alike—that the chance of war was lower during the period of detente than it was in the early and middle 1980s, although the former years saw many more crises than the latter. Since 1980 the superpowers have had few direct clashes in any area except rhetoric. During the early 1970s, by contrast, the Soviet Union aided a country (North Vietnam) that was fighting the United States; the United States attacked the Soviet ally and even inadvertently strafed Soviet ships; there were mini-crises over Cuba; there was a war between India and Pakistan that the United States, if not the USSR, thought had great Cold War significance; and the war in the Middle East created a sharp confrontation and an American nuclear alert. Yet we call this period one of detente and the later, less eventful, years ones of greater hostility and danger.

SYMBOLS AND POLITICS IN THE NUCLEAR ERA

Phenomenological studies of political and social life are familiar, if often obscure. In the same vein, but from a different intellectual back-

11. Stephen Kull, *Minds at War: Nuclear Reality and the Inner Conflict of Defense Policymakers* (New York: Basic Books, 1988).

12. Security Resources Panel of the Science Advisory Committee, "Deterrence and Survival in the Nuclear Age," Report to the President, November 7, 1957, in Marc Trachtenberg, ed., *The Development of American Strategic Thought: Basic Documents from the Eisenhower and Kennedy Periods* (New York: Garland, 1988), p. 33, emphasis omitted.

ground and of more direct relevance to our concerns here, Walter Lippmann, Harold Lasswell, and others have argued that much of politics is about symbols. As Lasswell put it, "any elite defends and asserts itself in the name of symbols of common destiny. . . . By the use of sanctioned words and gestures the elite elicits blood, work, taxes, applause, from the masses. When the political order works smoothly, the masses venerate the symbols; the elite, self-righteous and unafraid, suffers from no withering sense of immorality."[13] Symbols are the means and ends of politics both as they are valued in themselves and as they can be manipulated to influence others. Similarly, Lippmann noted that "the pictures in our heads" lead to "fictions" ("a representation of the environment which is in lesser or greater degree made by man himself") and "the insertion between man and his environment of a pseudo-environment. To that pseudo-environment his behavior is a response."[14]

By now, these notions are not new. Yet I would venture four propositions. First, this field is still very much an understudied one.[15] Second, the study of symbols in politics must be closely linked to political psychology—how people think about objects in the political arena. Indeed, one of Lasswell's important contributions was his stress on the relations between the two. His examination was in terms of ego dynamics, but other psychological approaches are also relevant. Third, symbols are central to international politics. Although nations struggle for power and the final arbiter of crucial disputes is military force, many conflicts involve not concrete gains and losses but, rather, issues

13. Harold Lasswell, *Politics: Who Gets What, When, How* (New York: McGraw-Hill, 1936), p. 29.

14. Walter Lippmann, *Public Opinion* (New York: Macmillan, 1922), p. 15.

15. Murray Edelman has done a great deal to call our attention to the need to analyze politics in terms of symbols. See his *The Symbolic Uses of Politics* (Urbana: University of Illinois Press, 1964); *Politics as Symbolic Action* (New York: Academic Press, 1971); *Political Language: Words That Succeed and Policies That Fail* (New York: Academic Press, 1977); and *Constructing the Political Spectacle* (Chicago: University of Chicago Press, 1988). A classic treatment is Thurman Arnold, *Symbols of Government* (New Haven: Yale University Press, 1935), and a good synthesis is Charles Elder and Roger Cobb, *The Political Use of Symbols* (London: Longman, 1983). For an appreciation of these elements in the purposes and effects of economic sanctions in international politics, see David Baldwin, *Economic Statecraft* (Princeton: Princeton University Press, 1985). David Sears and his colleagues have also argued that attitudes are strongly influenced by the symbolic aspects of issues. See David Sears, Carl Hensler, and Leslie Speer, "Whites' Opposition to Busing: Self-Interest or Symbolic Politics," *American Political Science Review*, 73 (June 1979), 369–84; Sears, Richard Lau, Tom Tyler, and Harris Allen, Jr., "Self-Interest vs. Symbolic Politics in Policy Attitudes and Presidential Voting," *American Political Science Review*, 47 (September 1980), 670–84; and Sears and Jack Citrin, *Tax Revolt* (Cambridge: Harvard University Press, 1982).

whose importance arise from the way national leaders have framed the questions. Fourth, and the point on which I want to concentrate, symbols and psychology are particularly important in the nuclear era. W. I. Thomas's famous dictum is especially true for nuclear weapons: "If men define situations as real, they are real in their consequences."

Because they can destroy civilization but may never be used, nuclear weapons cast a shadow that is simultaneously ephemeral and full of menace. The ability of each superpower to destroy the other has a number of ironic consequences with which we are familiar—for example, the most powerful force is not usable; what is usually considered offensive is now defensive and vice versa; making threats credible is both extremely important and extremely difficult; the superpowers are at the same time terribly insecure (because of the chance of total destruction) and very secure (because the chance of major war is lower than it has ever been in the past). But perhaps a more basic consequence of mutual second-strike capability is the unprecedented weakening of the links between the physical capabilities and much of the behavior of states; this attenuation allows an unusual opening for the play of psychology, symbols, and beliefs.

Thomas Schelling, Glenn Snyder, and others have noted the shift from defense to deterrence, or, to put it more broadly, from brute force to coercion. In previous eras, all-out wars could be won and many objectives could be reached physically—that is, superior force could keep the enemy's armies off a state's territory and push the state's armies onto the enemy's lands. When brute force is effective, little psychology or symbolism is needed, although it still can be useful. But when each side can destroy the other and neither can protect itself, states must bargain on the basis of ability to inflict and bear pain. Military power then can be converted into favorable political outcomes only by processes that are indirect and that must involve large elements of highly subjective assessments.

Another factor that explains the increased importance of symbols and psychology is the world's lack of experience with nuclear wars, which means that the beliefs on which we operate must be speculative. Nuclear strategy must remain hypothetical; arguments can be supported with rigor and logic, but there cannot be much evidence. Similarly, credibility plays a crucial role in strategic thinking—and yet cannot be objectively specified.[16] We must be preoccupied with how

16. See Patrick Morgan, "Saving Face for the Sake of Deterrence" in Robert Jervis, Richard Ned Lebow, and Janice Stein, *Psychology and Deterrence* (Baltimore: Johns Hopkins

others see the world and see us, and these perceptions are influenced by their theories about international politics and about us. The validity of many of these judgments is hard to determine. Indeed, they can create or destroy the reality they are trying to capture. That is, if the state knows that others perceive its threats as credible, it can stand firm in a given situation with relatively low risk. Conversely, in most instances in which it believes its threat will not be viewed as credible, the state will retreat. Sometimes, however, this belief may create its own counteracting dynamic: if a state needs to demonstrate that others are underestimating its resolve, it may act not only in spite of, but because of, others' beliefs.

Thus many questions of nuclear politics cannot be answered apart from the actors' ideas. For example, the belief that nuclear war cannot be kept limited would make a limited war impossible. (The belief that war could be kept limited is not a sufficient cause for that outcome, however; it is only a necessary condition.) Similarly, there is no objective answer to the question of which nuclear postures and doctrines are destabilizing apart from the highly subjective beliefs that decision makers hold about this question. In related ways, the question of credibility of threats cannot be discussed, even in principle, entirely on the basis of objective factors. Not only do each side's beliefs constitute an important part of the reality with which the other has to contend, but also states can collude or contend on the constructions of reality that frame these judgments. Similarly, to note a topic which I discussed in Chapter 5 and to which I return at the end of this chapter, the superpowers' beliefs about whether or not war between them is inevitable create reality as much as they reflect it. Because preemption could be the only rational reason to launch an all-out war, beliefs about what the other side is about to do are of major importance and depend in large part on an estimate of the other's beliefs about what the first side will do. Each side's judgment about whether the other thinks that war is likely strongly influences the chances of war or peace.

In this sort of world, the lack of objective answers to many crucial questions allows unusual scope for the power of the ideas we develop and the concepts we employ. Thus Herman Kahn talks about an escalation "ladder," implying that one can move up and down the rungs with some precision and that at least one side can choose

University Press, 1985), pp. 125–52, for the argument that the United States is more concerned with credibility than are other states.

the level of violence to which it will move or stay.[17] But the argument for this sort of control rests on a metaphor, not evidence. If one talks about an escalation "slippery slope" one gets a very different picture. But there is no way to determine which picture is more accurate, in part because how escalation would occur will be influenced by decision makers' expectations, which in turn are influenced by the terms and analogies they employ. Indeed, once a person has thought up a story or scenario that links events together, however improbable they may be individually, he or she will come to see those events as more likely.[18]

Nuclear weapons, then, have only increased the importance of symbols and psychology, not created it. While brute force operates on capabilities, not intentions, it still acts on people; morale and faith in one's weapons and tactics make men fight better. Similarly, armies are defeated not when everyone in them is killed but when they lose their effectiveness. Thus blitzkrieg tactics work primarily by interfering with the enemy's command and intelligence structures, disorienting and demoralizing him, and thereby undermining the will to fight at all levels. Even in battles of attrition, the unwillingness or inability of the soldiers to continue resisting, while of course related to the physical punishment the army has taken, is not directly predictable from it.[19]

Leaders always have to act on their beliefs about the world, and these beliefs often lack solid foundation. Thus in the 1930s England appeased Germany in part because of the prevailing belief that Hitler sought only minor modifications of the status quo, and at the start of World War I all the powers engaged in mobilization races and offensives because they incorrectly believed that the offense had a major

---

17. Herman Kahn, *On Escalation, Metaphors and Scenarios* (Baltimore: Penguin Books, 1968), p. 3.

18. See Amos Tversky and Daniel Kahneman, "Extensional versus Intuitive Reasoning: The Conjunction Fallacy in Probability Judgment," *Psychological Review*, 90 (October 1983), 293–315; Nancy Kanwisher, "Cognitive Heuristics and American Security Policy," *Journal of Conflict Resolution*, forthcoming.

19. Carl von Clausewitz stressed the psychological nature of warfare in *On War*, ed. and trans. Michael Howard and Bernard Brodie (Princeton: Princeton University Press, 1976); also see Robert Osgood, *Limited War* (Chicago: University of Chicago Press, 1957), pp. 61–62. Tim Travers demonstrates that one reason why British generals chose their tactics of direct frontal assault was the fear that their soldiers would not fight in any other configuration and the belief that only this approach would break the Germans' morale (*The Killing Ground* [London: Allen & Unwin, 1987]). For an analysis of the American Civil War that stresses the importance of morale and will, see Richard Beringer, William Hattaway, Archer Jones, and William Still, Jr., *Why the South Lost the Civil War* (Athens: University of Georgia Press, 1986).

advantage over the defense.[20] But the validity of beliefs like these had objective answers apart from what people thought, and the questions were at least subject to a final test. Although the British beliefs and the behavior based on them may have influenced Hitler and even altered his intentions, there finally came a point at which the menace he posed became clear. Similarly, by the winter of 1914 the powers discovered the potency of the defense. There was then an underlying substrate of reality that impinged on the decision makers.

Perceptions of Vital Interests

The question of what constitutes a vital interest is particularly sub-jective in the nuclear era. In the past, vital interests were those directly linked to the state's core values. Events outside its territory menaced the state if they threatened to deprive it of necessary resources, allies, or buffer zones. Thus, Britain could be attacked if a hostile power controlled the coast of Belgium, and the powers before World War I could not protect themselves if one of their major allies defected to the opposing coalition.

I do not want to claim that the earlier situations were simple and entirely objective.[21] The links between many events in third areas and the state's security were tenuous and debatable. But today the problem is both greater and less. It is less in that no matter what happens, each side can maintain its ability to destroy the other. But it is greater in that to the extent that defeats in third areas are taken as showing that the threat to use nuclear weapons under the most dire circumstances lacks all credibility, then these events—even if inherently trivial—im-pinge on the state's security. In the past, losing a limited war or re-treating in a confrontation could endanger the state because it decreased the state's physical ability to protect itself. This is rarely, if ever, true for the superpowers today. Instead, retreats or defeats in third areas can weaken the state's position on other issues only through influencing others' beliefs about the superpower's future behavior.[22]

20. For excellent analyses of the latter case, see Jack Snyder, *The Ideology of the Offensive* (Ithaca: Cornell University Press, 1984); Snyder, "Civil-Military Relations and the Cult of the Offensive, 1914 and 1984," *International Security*, 9 (Summer 1984), 108–46, and Stephen Van Evera, "The Cult of the Offensive and the Origins of the First World War," *International Security.*, 9 (Summer 1984), pp. 58–107.

21. See the discussion in Bernard Brodie, *War and Politics* (New York: Macmillan, 1937), chap. 8.

22. For a further discussion, see Glenn Snyder, *Deterrence and Defense* (Princeton:

Of major importance, then, are the perceptions of other actors, perceptions that can be influenced by what the superpower says and does. To an unusual degree, statesmen's beliefs create vital interests.[23] Interests are vital if others think they are, and a large component of others' beliefs is how they think the first state sees those interests. The extent to which these perceptions can be grounded in objective factors like geography and patterns of trade is not insignificant, but neither is it close to complete.[24] As a result, commitments now create interests at least as much as interests create commitments.[25] Because the bulk of the costs of retreats and defeats are the expected damage to the superpower's reputation, becoming committed to standing firm on a question gives the superpower a greater reason to stand firm. Indeed that is the purpose of the tactic of commitment, although the results are not always to the state's liking.

Perceptions of Success and Failure

In many cases it is hard to find objective indicators of whether a policy has succeeded or failed.[26] Thus there is a great deal of room for states to influence the interpretation of the outcomes, and that may be more important than the outcomes themselves. To return to an earlier example, how do we know whether Reagan's visit to Bitburg was a

---

Princeton University Press, 1961), pp. 30–40, and Jervis, "Deterrence Theory Revisited," *World Politics*, 31 (January 1979), 314–17. George Liska argues that "the greatest threat to international stability—and, thus, in the long run, to world peace—lies in the pervasive tendency to dilute concern for the real issues of politics by concentrating on nuclear weapons. The real issues continue to involve questions of territory, in the broad sense: control or influence over—or access to—geopolitical and geostrategic assets" ("The Geopolitics of U.S.–Soviet Conflict," in Simon Serfaty, ed., *U.S.–Soviet Relations* [Washington: Foreign Policy Institute, Johns Hopkins University, School of Advanced International Studies, August 1985], p. 67). This claim, which seems like common sense, is not satisfactory because it fails to explain why influence over various areas affects the superpowers' vital interests.

23. For a related argument, see Brodie, *War and Politics*, pp. 341–74.

24. Thus a statistical analysis of twentieth-century attempts at extended deterrence is able to explain only about one-third of the variance in outcomes by looking at the standard and important objective factors. See Paul Huth and Bruce Russett, "What Makes Deterrence Work? Cases from 1900 to 1980," *World Politics*, 36 (July 1984), 495–526.

25. For a similar conclusion, although based on slightly different reasoning, see Alexander George and Richard Smoke, *Deterrence in American Foreign Policy* (New York: Columbia University Press, 1974), pp. 550–65, and Robert Johnson, "Exaggerating America's Stakes in Third World Conflicts," *International Security*, 10 (Winter 1985–86), 42–43.

26. See, for example, the American debate over who "won" the Daniloff affair: Leslie Gelb, "Keeping Score," *New York Times*, October 1, 1986.

success or not? Did it show that German-American relations are especially close? Did it demonstrate that Reagan is a man of his word? Has it made the SS more respectable? These questions cannot be answered—even in principle—except by reference to people's answers to them. Thus to the extent that people believe the trip was a success, then indeed it was.[27]

There is, then, a great deal of room for false consensus effects—that is, if each person thinks that everyone else holds a certain view, then that view becomes the operating reality. Within a government or country, but sometimes between states as well, the "sheer repetition [of arguments and statements] may induce belief,"[28] especially when there are few ways directly to verify what is being said and when the truth of the statement depends on whether other people believe it.

Actors also often have significant room to establish the definition of the situation. After initially seeing and portraying the Reykjavik summit as a failure, President Reagan and his advisers decided to present it as a success. As one White House aide put it: At first "we were focusing on the one yard we didn't gain. Well, what about the 99 yards we did? We kept saying, 'Let's focus on that.' " Donald Regan's remark was more graphic: "Some of us are like a shovel brigade that follow a parade down Main Street cleaning up. We took Reykjavik and turned what was really a sour situation into something that turned out pretty well."[29] While somewhat self-serving, these accounts could have been a model for other episodes that were taken as American defeats largely because American leaders treated them as such. This may be true of the Berlin Wall. Of course the West could not have publicly welcomed this move without sacrificing West German faith, but neither did it have to proclaim the East German ability to halt the flow of refugees a major defeat. After all, the main issue from 1958 to 1961 was whether the Soviet Union could force the West out of West Berlin. Although

27. Generally, there is even more room for influencing the broader interpretations of events, such as whether a punishment is exceptional or typical or whether it connotes moral culpability. For an example of exceptional punishment, see Joseph Fried, "Howard Beach Defendant Given Maximum Term of 10 to 30 Years," *New York Times*, January 23, 1988; for an example of one connoting moral culpability, see David Johnston, "Nofziger Given 90 Days in Jail in Ethics Case," *New York Times*, April 9, 1988.

28. Robert Packenham, *Liberal America and the Third World* (Princeton: Princeton University Press, 1973), p. xix.

29. White House aide is quoted in Bernard Wienraub, "Reagan Triumphs from Failure in Iceland," *New York Times*, October 17, 1986; also see Leslie Gelb, "The Summit: New Issues," *New York Times*, October 25, 1986. Regan is quoted in Bernard Weinraub, "Criticism on Iran and Other Issues Puts Reagan's Aides on Defensive," *New York Times*, November 16, 1986.

only later did it become entirely clear that the Wall was a prelude to abandoning this campaign, such a possibility was obvious from the start. Thus the West could have portrayed the Wall as an admission of double failure by the East—it could neither keep its citizens in the country without force nor drive the West from its half of the city.[30] Similarly, most American leaders concluded that the Soviets "defeated" the West in Angola and, in confirmation of this portrayal, now support the rebels. But alternative interpretations are possible. Not only were most of the forces at work internal to Angola, but the Soviets sponsored an unsuccessful coup attempt against the regime of Agostinho Neto. Ordinarily this would have been sufficient to make the outcome seem, if not an American victory, at least one undesired by the Soviet Union. But American decision makers were so set on claiming—and seeing— events as showing weakness that they ignored the opportunity presented by the failed coup to alter either their policy or the judgments of who had gained and who had lost.

By contrast, President Eisenhower sought a solution to the Quemoy and Matsu problem by influencing the way events would be seen. He realized that the islands had no intrinsic value. The problem was that Chiang Kai-shek had staked his prestige on keeping them and so they had become psychologically important. The troops could be withdrawn if and only if doing so did not appear to be a defeat. Indeed, he argued, "if Chiang should develop a satisfactory alternative so that it would, under his leadership, be accepted in Formosa and in Southeast Asia as a shrewd move to improve his strategic position, his prestige should be increased rather than diminished."[31] This effort did not succeed, in part perhaps because he did not develop it further. Ronald Reagan did much better when he reduced the cost of withdrawing American Marines from Lebanon by portraying the move as one to further our goals. As he put it:

> Yielding to violence and terrorism today may seem to provide temporary relief, but such a course is sure to lead to more dangerous and less manageable future crises. Even before the latest outbreak of violence, we had been considering ways of reconcentrating our forces and the nature of our support in order to take the initiative away from the terrorists. Far from deterring

30. When the Kennedy administration defended itself against the charge that it had meekly accepted an unfavorable change in the status quo, its spokesmen took the line that East Berlin had been under effective Soviet control since the late 1940s.

31. Department of State, *FRUS, 1955–1957*, vol. 2., *China* (Washington, D.C.: Government Printing Office, 1986), p. 448.

this course, recent events only confirm the importance of the decisive new steps I want to outline for you now.[32]

Of course this redefinition could not eliminate all damage to America's reputation, but it did reduce it, especially for domestic audiences. Despite the numerous previous statements to the effect that, in the words of Secretary of State George Shultz, "If America's efforts for peaceful solutions are overwhelmed by brute force, our role in the world is that much weakened everywhere,"[33] Reagan's consistent post-withdrawal portrayal helped minimize the perceptions of weakness that the deployment itself was designed to forestall.

Of course the state will not always want an encounter to be seen as a victory. Defeats can be used to rally public opinion, which may explain the Angolan example. Futhermore, to claim victory can be to humiliate the other or to legitimate its claim to receive better treatment next time. Thus President Kennedy ordered his aides not to brag about the outcome of the Cuban missile crisis. During the confrontation he also understood that to convince the other side that it was facing a great loss was to increase the chance that it would strongly resist.[34] The state also may want to downplay the notions of winning and losing in order to stress the existence of mutual interests and pave the way for future cooperation. This probably was another of Kennedy's motives; it may also explain the Soviet foreign minister's response to a question from reporters about who won the conflict over the arrests of Gennadi Zakharov and Nicholas Daniloff: "Let us not speak in terms of winners and losers. If the meeting in Reykjavik is productive, mankind as a whole will be the winner."[35]

Murray Edelman argues that "political actions chiefly arouse or satisfy people not by granting or withholding their stable substantive demands, but rather by changing the demands and the expectations."[36]

32. New York Times, February 8, 1986; see also Reagan's press conference in New York Times, February 23, 1984.

33. George Shultz, "The Situation in Lebanon," U.S. Department of State Bulletin, 83 (December 1983), 44.

34. The political costs of losses are increased by psychological dynamics: see Daniel Kahneman and Amos Tversky, "Prospect Theory: An Analysis of Decision under Risk," Econometrica, 47 (March 1979), 263–91; Tversky and Kahneman, "Choices, Values, and Frames," American Psychologist, 39 (April 1984), 341–50; Tversky and Kahneman, "Rational Choice and the Framing of Decisions," Journal of Business, 59 (October 1986), S251–78.

35. Quoted in Christopher Wren, "Afganistan May Be Topic in Iceland," New York Times, October 3, 1986.

36. Edelman, Politics as Symbolic Action, p. 7.

While this claim is put too broadly, it often applies to judgments of success or failure. Because such judgments are usually measured against a baseline of expectations, defining that baseline can be crucial to how a situation is perceived. This is well understood by candidates in presidential primaries. In many cases, what is more important than the percentage of votes that a candidate receives is whether that percentage is greater or less than what was expected. Winning even one-third of the votes can be a major victory if people expected the candidate to do very poorly; getting a bare majority can be a failure for a front-runner.[37] In the same way, the strength of a state's protest will be measured in part against the actions it was expected to take.[38]

Similarly, detecting change is easier than inferring meaning and thus is often used as a surrogate for the latter. This is one reason why we often ask whether an actor did better this time than last time even if such changes are unimportant. Thus in examining the Daniloff-Zakharov-Orlov trade, politicians and reporters alike compared this outcome to similar cases in the past, often arguing that the United States "lost" because Soviet spies had previously been kept in jail longer and more dissidents had been released in the trade. Leaving aside the difficulties in deciding whether the circumstances of earlier cases really were the same, what is crucial for my argument is that many people jumped from the judgment that the Soviets did better this time to the conclusion that they "won"—that is, "set a precedent that would make Western governments think twice about arresting Soviet spy suspects."[39] But even if this trade was more palatable to the Soviets than earlier ones, it may not be so attractive as to tempt them to repeat the adventure. By the same token, the terms of the trade could have been worse than in previous cases without being excessively costly. But the baseline of the past establishes our expectations and so we concentrate on deviations from it even if logically they do not carry much meaning.

In a related process, whether one regards the American efforts to reduce terrorism as a success or failure depends in large part on one's beliefs of what a "normal" level of violence would be. Indeed, as people get accustomed to a certain amount of terrorism, it loses a great deal of its sting. After all, even at high levels, very few people are killed. Even in Israel, many more people die from automobile accidents than

37. For a further discussion of this and related cases, see Jervis, *The Logic of Images in International Relations* (Princeton: Princeton University Press, 1970), pp. 216–33.
38. See Bernard Gwertzman, "U.S. Ousts Attache of South Africa to Protest Raids," *New York Times*, May 24, 1986.
39. Serge Schemann, "A Limited Success for Gorbachev," *New York Times*, October 1, 1986.

from terrorism. Terrorism, then, for the most part affects people's psychology—they are deeply disturbed not only by the violence but also by the precautions required to minimize it. When such precautions come to be taken for granted—as we have come to accept airport security—they become less intrusive and less threatening. Indeed, what is intrusive and threatening cannot be defined objectively, apart from our feelings.

Echo Effects

Statements about potential threats and how to meet them can affect the speaker as well as the audience through "echo effects." A particular definition of the situation or construction of an event can become entrenched as it is repeated back to those who originally propounded it, even if they did not believe it in the first place. Furthermore, when interpretations act as self-fulfilling prophecies, the statements can become true if they are widely accepted, and the speakers will be correct to accept them if they have reason to believe that others do. Thus at least some of the people who deny the credibility of the American threat to use nuclear weapons in situations short of an all-out attack may not have originally believed these statements, instead expecting them to rouse the United States and its allies to make greater defense efforts. But if others accept this claim, then it may have to be taken as true by those who began the line of argument. Because credibility exists in the eye of the beholder, the beliefs of others not only measure but determine whether a stance or threat is in fact credible.

Statesmen are sometimes aware of the dangers and opportunities posed by echo effects. A member of the State Department Policy Planning staff in 1951 argued that the administration should be careful when it oversimplified Soviet intentions in its public statements so that

> we in the department and on the National Security Council do not become "hoisted by our own petard." We do not want to find ourselves in the position of the gambler at the race track who spread rumors about the excellent chances of a broken-down nag in order to improve the odds on the horse which he considered the likely winner who at the last moment, influenced by the clamors of the crowd who had been stimulated by his own propaganda, shifted his bet from the winner to the nag who crossed the finish line last.[40]

40. FRUS, 1951, vol. 1, National Security Affairs; Foreign Economic Policy (Washington, D.C.: Government Printing Office, 1979), pp. 166–67.

[191]

Morton Halperin and Tang Tsou argue that this effect occurred during the Quemoy and Matsu crisis. Proponents of taking a firm stand sought to bolster their position by presenting an exaggerated picture of the likely consequences of a retreat. As this version of the truth came to be accepted by the bureaucracy and the public, it became imbedded in common discourse and reduced American flexibility to a greater extent than the proponents of this line of argument had expected or desired.[41]

At other times, rather than one person or group spreading a version that others later accept, colleagues seek to develop their understanding of the situation they are confronting. This may be what was happening in the first years of the Eisenhower administration. Reading through the detailed minutes of the meetings of the National Security Council from 1952 to 1954 reveals a large number of arguments about the wording of position papers.[42] Many of the differences are so subtle that by reading only the final version one could not infer which paragraphs were seen as controversial and what the alternatives might have been. The debates, then, have an oddly academic quality, especially since the words are not specific enough to provide guidance to the bureaucracy. In part, contending factions within the NSC were engaging in tests of strength—the words themselves and even the ostensible issues mattered less than demonstrating who could win. But I think there also is a less conflictual and less frequently remarked-upon process at work—an attempt by the participants to arrive at a negotiated common view of the world that they will be willing to take as truth.

Similar echo effects have strongly influenced the kind of threats strategic analysts take seriously. Little attention is paid to chemical or biological warfare, not so much because of technical limits on the possibilities of such violence as because the strategic community has put it out of bounds. Positive feedback also is at work—the more a problem is considered important, the more attention it will receive, thus justifying the belief that it is worthy of attention. The reverse is also true. Within the area of nuclear strategy, "ground rules" for establishing what scenarios are to be taken seriously develop, and those scenarios that fall outside them are neglected. Thus for years after electromagnetic pulse was discovered, its effects were rarely incorporated into

41. Morton Halperin and Tang Tsou, "U.S. Policy toward the Offshore Islands," *Public Policy*, 15 (1966), 130–32. For reports of similar "blowback" from European audiences, see Richard Ullman, "Containment and the Shape of World Politics, 1947–1987," in Terry Deibel and John Gaddis, eds., *Containment: Concept and Policy*, vol. 2 (Washington, D.C.: National Defense University Press, 1986), pp. 622–23.
42. Department of State, *FRUS, 1952–1954*, vol. 2.

analyses and few forms of attack that heavily utilized it were studied. Similarly, in estimating casualties, most analyses employ assumptions that, while unrealistic, have become accepted over the years and so have become part of the reality the community has chosen to accept.

RESOLVE AND CREDIBILITY

In the nuclear age the ultimate threat is to risk if not start all-out war. But since the implementation of such a threat would lead to the destruction of the state as well as its adversary, it is not highly credible. Thus one crucial problem in the nuclear era is for countries to establish their resolve. To do so, the state must influence others' beliefs.

Of course others can try to judge the state's resolve by its previous behavior. The belief that they do make such judgments in part explains why the superpowers become deeply involved in issues and countries that can have little direct impact on their security. The Cold War is filled with conflicts and crises that involve at least some slight—usually vanishingly slight—chance of war and is interspersed with occasions on which one side or the other paid a significant price in terms of bloodshed—such as the Soviet Union in Afghanistan or the United States in Vietnam. But both logic and evidence raise questions about how much one can infer about the state's resolve from this behavior. Studies have failed to demonstrate a consistent impact of the resolution of one conflict on subsequent ones.[43] "Scaling up" from small issues and wars to nuclear confrontations is problematical because the costs and the stakes of the former are incomparably less than those of the latter. It seems unreasonable, for example, that anyone should draw inferences about how the United States might behave at the brink of nuclear war from how it behaved in Vietnam. Indeed, if fighting a small war like Vietnam would markedly increase the American ability to deter the Soviets from menacing its vital interests, then the war would have been a cheap way to protect the United States. This example shows that inferences about resolve can undermine rather than support themselves: if the United States felt that fighting a small war for a country of little intrinsic value would lead others to conclude that

43. Huth and Russett, "What Makes Deterrence Work?" p. 517, and Glenn Snyder and Paul Diesing, *Conflict among Nations* (Princeton: Princeton University Press, 1977), pp. 496–97. For contrary findings, see Robert Mandel, "The Effectiveness of Gunboat Diplomacy," *International Studies Quarterly*, 30 (March 1986), 68–69, Paul Huth and Bruce Russett, "Deterrence Failure and Crisis Escalation," *International Studies Quarterly*, 32 (March 1988), 29–46, and Paul Huth, *Extended Deterrence and the Prevention of War* (New Haven: Yale University Press, 1988), pp. 81–83.

it would display high resolve in a dangerous confrontation, then this action actually would not provide reliable evidence because the United States would fight the small war in order to create a favorable impression irrespective of whether or not it would run high risks in a nuclear challenge. In many instances, then, for a state to admit that it is behaving as it is in order to bolster its reputation should be self-defeating: there is no reason for others to see the behavior as typical of what the state will do in the future.

It can be argued that even if standing firm in a low-level dispute or fighting a small war yields no definite implications, retreating clearly undermines future credibility: the inference of refusal to pay costs is so direct that questions of the actors' beliefs or constructions of reality do not arise. But such an inference is erroneous, in part because if the actor who retreated believes that others believe the domino theory, he will feel especially strong incentives to prevail the next time in order to show that the theory is not correct, or at least does not apply to him. As the German foreign minister put it in 1911: "when our prestige ... is lowered we must fight."[44] Of course if others foresee this, they will expect a defeated actor to be particularly tough in the next confrontation. And if this is believed, then the domino theory cannot be right and so defeated actors should not have any special incentives in the next confrontation.

Lacking objective and reliable indicators of resolve, then, states are forced to do many odd things to convince others that they will stand firm in a major crisis. Kissinger argued:

> In my view what seems "balanced" and "safe" in a crisis is often the most risky. Gradual escalation tempts the opponent to match every move; what is intended as a show of moderation may be interpreted as an irresolution; reassurance may provide too predictable a checklist and hence an incentive for waiting, prolonging the conditions of inherent risk.... [In order to terminate a confrontation rapidly, a leader] must convey implacability. He must be prepared to escalate rapidly and brutally to a point where the opponent can no longer afford to experiment.[45]

This position is intriguing and may be correct, although it appears suspiciously like a generalization based on a superficial reading of the

---

44. Quoted in Ima Barlow, *The Agadir Crisis* (Chapel Hill: University of North Carolina Press, 1940), p. 327.
45. Henry Kissinger, *White House Years* (Boston: Little, Brown, 1979), p. 622.

Vietnam experience. But what is important here is that it rests—and logically must rest—on beliefs about how the other side is interpreting one's moves. The rules of inference that link the state's actions and the observers' predictions are created by the latter. States therefore try to act in ways that will produce desired impressions on observers, and observers try to judge what states will do next on the basis of the latter's previous behavior.[46] Circularity results as the behavior of the state depends on the expected inferences of observers and the latter have to judge how the state believes inferences are being drawn. The parties to the interaction then develop the definitions of reality that will guide them.

In much the same way, Ronald Reagan argued for the importance of aid to the Nicaraguan rebels: "Make no mistake about it. . . . The ability to succeed in [the summit] meeting will be directly affected by Gorbachev's perception of our global position and internal solidarity."[47] (Of course the president also wanted the aid because he saw the Sandinista regime as a threat to significant American interests. Indeed, this is part of the reason why he thought the Soviets would be impressed by his actions: they are more likely to see American passivity as weakness if they believe that Nicaragua is harming the United States.) Reagan's inference is difficult to verify because it is based on beliefs about how the Soviets draw inferences. It is at least questionable that their expectations of a range of American behavior would be greatly influenced by whether Congress voted aid to the Contras. But if they are, even those who believe both that America should not play a central role in the conflict and that broader inferences would be unwarranted might have to vote for the aid.

Credibility can in part be established by taking actions that risk escalation to higher levels of violence. Some actions do this by their physical effects—for example, delegation of the power to use nuclear weapons to local commmanders; direct menacing of the other's vital interests. But more often, risk is created by the subjective interpretations drawn by the participants. Thus how risky various actions are often depends on how others think about the problem. For example, during the Cuban missile crisis Robert Kennedy suggested that en-

46. President Eisenhower justified his reduction of American conventional forces by arguing, "The things we really need are the things that the other fellow looks at and respects"; these were nuclear weapons, not ground forces (Ambrose, *Eisenhower*, p. 144). For discussions of this general phenomenon, see Erving Goffman, *The Presentation of Self in Everyday Life* (Garden City, N.Y.: Doubleday, 1959), and Jervis, *Logic of Images*.

47. Quoted in Bernard Weinraub, "Reagan Will Seek $100 Million in Aid for the Contras," *New York Times*, January 22, 1986.

forcing the blockade would be terribly dangerous and "it was better to knock out the missiles by air than to stop a Soviet ship on the high seas."[48] On another issue, Bernard Brodie argued that there was "no basis in experience or logic for assuming that the increase in level of violence from one division to thirty [in a conventional war in Europe] is a less shocking and less dangerous form of escalation than the introduction of [tactical] nuclear weapons."[49] These assessments seem to me to be bizarre. But I do not see an easy way to prove that they are wrong. In part, the answer turns on physical arrangements such as both sides' command and control capabilities. But in large part it would depend on how people understood the behavior. The logic of strategic analysis simply cannot help us a great deal.

Unnecessary Capability as an Indicator of Resolve

The difficulty of establishing resolve helps explain one of the main arguments for the utility of nuclear superiority: superiority matters because others, especially the Soviets, think it matters. To a considerable extent, this is what many people have in mind when they say that a military posture is politically important although it lacks military utility. Harold Brown's argument is typical of this view: "The advantage to the Soviets of a possible lead in the primary measures of comparative capability is ill defined in terms of useful wartime capability.... But it might have some political value during peacetime or in a crisis. The perception of the United States–Soviet strategic balance has been and will be shifting away from that of U.S. advantage and becoming more favorable to Soviets. Such perceptions can have an important effect."[50] Two years later, he similarly argued that "the growing vulnerability of our land-based missile force could, if not corrected, contribute to a perception of U.S. strategic inferiority that would have severely adverse

48. Bromley Smith, "Summary Record of NSC Executive Committee Meeting No. 5, October 25, 1962, 5 p.m.," National Security Files, Box 315, p. 3, John F. Kennedy Library, Boston.
49. Bernard Brodie, "What Price Conventional Capabilities in Europe?" *Reporter*, May 23, 1963, p. 32.
50. U.S. House of Representatives, Committee on Armed Services, *Hearings on H.R. 8390 and Review of the State of U.S. Strategic Forces*, 95th Cong., 1st sess. (Washington, D.C.: Government Printing Office, 1977), p. 162. At least one Soviet commentator has taken a similar position. In reply to the argument that the USSR could engage in partial unilateral disarmament as long as it maintained second-strike capability, Aleksandr Bovin replied: "Theoretically, in a strictly abstract fashion, you are right.... But human logic does not exist outside psychological influence. A mathematically calculated, computerized universal catastrophe comes up against emotional objections and the insurmountable hope for survival" (*Foreign Broadcast Information Service*, April 22, 1987, p. CC8).

political—and could have potentially destabilizing military—consequences."[51] Although his successor sometimes implied that nuclear
superiority had military value, Weinberger too argued that "in some
sense, the political advantages of being seen as the superior strategic
power are more real and more usable than the military advantages of
in fact being superior in one measure or another."[52]

This phenomena is not unique to the nuclear age: it can exist whenever deterrence is seen as primary. Thus many of the decisions the
British made about the shape of their air force in the 1930s were geared
less toward military effectiveness than toward impressing the Germans. To this end, many of the rearmament plans slighted the reserves
and other support systems necessary to fight a war in order to create
a larger frontline force, or what was called a "shop-window force" (i.e.,
one in which everything was on display). In the cabinet debate in 1935,
the secretary of state for air did not dispute criticisms of the military
reliability of he current expansion plan

> but pointed to the crux of the matter, that military considerations
> as such really had little to do with the issue; . . . arguing that "the
> policy now being considered was designed largely as a gesture
> to check Herr Hitler's continual demands." . . . The program that
> resulted [from these deliberations] had no function other than to
> produce the same size front line as Germany was expected to
> have in April 1937. No notion of wartime use of such a force [or
> of the fact that Britain was more vulnerable than Germany and
> had more alliance commitments] . . . entered into the consid-
> erations.[53]

Later, when the British seriously contemplated the danger of war, they
paid more attention to forces that could protect them in the event of
war and constructed the air defense system that would prove itself in
the Battle of Britain.

Since it is doubtful that any systems could bring military victory in

51. Quoted in Herken, *Counsels of War*, p. 298.

52. Caspar Weinberger, *Annual Report for FY 1982* (Washington, D.C.: Government
Printing Office, 1981), p. 44. The reasoning is not dissimilar to President Kennedy's
explanation of why the Soviet missiles could not be permitted to remain in Cuba even
if they did little to alter the military balance (a judgment that is not beyond dispute):
deployment "would have politically changed the balance of power. It would have appeared to, and appearances contribute to reality" (*Public Papers of the President, 1962*
[Washington, D.C.: Government Printing Office, 1963], p. 898).

53. Malcolm Smith, *British Air Strategy between the Wars* (Oxford: Clarendon University
Press, 1984), pp. 156–57.

a nuclear war, it is not surprising that the approach shown in Britain in 1935 is dominant in the United States today, at least among civilian leaders.[54] Because the primary purpose of procuring many nuclear weapons is to demonstrate the willingness to fight, decision makers will not feel they need as many weapons when their resolve and credibility are high. Thus many people became concerned with the strategic balance only when defeat in Vietnam seemed likely. As victory was unattainable, the strategic buildup was needed as a substitute means to the same end—that is, the demonstration that the United States would safeguard important interests. Thus Colin Gray's argument: "The post-Vietnam, post-Watergate United States, particularly after January 1977 with a President near-universally regarded (justly or otherwise) as lacking the true 'Presidential timber,' was not a country that could presume the availability of superior political will as compensation for missing muscle."[55] For the same reasons, before the Scowcroft Commission presented its confused military rationale for the deployment of the MX missile, it stressed that "effective deterrence is in no small measure a question of the Soviets' perceptions of our national will and cohesion."[56]

The same logic indicates that when a state has either suffered a defeat or been unable to mobilize its resources effectively, its leaders will feel the need to reinvigorate the credibility of its threats by doing something difficult or dangerous. They will not care much about the particular issue or dispute; the point is not to reach a particular goal but to show that one can make the journey. This was largely true with the deployment of INF and the strong American reaction to the seizure of the *Mayaguez*. Coming as it did right after the fall of Vietnam, the latter was a welcome opportunity. As Kissinger explained, "The United States must carry out some act somewhere in the world which shows its determination to continue to be a world power."[57]

Obversely, a decision maker who feels strong may not require as many weapons as others do. This may explain why Eisenhower apparently came to accept with relative equanimity the prospect of Soviet

54. We know much less about the Soviet calculations. There is some evidence that they take war more seriously (see, for example, Gray, *Nuclear Strategy and National Style*), but this may be largely a reflection of the greater role of the military in the Soviet system and our tendency to compare American civilian pronouncements and attitudes with those of Soviet military leaders.

55. Colin Gray and Jeffrey Barlow, "Inexcusable Restraint: The Decline of American Military Power in the 1970s," *International Security*, 10 (Fall 1985), 39–40.

56. *Report of the President's Commission on Strategic Forces*, April 6, 1983, p. 16.

57. Quoted in Tom Braden, "Why Are We Looking for Problems?" *Washington Post*, April 14, 1975.

parity: "Eisenhower did not believe in nuclear blackmail. . . . He never believed for a moment that the Soviet government would deliberately choose a nuclear war, and so he saw no need for any American president to be moved by Soviet nuclear blackmail."[58] Knowing he would not be swayed, he did not feel the need for additional military forces. A somewhat different self-conception helps explain why President Reagan's nuclear program was very similar to that of his predecessors even though he claimed that they allowed a dangerous deterioration of America's posture. Furthermore, he argued that he had rectified the previous imbalance although the military picture actually had changed very little. Of course these claims can be dismissed as campaign rhetoric, but I think at least as significant was Reagan's feeling that Carter had been weak whereas he had displayed the willingness to use force. The United States, then, needed to increase its weapons in the earlier period and was safe with the same strategic balance under his leadership.

I will return to an intriguing implication of the importance of the impression one's military posture makes on others—that is, the possibility that because the problem is perceptual, one can deal with it by redefining the situation rather than by changing physical reality. Here I want to emphasize that people act in ways they believe to be wasteful or foolish because they think such actions will impress others. Steven Kull has analyzed this "perception theory" very nicely, and while I think he underestimates the extent to which some people believe that nuclear superiority has real military utility, it is fascinating to see that many proponents of superiority, when interviewed, are hard put to explain why their proposed posture would have military advantages.[59] Instead, they soon retreat to the claim that it is important because the Soviets think that the United States is less likely to stand firm if its leaders think that they are behind on various measures of the strategic balance. It is unclear whether this view holds that the Russians see real military advantages in superiority, that they simply have not thought matters through, or that superiority matters to them because they think it matters to the United States. Nevertheless, arguments that superiority is necessary because it will help deter the Soviets are self-perpetuating. These assertions not only describe what some people see as reality, they reinforce it.

58. McGeorge Bundy, *Danger and Security* (New York: Random House, 1988), p. 348.
59. Kull, *Minds at War.* Also see Lloyd Etheridge, "Nuclear Deterrence without the Rationality Assumption" (unpublished manuscript, Yale University, 1987).

For those who argue that nuclear superiority has only political, and not military, significance, the Soviet views are objectively incorrect in the sense that this capability would not allow the them to secure a military victory. If the United States were intimidated by the belief that the Soviets thought they had a real advantage, the Soviets could gain a bargaining advantage before a war; in an all-out war, however, the Soviet beliefs would be shown to be illusory. But because such a war is unlikely and what is important is peacetime bargaining, the fact—if it is a fact—of the Soviet belief is more consequential than its validity.

Many of the common measures of the strategic balance embody the thinking processes I am describing. Not only President Reagan but also more informed observers ask which side is "ahead" according to "static indicators"—numbers of weapons or measures built out of the numbers and characteristics of the weapons. Thus analysts who believe that military superiority can be meaningful compare each side's ability to destroy the other's hardened targets (e.g., missile silos, command and control bunkers). The assumption is that the United States needs to be, or be seen to be, ready to fight nuclear counterforce wars. But even if this assumption is correct, the question of which side is ahead still is inappropriate. To judge each side's ability to fight, one must match each side's capability to destroy targets against the targets the other side presents. Furthermore, one would want to do this for a variety of situations that differed on crucial dimensions (e.g., whether the country launched a first strike or was retaliating after absorbing a blow; whether the war was protracted or not).

This assessment is rarely made, however. Instead, analysts and leaders compare the two sides' counterforce capabilities, even though such a comparison is pointless. One could be far "ahead" of the other side and still not have enough to destroy the required targets (this was true, for example, for the United States until about 1970); one could be way "behind" and still have sufficient forces to knock out all the targets one would want to. Because these capabilities will never be matched against each other—counterforce capability fights the targets one seeks to destroy, not the other's counterforce capability—the idea of a "race" between them makes no sense. Thus even if one believes that deterrence comes from being able to deny the other side a military advantage from any move, asking who is "ahead" on measures like this yields answers that have meaning only if decision makers endow them with it. To the extent that statesmen believe that being "ahead" on any such measure influences either their resolve or that of the other side, then the measures take on meaning. But this is a world we have created for ourselves, not one that is derivable from the military significance of the weapons.

At first glance—and at second glance also—asking who is "ahead" seems pathological by leading to arms competition. But at least one benefit should be noted. Given the difficulty of meaningful indicators of resolve, looking at the strategic balance may be safer than searching for other tests of strength. Many commentators have noted that in the nuclear era crises may be the functional substitute for wars. But in fact crises are rare and arms competition may be a functional substitute for them. Arms competition is expensive, of course, but it takes place quite far from the brink of war. Better that the United States and the Soviet Union demonstrate their resolve by building new systems than by fighting in Vietnam or triggering crises in Berlin or Cuba.

NEED FOR HARD AND EXPENSIVE TASKS

Demonstrating resolve requires that the actions taken be costly or difficult. In this context, the expense of modern weapons systems is an advantage. If they were cheap, it would be necessary to buy many more of them to indicate the lengths to which one was willing to go in order to seem tough. The desire to trigger this inference process probably was at work in early July 1961 when Khrushchev announced that he would increase that year's defense spending by almost one-third. As Arnold Horelick and Myron Rush note, "such an increase could not be spent on a rational program within that year," and so the likely purpose was to demonstrate seriousness and resolve.[60] Similarly, a year earlier Eisenhower agreed to increase the defense budget by half a billion dollars; even though there was no military need for more arms, the increase perhaps "would carry sufficient credibility to create the psychological effect desired."[61] More recently, Secretary of Defense Weinberger argued that the "gigantic effort" of the large Reagan defense budget will favorably impress the Soviets and that had we not spent so much "their perception of our inaction could have tempted them to a catastrophic miscalculation."[62] In principle, of course, there is no reason why money has to be wasted on weapons. We and the

60. Arnold Horelick and Myron Rush, *Strategic Power and Soviet Foreign Policy* (Chicago: University of Chicago Press, 1966), p. 124.

61. Quoted in Ambrose, *Eisenhower*, p. 591.

62. Caspar Weinberger, "What Is Our Defense Strategy?" Remarks prepared for delivery to the National Press Club, Washington D.C., October 9, 1985, p. 3.

Soviets could agree on a different definition of the situation that would allow us to demonstrate resolve by sending each other gifts, potlatch fashion.[63]

Lives can also be spent to show resolve; the sacrifice can be more significant than whether the manifest goal is reached. Thus, contrary to what many Americans believe, the Soviets may have been more impressed by our willingness to spend thousands of lives for the unimportant country of Vietnam than they were by our eventual decision that the objective did not merit further bloodshed. President Eisenhower understood this when he argued, in a private memorandum to Secretary of State John Foster Dulles, that we and Chiang Kai-shek might not suffer if his forces on Quemoy and Matsu were defeated because "Chiang's prestige and standing in Southeast Asia would be increased rather than decreased as a result of the gallant, prolonged and bitter defense conducted under these circumstances."[64]

Difficult tasks as well as costly ones are the means of conveying messages. Thus the very obstacles to deploying INF probably served NATO well. Had there been no objections in Europe and the United States, there would have been no reason for the Soviets to have been impressed with the Western reaction. Indeed, under some circumstances states may create challenges for themselves so that, by overcoming them, they can demonstrate their skill, commitment, and resolve.

How, Not What

What is often important, then, is not what the outcome is but how it is achieved. Of course this is not unique to the nuclear era. Perception of threat is often triggered by the way in which the other side is behaving rather than by its specific demands.[65] Furthermore, in the past states often took actions to show they were capable of acting strongly rather than to reach particular substantive goals. Thus, in 1823, "the

63. For a discussion of how actors can demonstrate resolve by sacrificing things they value, see Jervis, *Logic of Images*, pp. 250–53. For a game theoretic analysis that reaches the same conclusions, see Barry O'Neill, "Game Theory and the Study of Deterrence of War," in Paul Stern, Robert Axelrod, Robert Jervis, and Roy Radnor, eds., *Perspectives on Deterrence* (New York: Oxford University Press, 1989).

64. *FRUS, 1955–57*, vol. 2, p. 450.

65. For a further discussion, see Jervis, "Perceiving and Coping with Threat," in Jervis, Lebow, and Stein, *Psychology and Deterrence*, and Raymond Cohen, *Threat Perception in International Crisis* (Madison: University of Wisconsin Press, 1979).

assertion by the French government of its right to act alone with respect to Spain was not initially accompanied with any firm indication of what its action would be." Some members of the French cabinet wanted to intervene to suppress the Spanish revolt; others opposed this course of action. All agreed that France did not need the approval of others because they were primarily bent on reestablishing France's rightful place as an equal to its former conquerors.[66] The similar goal of establishing French autonomy led de Gaulle to believe that the substance of the settlement of the Algerian dispute was less important than how it was reached. Independence would be granted, but only "from the height of [French] power." The French "would, therefore, put forth the effort required to make [them] masters of the battlefield."[67]

These phenomena are more common in the nuclear era because the outcomes, even of crises, can rarely directly affect the superpowers' security, which rests on their second-strike capability. Since states are most concerned with resolve and judgments of resolve, of crucial importance are the interpretations that actors make of each others' behavior. Thus the substance of an action or outcome is usually less important than the belief that it was not forced on the state. For example, during the deliberation over the MX, "Defense Secretary Brown argued with the President that the strategic triad should remain inviolate, if only to show the Russians that they could not make American nuclear strategy by pushing our deterrent out to sea."[68] Abandoning ICBMs might be tolerable; doing so because the United States was unable to muster the national determination to keep them was not. In the same way, if we woke up tomorrow morning to learn that half the American and Soviet warheads would not work, we would not feel much safer. But if the Soviets and Americans agreed to destroy half their warheads, most of us would feel safer. Not the changes per se, but the fact that they were reached by agreement, would be important. This reaction would not be foolish. Such an agreement would imply the existence of a common interest that could be brought to fruition by explicit cooperation and would entail the acknowledgment by each side that the other had a legitimate say in what it did.

66. Roger Bullen, "The Great Powers and the Iberian Peninsula, 1815–48," in Alan Sked, ed., *Europe's Balance of Power, 1815–1848* (London: Macmillan, 1979), p. 64.

67. Charles de Gaulle, *Memoirs of Hope: Renewal and Endeavor*, trans. Terence Kilmartin (New York: Simon & Schuster, 1971), p. 46. For reverse cases—instances in which others have sought to deny the state's right to have any say in an issue—see Norman Rich, *Why the Crimean War?* (Hanover, N.H.: University Press of New England, 1985), pp. 39, 194.

68. Herken, *Counsels of War*, p. 290.

Of course in many cases it is the state does not want inferences like these drawn. Thus in the same breath in which Henry Kissinger asked of the proposed INF treaty, "What is the purpose of symbolic agreements that you cannot explain in substance?" he attacked a proposed clause in the treaty that would have permitted the Soviet Union to retain some missiles in Asia exactly in these terms: "The Soviet Union does not need 100 warheads aimed at China, Japan, and Korea for military purposes. It has a surplus of warheads for that purpose. What it does need is our approval of that deployment."[69] Similarly, one reason for the nuclear alert in 1973 may have been to convince the Russians that while the United States was pressing the Israelis to abide by the cease-fire, it was not doing so out of fear of the USSR. When West Germany agreed to destroy its Pershing missiles, it also did not want to be seen as submitting to Soviet pressure: Chancellor Kohl explained instead that "I want to help the American President to successfully conclude" the INF agreement.[70]

The same importance of how a result was produced and why the parties acted as they did is revealed in the frequent cases in which states say they were not influenced by the other but were only acting as they would have in the absence of pressure. Most recently, Gorbachev said that the agreement to withdraw troops from Afghanistan "should not be regarded as a sort of present to President Reagan on the eve of his visit to the USSR," because the Soviet Union merely was "carrying out the plan outlined in our statement in February."[71] Related was President Reagan's insistence that America sold arms to Iran to establish its credentials with moderates, not to win the freedom of the hostages in Lebanon. Similar questions arose during the Cuban missile crisis and, more recently, in the TWA hijacking in June 1985. In the latter instance, once the Amal militia took control of the airplane it was clear that the hostages would be released and that the Palestinians captured in Lebanon by Israel would be freed; the bargaining was about the extent to which there would be a perceived connection between the two.

Similarly, the crisis over the Soviet missiles in Cuba was settled in

---

69. Henry Kissinger, "After Reykjavik: Current East-West Negotiations," *The San Francisco Meeting of the Trilateral Commission*, March 1987, p. 6.

70. Quoted in Serge Schmemann, "Bonn Would Scrap A-Missile in Reply to U.S.–Soviet Pact," *New York Times*, August 27, 1987.

71. Quoted in Paul Lewis, "Accord Completed on Soviet Pullout," *New York Times*, April 9, 1988. An alternative bargaining tactic would be to admit—or claim—that one's concession was designed with the other state in mind, thereby implicitly calling for a reciprocal concession.

part because Kennedy was willing to make a private promise to withdraw American missiles from Turkey in the near future. But this promise was neither public nor part of a bargain. The United States told the USSR that it was planning to take the missiles out in any event (just as Israel would have eventually released the prisoners) and so was not capitulating to Soviet pressure. As Bundy put it to Kennedy late in the deliberations: "It's one thing to stand [the missiles] down, Mr. President, in political terms, . . . as a favor to the Turks while we hit Cuba, and it's quite another thing to trade them out."[72] In the same way, the Soviets did not want to admit that Yuri Orlov and his wife were released as a trade for their spy, Gennadi Zakharov, in the aftermath of the Soviet release of an American journalist, Nicholas Daniloff. Secretary of State Shultz's formulation of what happened is interesting: "During the discussions held over the past 10 days [about Zakharov and Daniloff], Soviet Foreign Minister Shevardnadze has informed us that Yuri Orlov . . . will be allowed to leave the Soviet Union."[73] American critics of the exchange were quick to say that indeed Orlov would have been released in the near future anyway, and so the United States did actually trade Zakharov for Daniloff. A reverse twist occurred in the disagreement between the United States and Britain about the destroyers-for-bases deal before World War II. Largely in order to assuage domestic audiences, Roosevelt needed to portray the arrangement as a bargain and Churchill wanted it believed that Britain had offered the bases unilaterally, in order to increase British security. Churchill was reported to have put it this way: "if we are going to make a gift, well and good; if we are going to make a bargain, I don't want to make a bad one and this definitely is a bad one."[74] The conflict was not about what each state would get but about how its motives would be portrayed.

72. McGeorge Bundy, transcriber, and James Blight, ed., "October 27, 1962: Transcripts of the Meetings of the Excomm," *International Security*, 12 (Winter 1987–88), 53. It now appears that Kennedy probably would have been willing to pay the price of making a trade if that had been necessary to avoid the crisis becoming more dangerous: see ibid. and James Blight, Joseph Nye, Jr., and David Welch, "The Cuban Missile Crisis Revisited," *Foreign Affairs*, 66 (Fall 1987), 178–80.

73. "Excerpts from the Reagan and Shultz Statements," *New York Times*, October 1, 1986. When French hostages were released from Lebanon, the French foreign minister declared his country's stance was "to have contact with all states that could have an influence on the kidnappers and to have through these contacts a dignified policy that has nothing to do with bargaining" (quoted in Richard Bernstein, "2 Frenchmen in Lebanon Freed: Chirac Asks Syria for Its Help," *New York Times*, November 12, 1986).

74. Quoted in James Leutze, *Bargaining for Supremacy: Anglo-American Naval Collaboration, 1937–1941* (Chapel Hill: University of North Carolina Press, 1977), p. 124.

The Soviets are not the only audience for which the United States must perform. From the start, the United States has been concerned with convincing the Europeans that they would be protected. Indeed, when NATO was formed, the American decision makers were preoccupied not with the danger of Soviet invasion but with the need for and difficulties of European economic and political reconstruction. American leaders felt that Europeans would proceed with such efforts only if their morale was bolstered and their fears of the Soviets alleviated. This was to be the main function of the alliance. As George Kennan put it during the deliberations that led to the formation of NATO:

> The basic cause of insecurity in the minds of western Europeans is . . . really a lack of confidence in themselves. . . . By asking the Europeans to go in for economic recovery before achieving military security, we were in effect asking them to walk a sort of tightrope and telling them that if they concentrated on their own steps and did not keep looking down into the chasm of their own military helplessness we thought there was a good chance that they would arrive safely on the other side. And on this basis we made our economic aid available.
>
> Now the first of the snags we have struck has been the fact that a lot of people have not been able to refrain from looking down.[75]

He elaborated in a paper of late November 1948:

> [While] a military danger, arising from possible incidents or from the prestige engagement of the Russians and the western powers in the Berlin situation, does exist . . . basic Russian intent still runs to the conquest of western Europe by political means. In this program, military force plays a major role only as a means of intimidation.

75. Quoted in John Gaddis, *Strategies of Containment* (New York: Oxford University Press, 1982), pp. 73–74. As Gaddis notes (p. 85), Kennan's stress on the importance of psychology did not fit with his claim that the United States had to be concerned only about the centers of industrial might in the world; events in other areas might shake the confidence of the Europeans, and to a considerable extent this belief is the rationale for extending containment to areas of little intrinsic importance. Also see Timothy Ireland, *Creating the Entangling Alliance: The Origins of the North Atlantic Treaty Organization* (Westport, Conn.: Greenwood Press, 1981).

The danger of political conquest is still greater than the military danger. If a war comes in the foreseeable future, it will probably be one which Moscow did not desire but did not know how to avoid. The political war, on the other hand, is now in progress. A North Atlantic Security Pact will affect the political war only insofar as it operates to stiffen the self-confidence of the western Europeans in the face of Soviet pressures....

[The] preoccupation [with military affairs] is already widespread, both in Europe and in this country. It is regrettable; because it addresses itself to what is not the main danger. We have to deal with it as a reality; and to a certain extent we have to indulge it, for to neglect it would be to encourage panic and uncertainty in western Europe and to play into the hands of the communists. But in doing so, we should have clearly in mind that the need for military alliances and rearmament on the part of the western Europeans is primarily a *subjective* one, arising in their own minds as a result of their failure to understand correctly their own position. Their best and most hopeful course of action, if they are to save themselves from communist pressures, remains the struggle for economic recovery and for internal political stability.[76]

In many cases, of course, Kennan's view was a minority one, but not in this instance. Under Secretary of State Lovett agreed with the analysis just quoted and shortly before resigning as NATO's supreme commander, Dwight Eisenhower stressed that "one of the great and immediate uses of the military forces we are developing is to convey a feeling of confidence to exposed populations, a confidence which will make them sturdier, politically, in their opposition to Communist inroads."[77] Similarly, Foreign Minister Ernest Bevin's biographer notes that "Kennan's paper puts the real purpose of NATO . . . in terms Bevin would have endorsed."[78]

76. Department of State, *FRUS, 1948*, vol. 3, *Western European Unity and Defense* (Washington D.C.: Government Printing Office, 1974), p. 285, emphasis in the original.

77. Ibid., p. 284; Dwight David Eisenhower, *White House Years*, vol. 1, *Mandate for Change, 1953–56* (Garden City, N.Y.: Doubleday, 1963), p. 23, quoting his contemporary letter to Lucius Clay.

78. Alan Bullock, *Ernest Bevin: Foreign Secretary* (Oxford: Oxford University Press, l985), p. 645. Most other European perspectives were consistent with this view: see Joseph Becker and Franz Knipping, eds., *Power in Europe? Great Britain, France, Italy, and Germany in a Postwar World, 1945–50* (New York: Walter de Gruyter), 1986.

Bevin also believed that Communist propaganda, ostensibly devoted to peace was in fact aimed at playing on and exploiting the European peoples' fear of war and thereby forcing the Western Powers to seek four-power agreement on the old terms of unanimity or nothing. Bevin's purpose was to reduce that fear, and thereby retain the Western powers' freedom to act on their own. NATO had to take the form of an alliance to be effective, but its *purpose* was less military than political and psychological, concerned with underpinning Western Europe's will to resist pressure and the exploitation of its fears. This was certainly true in the initial years when the forces at NATO's disposal were only capable of fighting a delaying action and if war had broken out with the Soviet Union it could only have been won by the United States' use of atomic weapons.[79]

Time and again American diplomats stressed the need to help Europe resist Soviet pressure and the crucial importance of increasing "their confidence that they can successfully do so."[80] Again Bevin's view was identical: "The essential task was to create confidence in western Europe that further Communist inroads would be stopped."[81] As John Hickerson, the director of the Office of European Affairs, put it: "A stiffening of morale in free Europe is needed. . . . The problem at present is less one of defense against overt foreign aggression than against internal fifth-column aggression supported by the threat of external force, on the Czech model."[82] This quotation explains part of the reasoning for this analysis: the event that triggered the formation of NATO was the Czech coup of February 1948, an incident in which the combination of internal subversion and foreign pressure led to the collapse of the will to resist. Given the economic weakness in Europe, the strength of the local communist parties, and the undercurrent of pessimism, American leaders feared a repetition of February 1948 more than of September 1938 or September 1939.

Years later, when Eisenhower was being briefed on Kennedy's plan to increase troop levels in Europe and Berlin in response to Soviet pressure on that city, he "doubted whether the measures we were

79. Bullock, *Bevin*, p. 687. emphasis in the original.
80. *FRUS, 1948*, vol. 3, p. 62. The same phrase appears in NSC 9 and 9/3 (ibid., pp. 85, 140).
81. *FRUS, 1947*, vol. 2, *Western Europe* (Washington, D.C.: Government Printing Office, 1972), p. 816.
82. *FRUS, 1948*, vol. 3, p. 40; also see pp. 183–84.

taking would in any way affect Khrushchev's intentions but they would be of tremendous importance in impressing our Allies of [sic] our resolve. General Eisenhower believed that our build-up would cause Khrushchev to initiate a larger build-up of ground forces in order to stay ahead of us." [83] Thus even at what seems like the height of military threat, at least some leaders thought that the main role of military measures was the symbolic one of steadying our allies' nerves.

Of course some people saw some danger of Soviet attack: as one joint American-European paper in 1948 put it, "while there is no evidence to suggest that the Soviet government is planning armed aggression as an act of policy, there is always the danger that, in the tense situation existing at the present time, some incident might occur which would lead to war." Thus "the immediate purpose [of forming an alliance] is, in the first place, to prevent a Soviet attack." [84] Even George Kennan said that he and Charles Bohlen did "not mean to imply that there was no danger of war nor [sic] the threat of war." [85] European leaders more frequently claimed that, in the words of the British ambassador, "the threat was real." [86] The French were particularly outspoken on this point, but it is far from clear whether their main worry really was the Soviet Union or Germany. [87] Still, overall neither the main danger nor the main solutions seemed military.

How, then, did NATO become a major military force? Part of the answer is that both American and European fears increased after the start of the Korean War. It was almost surely incorrect, but certainly not foolish, for decision makers to reason that if the Soviet Union sanctioned an attack on South Korea, a country of little value to them (although also of little value to us), it might try to seize the more important objective of West Europe. Thus Dean Acheson said: "The real significance of the North Korean aggression lies in this evidence that, even at the resultant risk of starting a third world war, communism is willing to resort to armed aggression, whenever it believes it can win. In view of the threat presented by communism at many points

---

83. Allen Dulles, "Memorandum for the President," August 22, 1961, National Security Files, box 82, folder "Germany, Berlin, General," p. 6, Kennedy Library; also see p. 5. Eisenhower went on to note that American troops had been sent to Europe to provide security until the Europeans were back on their feet, but "because we have had our troops there, the Europeans have not done their share."

84. *FRUS, 1948*, vol. 3, p. 239. It should be noted that the document also says that the second purpose "is to restore confidence among the people of Western Europe."

85. Ibid., p. 177.

86. Ibid., p. 153.

87. See, for example, ibid., pp. 152, 206, 218.

on its borders, the nations thus threatened must immediately increase their individual and collective military strength."[88]

But this is not the entire explanation for the transformation of NATO from a treaty of guarantee to an organization with a complex infrastructure and a functioning army. In the past, stimuli more powerful than an attack by a client state in a distant theater have had less impact and the buildup of defenses in Europe continued long after the most alarming interpretations of the Korean War had been discredited. Indeed, the rearmament goals and measures adopted in the months following the North Korean attack would not add to Western strength for a number of years. If there was a significant danger of aggression in the near future, the Western actions could do no good and might be provocative.

To a considerable extent, the cause of the transformation was the peculiar dynamic of reassurance. In large part, American officials talked themselves into acting on the basis of heightened fears. The formation of NATO could not be publicly explained by the need to reassure jittery Europeans; the idea of making a military commitment when there was little military threat was hardly politically palatable. Furthermore, to announce that the danger was slight but that the United States had to act as though it were grave in order to help its friends get on with the real tasks would have been self-defeating by revealing the nature of the game the United States was playing. Thus, Alan Bullock notes that Bevin could not make public his true beliefs about the function of the alliance: "The effectiveness of NATO in restoring confidence on the European mainland depended on taking it at its face value, as a guarantee against armed attack."[89]

Of course decision makers can hold private views that are very different from the way they talk and act in public, but consistency between the two is likely to grow over time, especially when the situation is ambiguous. We usually think that beliefs determine behavior, but when people's views are not central to them, causation often runs in the opposite direction. That is, people act for a variety of reasons and under many impetuses and then infer their beliefs from the way they behaved in order to provide themselves with good reasons for their own actions.[90] Decision makers who acted as though there were a significant Soviet military threat then found themselves accepting this view.

88. U.S. Senate, *Hearings Before the Senate Committee on Appropriations, Supplemental Appropriations for 1951*, 81st Cong., 2d sess., (Washington, D.C.: Government Printing Office, 1950), p. 272.

89. Bullock, *Bevin*, p. 688.

90. For the argument that decision makers often form their beliefs on the basis of

Furthermore, once decision makers told Congress, attentive publics, and their subordinates in the bureaucracy to take the military threat seriously, the pressures on them to do so were bound to increase. The problem is nicely brought out by the statement of the chairman of the Joint Chiefs of Staff, Omar Bradley, in April 1949:

> It must be perfectly apparent to the people of the United States that we cannot count on friends in Western Europe if our strategy in the event of war dictates that we shall first abandon them to the enemy with a promise of later liberation. Yet that is the only strategy that can prevail if the military balance of power in Europe is to be carried on the wings of our bombers and deposited in reserves this side of the ocean. It is a strategy that would produce nothing better than impotent and disillusioned allies in the event of war.[91]

If the military establishment is told to prepare to counter a threat, it will call for the necessary resources. Even in the United States, which has tended not to take war seriously, once a military task is set, planning takes on its own momentum.[92]

The same process was at work thirty years later in the INF deployment. First opposed by the Carter administration because there was no military requirement for such weapons, deployment came to be favored almost exclusively on political and psychological grounds. But again, it was not politically legitimate to say that the United States was providing weapons of little military utility in order to meet the insecurities of the allies. Thus military rationales had to be provided. They developed a life of their own and so asymmetries between the NATO and Warsaw Pact nuclear forces then came to be seen as increasingly dangerous. This view helps explain why many Europeans felt that the withdrawal of these missiles, even though accompanied by larger reductions in Soviet forces, left them more vulnerable than they had been several years before.

Indeed, the continued stress on the military threat to Western Europe forms the basis for many aspects of U.S. defense policy, particularly

---

what they say and do, see Deborah Larson, *Origins of Containment: A Psychological Explanation* (Princeton: Princeton University Press, 1985). For the psychological theory on which this is based, see Daryl Bem, "Self-Perception Theory," in Leonard Berkowitz, ed., *Advances in Experimental Social Psychology*, vol. 6 (New York: Academic Press, 1972).

91. Quoted in Robert Osgood, *NATO, The Entangling Alliance* (Chicago: University of Chicago Press, 1962), p. 44.

92. See Colin Gray, *Nuclear Strategy and National Style*.

the strengthening of conventional forces and the deployment of extensive counterforce capability. (It should be noted that many of these American efforts meet European resistance, weaken the political cohesion of the alliance, and so may make American threats less rather than more credible.) But the perceptions of threat are largely generated by the efforts needed to meet it, rather than vice versa. The last major East-West crisis in Europe occurred almost a quarter of a century ago and it has been fifteen years since the signing of the agreements concerning Berlin and Germany, which seem to have shelved if not solved the major European disputes of the Cold War. The perception of threat has not diminished, however. Quite the contrary: recent years have seen a concern with a variety of possible Soviet military attacks on Europe even though the Soviets have refrained from disturbing the status quo and it is increasingly hard to imagine a motive strong enough to impel a Soviet attack. By almost any standard, the danger to Western Europe is much less than it was when NATO was formed, a time when the American leaders thought the military threat was slight. But the United States is so accustomed to taking the threat seriously that it rarely imputes any significance to the 1971 agreements or to the lack of disturbing Soviet pressures. It has become trapped in a world largely of its own making. The need to reassure the Europeans required credible threats; the problem had to be called a military one; the military definition led to behavior and then to justifying beliefs that fundamentally transformed the original conception of the situation.

IMPRESSING OURSELVES

Sometimes the audience to be impressed is ourselves: a country must exercise national will in order to provide what can be called self-reassurance, to show itself that it is willing to stand up to threats and thereby to generate the confidence that foreign policy requires. Paul Nitze stressed this factor when he explained that were he to revise NSC–68 today, he would "put even more emphasis on the importance of American will and resolve" which is "still a problem, and will be forever."[93] Henry Kissinger puts the need for limited options and strategic

---

93. Quoted in Herken, *Counsels of War*, p. 330. Other countries may use nuclear weapons to impress themselves, but in quite a different way. McGeorge Bundy's judgment about the British and French nuclear program is convincing: "I am persuaded that the basic objective, historically, for both the British and French governments, has been to have a kind of power without which these two ancient sovereign powers could not truly be themselves. This requirement has been clear for each government at every

defense in closely related terms: "It is not possible indefinitely to tell democratic publics that their security depends on the mass extermination of civilians, unopposed by either defenses or a mitigating strategy, without sooner or later producing pacifism and unilateral disarmament."[94]

Others believe it is the top decision makers themselves who need reassuring. Thus Secretary of State Alexander Haig argued that "perceptions of the military balance . . . affect the psychological attitude of both American and Soviet leaders, as they respond to events around the globe."[95] Harold Brown also spoke of the influence of the nuclear balance on "international perception (Soviet, third party, and our own.)"[96] Similarly, while arguing that the outcome of confrontations between the United States and the USSR logically should not be influenced by the balance of military power on the scene because what is most important is the danger of escalation, Bernard Brodie admitted that "it may be that a local or even an overall superiority in ships, aircraft, and other arms may be necessary to give the President of the United States backbone to face up to crises."[97]

---

moment of choice from 1945 onward, and it is not a matter of deterrent strategy as such. It is rather a matter of what Britain and France must have, as long as others have it, in order to meet their own standards of their own rank among nations" (Bundy, *Danger and Survival*, p. 501).

94. Kissinger, "After Reykjavik," p. 4, also see p. 7 and his interview with Michael Charlton, *From Deterrence to Defense* (Cambridge: Harvard University Press, 1987), p. 34. Fred Iklé's position is similar; see "Nuclear Strategy: Can There Be a Happy Ending?" *Foreign Affairs*, 63 (Spring 1985), 822–23. Also see the report of the Commission on Integrated Long-Term Strategy, *Discriminate Deterrence* (Washington, D.C.: Government Printing Office, 1988), p. 2. The lack of sympathy with and limited understanding of the American political processes that is apparent from Kissinger's memoirs is also revealed by his first book, as Paul Nitze noted in "Limited War or Massive Retaliation?" *Reporter*, September 5, 1957, p. 41.

95. Alexander Haig, "Peace and Deterrence," April 6, 1982 (U.S. Department of State, *Current Policy*, no. 383), p. 3. Also see the comments of many of the officials interviewed in Kull, *Minds at War*.

96. Harold Brown, in U.S. House of Representatives, Committee on Armed Services, *Hearings on H.R. 8390 and Review of the State of U.S. Strategic Forces*, p. 162.

97. Brodie, *War and Politics*, p. 416. In this connection Kissinger's remark about the 1973 Middle East confrontation is particularly interesting: "I have seen statements that in 1973, the United States was affected in the conduct of the Middle East crisis by its fear of the Soviet Navy. This may have been true of our Navy; it wasn't true of our government. . . . We all suffered from the illusion that our Navy was far superior to the Soviet Navy, and we conducted ourselves accordingly" (quoted in Alan Dowty, *Middle East Crisis: U.S. Decision-Making in 1958, 1970, and 1973* [Berkeley: University of California Press, 1984], p. 260). Better crafted impression management would have tried to lead the Soviets to believe that the United States stood firm not because of its advantage in the local balance—which might favor the Soviets in the next confrontation—but because it is willing to run risks to protect its allies even if local conditions are not propitious.

The need for self-reassurance may help explain why decision makers often talk confidentially of their willingness to use nuclear weapons only when the threats that might trigger this awful response have faded. That this is done in secret indicates that the reason cannot be to impress adversaries or allies. Thus at an NSC meeting four months after the armistice in Korea had been signed, Eisenhower "expressed with great emphasis the opinion that if the Chinese Communists attacked us again we should certainly respond by hitting them hard and wherever it would hurt most, including Peiping itself."[98]

Even for those who have become accustomed to the strange arguments being analyzed here, this position is particularly odd. People are not trying to fool others or cater to others' incorrect beliefs; they are trying to fool themselves. Just as a person might take a drink to bolster his courage, so a decision maker might develop military forces he knows are useless in order to bolster his own resolve. If decision makers are emboldened by the extra weapons, then procuring them will indeed influence their behavior. But one wonders how long statesmen can play this trick on themselves without the effect wearing off or their coming to believe in the military efficacy of the weapons and the intrinsic significance of the actions. Such a transformation, however, is not likely to be complete and the nagging awareness of the continuing fact of mutual vulnerability will keep breaking through, thus limiting the extent to which they can consistently use this technique.[99]

IMPLICATIONS

This analysis of the psychological and symbolic nature of current nuclear issues yields five implications: many strategic policies create their own difficulties; there are opportunities for avoiding such pitfalls; a good deal of strategic planning operates autonomously on the basis of self-defined problems; many of the possibilities for and arguments

98. *FRUS, 1952–1954*, vol. 15, *Korea* (Washington, D.C.: Government Printing Office, 1984), pt. 2, p. 1638. Perhaps a bit less reliable is Khrushchev's claim to believe that "when we delivered our... stern warning to the three aggressors [in the 1956 Suez Crisis] ... they took us very seriously. I've been told that when Guy Mollet received our note, he ran to the telephone in his pajamas and called Eden. I don't know if this story is true, but whether or not he had his trousers on doesn't change the fact that twenty-two hours after the delivery of our note the aggression was halted" (*Khrushchev Remembers*, trans. and ed. Strobe Talbott [Boston: Little, Brown, 1970], p. 436).

99. For a discussion of the contradictions that an awareness of vulnerability introduces into the belief systems of those who stress the importance of military superiority, see Jervis, *The Illogic of American Nuclear Strategy* and Kull, *Minds at War*.

against arms control must be seen in psychological, not military terms; beliefs about whether war is inevitable are especially important in determining whether peace will be maintained.

Self-inflicted Wounds

Many commentators have noted the American propensity to "shoot itself in the foot" in describing and developing its strategic programs. I think the reason for this is not incompetence but the reflective nature of nuclear politics in which psychological effects loom so large.[100] The need for new strategic systems is largely motivated by the felt need to demonstrate national will. But an explicit defense in these terms not only would be unacceptable to public opinion but also would be self-defeating. To announce that one is doing something not because it is needed but because it will impress others is to nullify the desired effect. So officials have to claim that the systems are needed to catch up with the Soviets and remedy pressing military deficits. In one way this approach makes the world safer: if statesmen recognized and acknowledged that most new systems could not serve a military function, then they would have to search for new, and perhaps more dangerous, ways to demonstrate resolve and credibility.

Nevertheless, this way of thinking often creates great difficulties. It requires the state to stress, and often exaggerate, its own weakness. Arms-control negotiations increase the incentives to do so. Because of the norm of fairness, the superpowers agree that any treaty should be based on equality. Thus in order to increase the pressure on the other side to make reductions, each state seeks to portray the existing strategic balance as unfavorable to itself. But to the extent that resolve and will are seen as linked to the strategic balance, these tactics have the unfortunate consequence of undercutting the state's threats.

Furthermore, the obvious danger is that the state will fail the test it has set for itself. Having declared that its security will suffer unless a self-defined problem is remedied, it must then cope with it or appear militarily weak and politically irresolute. The most obvious example is Minuteman vulnerability. By saying that a Soviet attack that would destroy most of its ICBMs would deprive it of significant options, the United States put itself in a position in which an inability to develop a secure basing mode would be taken as a dangerous failure. Thus

---

100. Thurman Arnold's claim is particularly appropriate here: "The history of the symbols of government is a succession of romantic but unnecessary sacrifices of human life or comfort in their honor" (*Symbols of Government*, p. iv).

President Carter responded to some of his advisers' arguments for deploying the MX "by saying that much of the perception of Soviet superiority had been created by 'this group.' "[101] Indeed, the very awareness of the manufactured nature of the challenge may have contributed to Carter's lack of enthusiasm for having to solve it.

Opportunities

There is a more fortunate side to this situation, however. As many of our dilemmas arise not out of military danger but out of our constructions of reality, there is often scope for creative solutions that are not costly or highly threatening to the other side. When states care less about concrete outcomes than about the images others hold and the interpretations they draw, as is frequently the case, tactics that are foreign to traditional Realist prescriptions may be quite effective.[102] Thus by issuing a report and accepting many of the long-standing arguments of the opponents of the MX, a blue-ribbon commission disposed of many of the worries about Minuteman vulnerability, thereby accomplishing a task that otherwise would have required the expenditure of billions of dollars. Similarly, President Reagan was able to defuse much of the anxiety about American nuclear inferiority by arguing that he had rectified the earlier imbalances.[103] No examination of the objective military situation would confirm this; the nuclear balance remained very much the same as it was when he took office. But the president's claims were an effective substitute for building large numbers of missiles, which would have been more costly and more threatening than our current programs.

Furthermore, although Reagan's claim was not true in terms of weapons, it may have had a more important kind of validity. By believing that there was no significant gap, Reagan was not inhibited by perceptions of inferiority. Interesting in this respect was his reaction to the Soviet forward deployment of submarines in the Atlantic (which in turn was a response to NATO's deployment of INF): "If I thought there was some reason to be concerned about them, I wouldn't be

101. Herken, *Counsels of War*, p. 299.

102. See the discussion of "the gentle art of reframing" in Paul Watzlawick, John Weakland, and Richard Fisch, *Change* (New York: Norton, 1974), pp. 92–109.

103. The public seems to have at least partly accepted his claim: the percentage of people who believed that the USSR had nuclear superiority dropped from 41 percent in 1982 to 27 percent in 1984 (*Voter Options on Nuclear Arms Policy*, Public Agenda Foundation and the Center for Foreign Policy Development [Providence: Brown University, 1984], p. 20.)

sleeping in this house tonight. They are there, but it is not that much of a change. You are in for a dime or in for a dollar. There has been no essential change in the strategic situation. The numbers don't change much. It is not a significant escalation. This isn't really anything new. I don't think they pose any particular threat at all."[104] This sort of confidence can be stabilizing by enabling the state to protect its important interests. But it can also form the basis for offensive actions. In explaining American assertiveness in the Third World, administration officials argued, "President Reagan believes that he has succeeded in bringing about a more favorable Soviet-American balance of power, thus enabling him to act with greater freedom and decisiveness around the world."[105]

Although not automatically self-validating, a posture of confident and consistent declarations that an outcome is a victory can go a long way to accomplishing a state's major goals of safeguarding its reputation. Obviously, complete sleights of hand are not possible—Khrushchev could not convince many people that the Cuban missile crisis was a Soviet victory because he had forced the United States not to overthrow Castro—but often there is significant room for alternative interpretations. By their expositions and actions, statesmen can influence the way others understand an interaction. For example, most people saw the maneuvers in the Horn of Africa as a defeat for the United States and a victory for the Soviet Union, but this may be largely because they accepted the definitions supplied by American leaders. The events were more ambiguous. The Soviet Union gained influence in Ethiopia, but it lost influence—and a naval base—in Somalia. Furthermore, the fighting between the two African countries was brought to a halt. That Cuban troops were needed to defeat a misguided Somali invasion was unfortunate but not of major importance to an America that opposes the use of force to change international boundries. Thus if U.S. leaders had portrayed the events as a regional squabble that was satisfactorily settled, few would have seen them as a Soviet-American confrontation, let alone an American defeat.

In many cases states can similarly define their interests, motives, and behavior in ways that can enable them to avoid challenges. Schelling argues, "If you are . . . invited to play chicken and say you would rather not, you have just played."[106] But this is not always true. Often a challenge has great significance only when it is treated as such. To

104. Quoted in New York Times, May 22, 1984.
105. Leslie Gelb, "Reagan's Maneuvers," New York Times, March 27, 1986.
106. Schelling, Arms and Influence, p. 118.

take an eighteenth-century example that is arcane but not trivial, by arriving late for audiences between the Polish king and the ambassadors, the Russian ambassador was able to avoid the choice between provoking a crisis with the Vatican or suffering a humiliating defeat over protocol by draining of significance the fact that the king spoke to him only after first talking to the pope's representative.[107] Because many of their vital interests are such only because of an agreed-upon definition, the superpowers are usually free to pick and choose among the situations that could be seen as challenges. Just as congressional opponents of a symbolically objectionable but subtantively harmless bill can sometimes gut it of meaning by voting for it,[108] so the French avoided having to retaliate against a Libyan air attack on southern Chad (which followed a French strike against a Libyan base) by labeling it a "mistake." "It was a matter of several bombs, dropped from high altitude and falling in some sand dune," a French spokesman said. "It would be inappropriate to operate a system that consisted of replying each time a bomb fell in the sand."[109] The most obvious major instance of a state's taking the opposite course was the Cuban brigade, whose presence no foreign audience would have seen as noteworthy had it not been for the American interpretation. On the other extreme was the Soviet placement of missiles in Cuba, which would have been seen as a challenge no matter how the United States defined it in October, partly because the United States had earlier forbidden such a move. But a great many issues in superpower politics are closer to the former end of the continuum than to the latter.

The Momentum of Strategic Planning

A third implication of the way in which our beliefs can create reality is more disturbing: war planning can take on a life of its own. When he was briefed on Kennedy's contingency plans for Berlin shortly after he retired, Eisenhower remarked that "long ago he had learned that plans are worthless but planning is everything."[110] Eisenhower was thinking of the useful functions of the planning process, but it has a

107. Lawrence Wolff, "A Duel for Ceremonial Precedence: The Papal Nuncio versus the Russian Ambassador at Warsaw, 1775–1785," *International History Review*, 7 (May 1985), 235–44. For related examples, see Jervis, *Logic of Images*, pp. 201–24.

108. For a recent example, see Jonathan Fuerbringer, "Plan on Gulf Role Stalls in Senate," *New York Times*, October 1, 1987.

109. Quoted in Richard Bernstein, "France Plays Down Latest Libyan Air Raid in Southern Chad," *New York Times*, January 9, 1987.

110. Dulles, "Memorandum for the President," p. 8.

dark side as well. Civilian leaders need only set general guidelines for the requirements of deterrence, but the military has to take these requirements seriously and design forces and plans to fight a war if need be. Furthermore, since the question of how much and what kind of destruction would be sufficient to deter the Soviets cannot be answered with certainty, our own thinking about these matters tends to set the standards we try to meet.

A number of troublesome consequences follow. First, as analysts become accustomed to casualty levels that initially seemed horrifying, the requirements for deterrence increase. In the early years of the Cold War, Americans felt quite secure even though the United States did not possess the ability for what would later be called "assured destruction." Indeed, in the early 1950s, enthusiasm for a counterforce strategy waned when the analysts at the RAND Corporation found that such an attack would kill up to two million Soviet civilians.[111] In the same way, in 1961 analysts calculated that Soviet retaliation in the event of an American first strike would kill between two and three million Americans in the best case and ten to fifteen million in the worst case. This estimate was more than sufficient to deter the United States from launching such a strike, even during the provocation of the Cuban missile crisis.[112] Now, such numbers seem very low; if the USSR or the United States thought it could destroy the other at a cost of casualties below fifteen million, one could not dismiss the possibility of a first strike, especially in a crisis.

Just as the number of casualties believed required for deterrence has increased, so has the number of other targets that American analysts feel need to be held in hostage. Part of the reason is that the number of targets themselves has increased as the Soviets have proliferated military installations and leadership facilities. But another part of the reason is that as people worked through the possibilities of having to fight a war, they found that there was no natural limit to the targets they could want to destroy. When President Eisenhower was told that the air force wanted the Minuteman factories to be able to turn out four hundred missiles a year, George Kistiakowsky reports that the President "remarked in obvious disgust, 'Why don't we go completely crazy and plan on a force of ten thousand?'"[113]

The military is usually blamed for this state of affairs, but the attri-

---

111. Herken, *Counsels of War*, pp. 301–2.

112. Fred Kaplan, *The Wizards of Armageddon* (New York: Simon & Schuster, 1983), pp. 299–306.

113. George Kistiakowsky, *A Scientist at the White House* (Cambridge: Harvard University Press, 1976), p. 294. Also see Ambrose, *Eisenhower*, pp. 432–33, 493.

bution is unfair. Generals are charged with taking the possibility of war seriously, and once they are told that deterrence requires the ability to hold at risk various categories of targets, doing their job responsibly leads to this kind of escalation. The problem arises because the civilian leadership has not "been able to disavow the prospect, however skeptically it may have viewed that prospect, of the controlled use of nuclear weapons. Equally, no administration has been able to disavow the prospect of emerging from a nuclear conflict with some kind of meaningful victory. Unable to disavow these prospects, no administration has been able to disavow the force structure that might make possible fighting a limited nuclear war."[114]

The military is merely trying to develop forces and plans to meet this logic. But the civilian decision makers, although they have accepted the premises, understandably recoil from the consequences. Thus former secretary of defense "Schlesinger concluded that PD-59 'took logic too far' by spinning out theoretical concepts 'in a way that was still barely plausible on paper but in my guess is not plausible in the real world.' " Similarly, after he left office, Harold Brown said, "We started down the path [of developing plans for how to fight a nuclear war] and got into that morass and PD-59 was the result."[115] But once these civilian leaders set the premises and began the chain of logic, they should not have been surprised that the military took the orders seriously. The search for what Schlesinger called "implementable threats" and the attempt to answer the question of what the United States should do if every kind of deterrent should fail inevitably leads to the proliferation of requirements, options, and targets.[116] Since there is no basis in experience that allows cautious statesmen flatly to dismiss any of the unlikely possibilities that creative analysts can imagine, the dynamics of thinking about contingencies prompts ever more complex countermeasures. But even these can never meet all the dangers that we can conjure up. To limit this process, we do not need to limit the military. In-

114. Robert Tucker, "The Nuclear Debate," *Foreign Affairs*, 63 (Fall 1984), 9. Also see David Rosenberg, "Reality and Responsibility: Power and Process in the Making of United States Nuclear Strategy, 1945–1965," *Journal of Strategic Studies*, 9 (March 1986), pp. 49–50.

115. Quoted in Herken, *Counsels of War*, pp. 301–2.

116. Quoted in U.S. House of Representatives, Committee on Armed Services, *Hearings on Military Posture*, pt. 1, 93d Cong., 2d sess. (Washington, D.C.: Government Printing Office, 1974), p. 49. Also see Schlesinger's testimony in U.S. Senate, Subcommittee on Arms Control, International Law and Organization of the Committee on Foreign Relations, *Briefing on Counterforce Attacks*, 93d Cong., 2d sess. (Washington, D.C.: Government Printing Office, 1975), p. 44.

stead, we need to limit the unreasonable demands that are created by the way we have posed the question.

The obvious response is that these requirements are set not by our conceptualizations, but by Soviet perceptions and beliefs. The question of the nature of Soviet military doctrine is a large, complex, and highly contested one. But sufficient for the argument here is the claim, with which I believe most Soviet experts would agree, that while the Soviets do not embrace the "assured destruction" doctrine, neither do they think in terms of controlled and limited nuclear wars.[117] Although it can be argued that the American commitment to Europe requires what Herman Kahn called a "not incredible first strike capability," it is much more difficult to trace the drive for an ever-increasing array of options to the requirements imposed on the United States by its interests and its adversaries. The problem has been self-generated. We need these options to convince ourselves that we can cope with most of the nuclear threats we can think of.

Much of the same logic is at work in NATO defense planning, but with an added twist. For those who are unwilling to rely on the deterrent created by the presence of American forces in Europe and the attendant linkage to the United States strategic nuclear forces, the problem of how to protect Europe is extremely difficult, if not insolvable. But the military is given the task of trying to determine the best defense. It does not have the luxury of arguing that the Soviet incentives to attack are weak at best and that only a little deterrent is sufficient. Having to take the problem seriously, military analysts will see that NATO's posture—whatever it happens to be—will be inadequate, and thus they will call for changes. The problem is that while the Europeans are never completely satisfied with existing arrangements, alterations of established policies usually upset them even more, in part because of ambivalent feelings about American leadership. Thus new efforts generally increase friction within the alliance and feed American beliefs that the allies are ungrateful "free riders." At least to some extent, the result is to weaken the links between the United States and Europe, links that provide the main element of American deterrence.

Arms Control—A Psychological Endeavor

The final implication concerns arms control and has two parts to it, reflecting from different perspectives the dominant role of symbolic

---

117. For a further discussion, see Jervis, *The Illogic of American Nuclear Strategy*, pp. 103–9. This is the conclusion of many hawks as well as doves. See, for example, Gray, *Nuclear Strategy and National Style*.

and psychological factors in these endeavors. Almost everyone, opponents and proponents of arms control agreements alike, agrees that the United States should not seek an agreement merely for the sake of agreeing. What matters is the substance of the arrangement, whether it makes the world more stable, whether it gives the Soviet Union a dangerous military superiority, whether it lends itself to a break-out by either side. While there is something to this, the argument here indicates that within a wide range of outcomes, it is indeed the existence or lack of existence of a treaty that has more impact than its terms.

This explains one of the puzzles noted at the beginning of this chapter: many of those who are most concerned about Soviet power are not worried about the danger that in the absence of an agreement, the Soviets could deploy large numbers of SS-24s and SS-25s, thus greatly increasing their lead over the United States in prompt counterforce capability and even pulling ahead in warheads. The conundrum seems to be heightened but actually can be unraveled by noting that this characterization refers only to the civilian officials in the Department of Defense, especially during the Reagan administration. The military officers indeed are worried about the additional new Soviet missiles and, for this reason, many of them are favorably disposed toward arms control, including maintaining SALT II's restraints. Similarly, the civilians rather than the military are the strongest proponents of SDI and are the staunchest opponents of an ASAT ban.[118]

The military, being concerned about capabilities, is at least open to arms control because many proposals would limit Soviet deployments more than American ones. Similarly, since the United States relies on satellites for communications and intelligence more than the Soviet Union does, many officers would like to see ASATs banned. They are also unenthusiastic about SDI because they are skeptical that it could work. (They also know that the enormous spending that would be necessary would result in budget cuts for established systems. In addition, they tend to be unenthusiastic about defensive technologies and strategies in general.)

The reason that many of the top civilians under Reagan reached opposite conclusions was not that they were judging the military questions differently but that they placed American resolve and will higher in importance than the military balance. Arms-control agreements are

---

118. Strobe Talbott, *Deadly Gambits* (New York: Knopf, 1984); Bill Keller, "Military Chiefs Favor Abiding by Soviet Pact," *New York Times*, June 26, 1985, and discussions with military and civilian officials. Of course, neither the civilians nor the military are entirely united on these issues.

bad, not because they produce a less favorable military balance than would otherwise result, but because they produce psychological demobilization and undermine our readiness to compete with the Soviets. Zbigniew Brzezinski is surely right when he points to the possibility of "arms control without détente." Yet for many people, the two are linked. Thus arms-control agreements are bad because they will reduce the American willingness to stand up to the Soviet Union. Richard Perle has been explicit on this point: arms control "is a soporific. It puts our society to sleep. It does violence to our ability to maintain adequate defense." "Democracies will not sacrifice to protect their societies in the absence of a sense of danger. And every time we create the impression that we and the Soviets are cooperating and moderating the competition, we diminish that sense of apprehension."[119]

Many leaders in the Reagan administration, therefore, preferred a world of unregulated competition in which the United States was "behind" the Soviet Union in various indicators of strategic power to a world in which the balance was more even but was reached through agreements. Thus while an ASAT ban might be good from a strictly military standpoint, it would be bad psychologically. Similarly, for many officials the main goal of the SDI program is not to deploy a working ABM system, but to break the ABM treaty,[120] thereby symbolizing a correct American understanding of the Soviet Union, producing in the American public the necessary resolve to meet the Soviet threat, and showing adversaries and allies that the United States is equal to the challenge. While I hope it is clear from the rest of this discussion that I disagree with these conclusions, it also should be clear that I am in sympathy with the stress on the dominance of the psychological factors over purely military ones.

Kenneth Adelman shows an insensitivity toward this dimension of politics when he argues that arms control has suffered from the degree of public attention it has received. "Should arms control ever approach the public inattentiveness with which trade negotiations or civil aviation talks have been met, it would yield richer results."[121] Related is the common argument that arms control is relatively unimportant because it has little effect on the substance of world politics. But these

---

119. Perle's first quotation is from Talbott, *Deadly Gambits*, p. 348; his second is from *Defense Monitor*, 16, no. 4 (1987), 3.

120. Thus when an antimissile laser was tested in space, critics said its power was "too weak for anything significant but breaking the ABM Treaty" (William Broad, "Anti-Missile Laser Given First Tests for Use in Space," *New York Times*, January 3, 1988).

121. "Arms Control with and without Agreements," *Foreign Affairs*, 63 (Winter 1984–5), 243.

claims are superficial. Arms control matters because people take the agreements to symbolize the state of Soviet-American relations. Thus when President Eisenhower sought to eliminate or limit nuclear testing he "did not want to act unilaterally," although doing so could at least end fall-out. "He wanted an agreement, almost any kind of agreement, that could serve to start the process of trust and accommodation."[122] Arms agreements show that the United States and the USSR realize that arms levels are a matter of mutual concern that must be negotiated rather than being produced by unilateral decisions. They acknowledge that the Soviet-American competition is not total, that what is often more important than unilateral advantage is reaching settlements that are good for both sides, and that limiting national autonomy can help reach common objectives.

Belief That War Is Inevitable   The most important goal of arms control is to reduce the threat of war. Many analysts have argued that over the past years we have lost sight of this goal and have come to focus on reducing the numbers of weapons on each side instead of concentrating on their destabilizing characteristics—especially their abilities to destroy the other side's strategic systems. This argument overstates the importance of crisis stability seen in purely military terms, however. The danger of war is more strongly affected by the political climate in general and beliefs about the inevitability of war in particular.

A major cause of many past wars was the belief that armed conflict could not be avoided. Given the incredible cost of war today, such a belief both is less likely to form and is probably a necessary condition for war. This was part of Eisenhower's opposition to putting bombers on air alert and explains his reply to a newsman's question about his secretary of defense's testimony that the United States might launch a preemptive first strike: "I don't think we ought to be thinking all the time, every minute, that while we are sitting here, we are very apt to get a bombing attack on Washington. [By such ways of thinking] I believe we create more misapprehension than we do understanding."[123]

It is hard to conceive of either side launching a major strike as long as it believed there was a chance that peace could be preserved if it did not do so. Thus creating an atmosphere in which people believe that war is extremely unlikely would be a major contribution to peace. This is not unique to the nuclear age. James Joll argues that imperialism

---

122. Ambrose, *Eisenhower*, p. 522.
123. Ibid., p. 518.

was an important, but indirect, cause of World War I. The decisions of 1914 were conditioned by the feelings that war was inevitable "and to the creation of that mood the rhetoric even more than the reality of imperialism had contributed much."[124] This dynamic helps explain another of the puzzles noted earlier: the sense of threat was low during the period of detente even though there were many conflicts, and it was higher in the early 1980s even though there were no confrontations. Partly through heightened rhetoric, partly through the absence of serious discussion of arms control, people came to feel that war was not impossible in the later period.

If war can come by a self-fulfilling prophecy, then the danger of war can build on itself; the reality is created by the participants' beliefs. It makes sense for people to be worried if others are. Indeed, in a crisis each side would try to guess whether the other thought war was inevitable, which would mean guessing whether the other thought the state thought war was certain. A positive answer is much more likely if the crisis arises in a period in which war is seen as a real possibility. The background mood can thus be crucial, as it was in 1914. In setting these expectations, symbols play a large role. Here arms-control agreements can be particularly important by reinforcing the belief that Soviet-American relations can be managed peacefully. The main purpose of such treaties is to control our expectations and beliefs, not our arms. The former rather than the latter will determine our fates.

124. James Joll, *The Origins of the First World War* (London: Longman, 1984), p. 168.

[7]

Conclusions: Winning and Losing—
Clausewitz in the Nuclear Era

In war, there is no substitute for victory.
—*General Douglas MacArthur*

Winning isn't the most important thing, it's the only thing.
—*Vince Lombardi*

Tying is like kissing your sister.
—*Anon.*

The highest wisdom is not to be concerned exclusively for oneself, especially when this is to the detriment of the other side. It is necessary that everyone feel equally secure, since the fears and anxieties of the nuclear age give rise to unpredictability in policies and concrete actions.
—*Mikhail Gorbachev, speech to the CPSU Central Committee, February 25, 1986*

THE PRIMACY OF POLITICS

The objective of war, surely, is to win, not because—or at least not only because—of a competitive instinct or primordial drive to dominate, but because statesmen seek a variety of objectives that can be furthered by victory. This is true not only of total war, but of limited uses of violence and the threat of force as well. These assertions, however, which seem like common sense, have been undermined by mutual vulnerability. As I noted in the first chapter and as both American and Soviet leaders have acknowledged, military victory in an all-out war is now impossible. Thus other kinds of victories must be sought. Attempts to establish excessive unilateral advantage, always dangerous in international politics, are now almost surely self-defeating. Clause-

[226]

witz's central point that armed violence makes sense only if it serves political ends must remain our guiding insight; military advantage can threaten our goals and values.

Today more than ever we need to keep political goals uppermost in our minds and remember that military advantage is not an end in itself. For one superpower to win in competitive terms means that the other must lose. Given the enormous resources that both sides can employ, the side that is losing is likely to be able to resist strongly. Even if such resistance cannot directly overturn the verdict of the previous inter-action, for example, by changing the course of a limited war, it can increase the costs and risks the other confronts. Of course, the risks in a confrontation menace both sides. But because states tend to be more strongly motivated to protect the values that they already have than they are to gain new ones, states are especially likely to make major efforts and run significant risks in order to avoid defeats.[1] Pro-tecting the status quo, therefore, usually is easier than changing it; negative victories are more likely than positive ones.[2] The corollaries are that self-interest leads the superpowers to act with restraint and with respect for the other's vital interests and that, if wars are to be kept limited, not only the weapons used but also the objectives sought must be limited. If the latter are not restrained, neither will the former be, and the results will be disastrous. These arguments are familiar, but as is the case with the concept of the nuclear revolution, their implications have not been fully understood.

For the United States, the results are generally desirable. While force cannot safely be used to change the most important aspects of the status quo, general political trends are slowly producing a world that is more consistent with American values than the one we now live in. Most strikingly, domestic changes in the Soviet Union of the kind that George Kennan placed his faith in at the beginning of the Cold War may both reduce East-West tensions and ameliorate the characteristics that have made the USSR abhorrent to the United States. Furthermore, most Third World countries, although hardly embracing democracy, have not become irrevocably authoritarian. The Communist political model has little appeal for them; the Communist economic model has

---

1. See the discussion in Chapter 1.
2. For discussions of when states are particularly likely to challenge the status quo in the face of the defender's commitments, see Alexander George and Richard Smoke, *Deterrence in American Foreign Policy* (New York: Columbia University Press, 1974); Richard Ned Lebow, *Between Peace and War* (Baltimore: Johns Hopkins University Press, 1981); Robert Jervis, Richard Ned Lebow, and Janice Stein, *Psychology and Deterrence* (Baltimore: Johns Hopkins University Press, 1985).

none.[3] Conflicts within the Third World cost the states involved blood and treasure, but they rarely menace the United States. This argument is highly speculative, but it is much more plausible than the recurring view that in the absence of war the Soviet Union can employ cunning, example, and subversion steadily to undermine Western influence and values.

Indeed, in our focus on the conflicts between the United States and the USSR it is easy to fall into the error of believing that the only common interest they share is avoiding a major war. In fact, they are both quite satisfied with the current situation. While each would prefer to see changes in the other's domestic system, the main gain from defeating the other in war—were that possible—would be an end to the fear that the other might soon trigger another war. (Reaching this objective, of course, also would require the state to see that the adversary did not regain nuclear weapons.) That each has so much to lose in a war and so little to gain produces what John Mueller calls "general stability."[4]

International Stalemates

The basic dynamics of international politics usually act to limit the extent to which a country can reach its objectives at the expense of others. Nuclear weapons have magnified many of these characteristics. As observers starting with Thucydides have pointed out, in a world of independent states, each will act to check the most objectionable efforts of others. As a result, most attempts to make excessive gains have been self-defeating. This is the basic lesson of the balance of power. A state that seeks domination may gain a series of successes, but doing so will lead others to see the state as such menace that they must temporarily submerge their quarrels to defeat it lest they be permanently in its thrall. By seeking dominance rather than accepting lesser objectives, Napoleon's France and Hitler's Germany sacrificed the positions they had earlier established.

Perhaps these outcomes were not predetermined. The defending coalitions were not easy to form and maintain, after all, and in the third century B.C. the Chinese state formed out of the failure of the

3. For an argument that these arguments conflate Communist appeal and Soviet power, see Colin Gray, *The Geopolitics of Super Power* (Lexington: University Press of Kentucky, 1988), p. 178.

4. John Mueller, "The Essential Irrelevance of Nuclear Weapons," *International Security*, 13 (Fall 1988), 55–79, and Mueller, *Retreat from Doomsday: The Obsolescence of Major War* (New York: Basic Books, 1989). Also see Kenneth Waltz, *Theory of International Politics* (Reading, Mass: Addison-Wesley, 1979), p. 190.

balance of power.[5] The attempts to dominate Europe might have succeeded if the would-be hegemon had adopted somewhat different tactics. But tactical excesses, such as Hitler's declaration of war against the United States, may not be accidental. The drive to risk all in order to try to remake the world is not likely to coexist with cautious calculation.

Even on a smaller scale, states that keep increasing their power and continually encroach on the interests of others are likely to meet increased resistance. Although states sometimes "bandwagon" and move to align themselves with rising powers, more often they balance against such threats.[6] Of course not every action calls up an immediate and equal counteraction. For example, taking advantage of their geographic isolation, in the nineteenth century both the United States and Russia annexed their hinterlands with little resistance from other states.[7] But the fact that the world consists of independent states that seek goals that conflict with those of each other means that states will rarely be able to gain most of what they want. Furthermore, to succeed too well is often to invite others to increase their efforts to combat, contain, and control the state. Realist scholars such as Hans Morgenthau understood these dynamics when they advocated restraint, the use of quiet diplomacy, and the sacrifice of peripheral interests when necessary in order to respect the vital interests of others and minimize conflict with them.[8]

Security might seem like a modest objective, but even the attempt to ensure that others will not be able to menace the state may be self-

---

5. For an intriguing interpretation of the dynamics of the anti-Napoleonic coalitions, see Paul Schroeder, "The Collapse of the Second Coalition," *Journal of Modern History*, 59 (June 1987), 244–90. He argues, "Far from being a clear goal on which everyone could unite, the concept of military victory proved profoundly ambiguous and divisive." The coalition could be kept together only following "a broad change in the collective mentality of European statesmen.... That change would involve two things above all: first, a recognition that the prime question was not, How can we defeat France? but How can we achieve a durable, tolerable European system overall? and, second, the willingness and ability of leaders to put that system together, not by the dictates of one or more dominant powers, but by patiently reconciling and satisfying the individual aims of the coalition's members during the course of the war and as a condition of each state's entering the coalition and fighting in it" (ibid., pp. 288–89).

6. See Stephen Walt, "Alliance Formation and the Balance of World Power," *International Security*, 9 (Spring 1985), 3–43; Walt, *The Origins of Alliances* (Ithaca: Cornell University Press, 1987); Waltz, *Theory of International Politics*; Jack Snyder and Robert Jervis, eds., *Dominoes and Bandwagons: Strategic Beliefs and Superpower Competition in the Eurasian Rimland* (New York: Oxford University Press, forthcoming).

7. If Russia had ventured further, it probably would have had to fight Britain.

8. Hans Morgenthau, *Politics among Nations*, 5th ed., rev. (New York: Knopf, 1979), pp. 550–58.

defeating. International politics is characterized by the security dilemma. Absolute security for one state generally means absolute insecurity for others; the attempt to free the state from foreign dangers generally leads others to take counteractions that are likely to reduce the state's security to a lower level than it was before it launched its efforts. In some cases, the result can be a spiral of misperceptions, hostility, and war. When statesmen understand these dynamics, they do not try to maximize their power to make them safe; they seek to maximize their security.[9]

SECURITY, BALANCING AND NUCLEAR WEAPONS

Nuclear weapons have compounded the difficulties facing a state that would seek complete victory. The danger of escalation, combined with the obvious impossibility of winning a total war, means that statesmen realize that serious challenges to the adversary's vital interests can lead to disaster. Furthermore, as I discussed earlier even the possession of military advantage at the site of the dispute does little to reduce the danger involved.

Great Victory—Great Defeat

Particularly in the nuclear era, the sequel to a great competitive victory is likely to be a great defeat. Contrary to the waves of optimism and pessimism that have swept each of the superpowers as they have made periodic advances or retreats, this dynamic has produced a high degree of stability. Neither side has been able to make steady gains at the expense of the other, either in the arms competition, in conflicts in the Third World, or in Europe.

The question of what determines the course of the arms race—and indeed whether there is an arms race—is contentious, posing as it does difficult empirical and theoretical problems as well as being closely linked to analysts' policy references and views of their own countries. Most important here, however, is the simpler point that neither superpower will allow the other to gain what it thinks might be a decisive advantage. As opposed to earlier times, when states required allies in

9. Waltz, *Theory of International Politics*, p. 126, and Waltz, "Reflections on *Theory of International Politics*: A Response to My Critics," in Robert Keohane, ed., *Neorealism and Its Critics* (New York: Columbia University Press, 1986), pp. 333–34. Similar implications can be drawn from Edward Luttwak's discussion of the paradoxical nature of strategy in *Strategy: The Logic of Peace and War* (Cambridge: Harvard University Press, 1987).

order to avoid domination by a would-be hegemon in an era of nuclear weapons and bipolarity, superpowers rely more heavily on internally generated resources. Each superpower further knows that the other is the only state that can menace its security, and so each must be vigilant and able to meet increases in the adversary's capabilities. Thus from the beginning Stalin saw that nuclear weapons were enormously powerful and vowed to build them. Given Soviet economic and scientific weakness, doing so was not quick or easy. But the American nuclear monopoly was intolerable and could not be permitted to last indefinitely. This is clear not only in hindsight. As Dean Acheson put it in a memorandum to the president in 1945, "It is impossible that a government as powerful and power conscious as the Soviet Government could fail to react vigorously to this situation. It must and will exert every energy to restore the loss of power which this discovery has produced."[10]

Similarly, the American possession of a second-strike capability could and would be emulated. It is unclear whether the Soviets would have produced a smaller ICBM force if the United States had not engaged in an accelerated buildup in the early 1960s when it was already far ahead of the Soviets, but the American program probably ensured that the Soviets would seek at least a comparable force. For the same reasons, the logic of the competition makes it hard to imagine either side's abstaining from procuring a potent weapon like MIRVs once the other side moved forward with the innovation. The question President Truman asked when deciding whether to try to build the hydrogen bomb was not unique to this situation: "Can the Russians do it?" When his advisers replied in the affirmative, he declared: "In that case, we have no choice. We'll go ahead."[11]

Internal balancing, then, allows each side to deny the other long-term important advantages.[12] The frequent arguments that the United

10. U.S. Department of State, *Foreign Relations of the United States, 1945*, vol. 2, *General: Political and Economic Matters* (Washington, D.C.: Government Printing Office, 1967), p. 49 (hereafter cited as *FRUS*). Acheson's next sentence bears on another important issue: "It will do this [pursue nuclear weapons], if we attempt to maintain the policy of exclusion, in an atmosphere of suspicion and hostility, thereby exacerbating every present difficulty between us."

11. R. Gordon Arneson, "The H-Bomb Decision," *Foreign Service Journal*, May 1969, p. 27.

12. This is recognized in Henry Kissinger, "Foreign Policy and National Security," *International Security*, 1 (Summer 1976), 186–87. Years earlier, Samuel Huntington argued that qualitative, as contrasted with quantitative, arms races were stabilizing and led to peace. This is just the sort of competition expected in a bipolar system composed of modern states; see Huntington, "Arms Races: Prerequisites and Results," in Carl J.

States "allowed" the Soviet Union to pull even with it in the early 1970s are misguided. Short of launching a preventive war, the United States could not have prevented the Soviet Union from drawing on its own resources in order to develop a potent and robust second-strike capability.[13] The United States of course could have increased its own forces, but this would only have briefly postponed the time when the Soviet Union had a force that could diminish the credibility of the American threat to strike first in protection of its allies.[14] Nuclear arms are not so expensive and the American lead in technology is not so great that the Soviet Union cannot develop important systems that are available to the West.

Similarly, American domestic politics and competing priorities do not prevent it from reacting to perceived Soviet advantages. Thus when in the late 1970s and 1980s American decision makers came to believe that the Soviet strategic programs had reached a dangerous point they instituted a buildup that made them feel more secure again. The details of these efforts are strongly influenced by the course of domestic politics and debates about whether they are needed, but in view of the resources that each side can mobilize, it would seem that neither could gain a useful and lasting competitive advantage. Indeed, for either side to show that it has such an advantage is almost certain to ensure that the other will try to neutralize it.

Related dynamics have prevented either the United States or the USSR from gaining dominance in the Third World. Standard arguments about the prevalence of domino effects would have us believe that gains for one side and losses for the other produce further changes of the same kind as Third World countries scramble to "get on the bandwagon" of the winning side. But equilibrating negative feedback has been more common than amplifying positive feedback.[15] The Soviet reversal of fortunes in Egypt in 1972 did not lead to a further diminution of Soviet influence among the Arabs. Even if a Soviet withdrawal from

---

Friedrich and Seymour Harris, eds., *Public Policy*, (Cambridge: Harvard University, Graduate School of Public Administration, 1958), pp. 41–86, and Huntington, "The Renewal of Strategy," in Huntington, ed., *The Strategic Imperative* (Cambridge: Ballinger, 1982), pp. 41–42.

13. Eisenhower and Dulles made this clear to those within their administration who called for more belligerent action in the period before the Soviets acquired parity. See Marc Trachtenberg, " 'A Wasting Asset'? American Strategy and the Shifting Nuclear Balance, 1949–1954," *International Security* 13 (Winter 1988–89), 5–49.

14. For a thorough discussion of the American response in this period, see Warner Schilling, "U.S. Strategic Nuclear Concepts in the 1970s: The Search for Sufficiently Equivalent Countervailing Parity," *International Security*, 6 (Fall 1981), 49–79.

15. See the literature in note 6 above.

Afghanistan is followed by the establishment of an anti-Soviet government, it probably would not reduce Soviet influence in other Third World countries. The American defeat in Indochina did not, contrary to so many predictions, lead to further defections in the area, let alone to increased Soviet pressure on Europe. The Soviet victories in Angola and Ethiopia—if the outcomes of these situations can be so described, and I am doubtful that they can—did not produce further Soviet victories or even an increase in Soviet influence over these country's neighbors. Even the Cuban revolution did little to spread Soviet power in Latin America.

Several mechanisms explain this pattern. First, local victories often increase the neighbors' sense of threat. Although this can lead to bandwagoning, nationalism and the drive for autonomy are likely to lead Third World countries to resist as long as they believe that their increased efforts, combined with assistance from the other superpower, can be effective. Second, superpowers usually react to defeats by increasing rather than decreasing their efforts.[16] Thus the United States has paid more rather than less attention to Africa in the wake of the Soviet adventures there, and American support for the regime in El Salvador would be less were it not for the earlier Sandinista victory. Third, a superpower that has suffered a reverse in the Third World may react on the global level, especially if a local response is impossible or inappropriate. In part because statesmen believe that domino dynamics will operate unless they act strongly, they usually will find a place to assert themselves after having suffered a defeat. Thus one reason why President Kennedy reacted so sharply in the Berlin crisis of the summer of 1961 was that he feared that his behavior in Laos and the Bay of Pigs had generated the impression that he was weak.[17] The American responses to the Soviet adventures in Africa five years later were much less dramatic, but not much less significant: support for detente eroded, the Vietnam syndrome faded, and American public opinion turned toward greater defense spending.[18]

16. This and the previous point are documented by Walt, *Origins of Alliances*, e.g., on pp. 66–67.

17. For a further discussion of the paradox that decision makers who believe in the validity of the domino theory must act to invalidate it, see Robert Jervis, "Domino Beliefs and Strategic Behavior," in Snyder and Jervis, eds., *Dominoes and Bandwagons*.

18. Furthermore, the Soviets have found their Third World friends to be unreliable and expensive. See Elizabeth Valkenier, "Revolutionary Change in the Third World: Recent Soviet Assessments," *World Politics*, 38 (April 1986), 415–34. For an exhaustive discussion of Soviet debates about policy toward the Third World, see Jerry Hough, *The Struggle for the Third World* (Washington, D.C.: Brookings Institution, 1986).

When we shift our attention from the long-run consequences of Soviet-American conflict in the Third World to immediate outcomes of wars between Third World states that are allied to the superpowers, we see other mechanisms that inhibit complete victory or defeat. Even in the absence of explicit treaties, superpower involvement provides at least a degree of extended deterrence to clients: attacks on and limited defeats of them are possible, but if the balance tilts too far, superpower intervention is likely.

Two interrelated restraints are at work. First, each superpower will devote significant resources—and run significant risks—to see that its clients are not excessively damaged. The superpowers develop close ties to Third World countries only when they have significant interests at stake and close ties themselves increase their interests. Second, because each knows that this is true for the other superpower as well, it cannot easily permit its client to win too complete a victory. These dynamics are illustrated by the 1973 Middle East war in which the United States and the USSR worked together to enforce a settlement. American officials realized that they could not permit a full-scale Israeli victory because of the danger of Soviet intervention and the cost of undesired Arab reaction. Kissinger flew to Moscow not because the U.S. ally was losing, but because it was winning too much. So the United States should not have been surprised when the continued Israeli efforts to press its advantage led the Soviet Union to threaten to intervene. Neither is it surprising that the United States responded, not only with a well-publicized but probably less than crucial nuclear alert to deter the Soviet Union, but also with continued pressure on Israel to ensure that the latter complied with the cease-fire rather than making gains that would have dangerously increased the Soviet incentives to send troops. Similarly, as long as the United States strongly supported Israel, the Soviet Union could not have gained by a full-scale Arab victory that would have shattered detente, brought direct American intervention, and made it likely that the Arabs would demand the same support from the Soviet Union. The very danger of wider war that comes from superpower involvement in local conflict thus gives each side powerful reasons to see that such conflicts do not produce a result so unacceptable to the superpower whose ally is losing that it sees little choice but to take stronger action.

On occasion, the superpower that moves quickly to back one side in a Third World conflict can deter its adversary from strongly supporting the other side. But more often the competitive dynamics operate in the opposite way—each superpower is more likely to get involved in Third World conflicts if the other side is involved. For either side to weigh in is to create a test of strength that the adversary will have trouble declining; the superpowers are less likely to tolerate undesired political and social changes in the Third World if they believe that the forces at work are not indigenous. As Henry Kissinger told the Egyptians after the 1973 war: "Do not deceive yourselves, the United States could not—either today or tomorrow—allow Soviet arms to win a big victory . . . against American arms. This has nothing to do with Israel or with you."[19] This dynamic is particularly clear in cases in which the alignments between superpowers and clients are little more than accidental. For example, it mattered little to the United States which faction won the struggle in Angola; it mattered much more that the side the Soviets supported won. Had the Soviets supported Savimbi, the United States probably would have backed the MPLA. Thus local victory may be less rather than more likely if the superpower uses its own troops. When the United States decided not to try to save the French at Dien Bien Phu, it simultaneously decided that it would intervene if Chinese troops entered the war. Similarly, the North Vietnamese victory in 1975 probably would not have been possible if it had required Chinese or Soviet troops. To put it more generally, states are often more concerned with *how* an outcome is brought about than exactly *what* that outcome is.[20] As a result, countervailing forces are more likely to be called into play when the superpower's role is believed to be great.

Although we can only speculate about the matter, I would argue that the aftermath of a major Soviet politico-military victory in Western Europe (e.g., pushing the West out of West Berlin; gaining some territory in a limited war) probably would be a vast strengthening of the NATO alliance, not its dissolution.[21] The nature of the Soviet menace would be clear to all. Western resources would be more than adequate for the task; the only questions would involve Western confidence and dedication to preserving freedom. Thus while such a Soviet victory would certainly be bad for the West, it probably would not be in the Soviet Union's interests either. An analogy might be the Communist attack on South Korea, which was the most disastrous Soviet move of

19. Quoted in Walt, *Origins of Alliances*, pp. 155–56. Also see the discussion in Alexander George, "U.S.–Soviet Efforts to Cooperate in Crisis Management and Crisis Avoidance," in Alexander George, Philip Farley, and Alexander Dallin, eds., *U.S.–Soviet Security Cooperation* (New York: Oxford Univesity Press, 1988), pp. 584–85.

20. For a further discussion, see Robert Jervis, "Perceiving and Coping with Threat," in Jervis, Lebow, and Stein, *Psychology and Deterrence*, pp. 14–18.

21. Surprisingly enough, this was Dean Acheson's view: "Wishing Won't Hold Berlin," *Saturday Evening Post*, March 7, 1959, p. 86.

the Cold War. Whether the United States gained by the changes in world politics that followed the attack can be debated, but the Soviet Union lost very badly as American military capability increased radically, NATO became transformed into a functioning military alliance, the United States sprinkled security guarantees around the globe, and Sino-American tensions increased with the result that the Soviet Union faced Chinese demands for costly support and the danger of being drawn into a Sino-American war.

An awareness of dynamics like these influenced President Kennedy's behavior in the last phases of the Cuban missile crisis. As he said, "we tried to make [the Soviets'] setback... not the kind that would bring about an increase in hostility but perhaps provide for an easing of relations."[22] Three related aspects of Kennedy's behavior were particularly important. First, although he was determined to have the Soviet nuclear weapons removed, he was willing to tolerate an outcome that was less than a complete victory: he was willing to make concessions and he resisted the urgings of some of his advisers to push for additional objectives, such as the removal of Castro. Although the detailed incentives were different, his understanding echoed Bismarck's after the defeat of Austria in 1866: "In positions such as ours..., it is a political maxim after a victory not to inquire how much you can squeeze out of your opponent, but only to consider what is politically necessary."[23] Until recently, it appeared that the major concession Kennedy had been willing to make was the secret promise to remove American missiles from Turkey. But it now appears that, had this inducement been insufficient, Kennedy would have been willing to make this a public bargain.[24] Second, Kennedy "laid down the line... all [his advisers were] to follow—no boasting, no gloating, not even a claim of victory. We had won by enabling Khrushchev to avoid complete humiliation—we should not humiliate him now."[25] Third, in the aftermath of the crisis the United States not only refrained from seeking unilateral

22. Quoted in Arthur Schlesinger, Jr., *A Thousand Days* (Boston: Houghton Mifflin, 1965), p. 841.

23. Quoted in Robert Osgood, *Limited War* (Chicago: University of Chicago Press, 1957), p. 72.

24. The account, which comes from Dean Rusk, cannot be verified in the written record, but there is little reason to doubt it. See James Blight, Joseph Nye, Jr., and David Welch, "The Cuban Missile Crisis Revisited," *Foreign Affairs*, 66 (Fall 1987), 179. From the start of the crisis, Kennedy realized he would have to make some concessions. See Arthur Schlesinger, Jr., *Robert F. Kennedy and His Times* (Boston: Houghton Mifflin, 1978), p. 514–16 and Alexander George, David Hall, and William Simons, *The Limits of Coercive Diplomacy* (Boston: Little, Brown, 1971), pp. 100–3.

25. Theodore Sorensen, *Kennedy* (New York: Harper & Row, 1965), p. 717.

advantage, but made important conciliatory overtures toward the Soviet Union (although not toward Castro). The American University
speech in June 1963, the "Hotline" agreement, and the Test Ban Treaty
were the results.

These three elements were reflections of Kennedy's belief that "every
setback has the seeds of its own reprisal, if the country is powerful
enough."[26] He realized that a greater victory in the short-run would
leave both sides worse off in the future. A sensible appreciation of
American interests and an understanding of the dynamics of conflict
and cooperation led to fruitful moderation. Kennedy's firmness
showed the Soviets that they could not safely move against important
American interests; his restraint may have demonstrated that he would
not take undue advantage of their weakness.

IMPLICATIONS FOR LIMITED WAR, COERCION, AND CRISIS MANAGEMENT

The principles discussed so far are reflected in the theory and practice
of limited war.[27] The tension between common and conflicting interests, the inability to gain all of what the state seeks, and the risk of
widespread devastation all come to the fore when violence is used.
The requirement to limit the means employed during the war neces-
sitates parallel restrictions on the objectives that can be sought. When
the adversary's vital interests are not at stake, the state may be able to
reach most of its objectives because the other side will tolerate that
outcome. Thus the Soviet Union can crush the forces it fears in Eastern
Europe, the United States can win complete victory in Grenada, and
North Vietnam can conquer South Vietnam (although, as we noted,
the United States might well have intervened again had Soviet or

---

26. Quoted in Schlesinger, *A Thousand Days*, p. 841. It would be tempting to add
that, despite Kennedy's understanding, his policy produced such a sequel in the form
of the Soviet missile buildup. But the Soviet plans seem to have been in place before
the missile crisis and there is no evidence that they would have produced fewer weapons
had the confrontation not occurred or had a more favorable outcome. For an extension
of the arguments for moderation to peacemaking, see Nissan Oren, "Prudence in Victory," in Oren, ed., *Termination of Wars: Processes, Procedures, and Aftermaths* (Jerusalem:
Magnes Press, 1982), pp. 147–63.

27. Although some of the details in Osgood, *Limited War*, are dated, this study remains
perhaps the best. Also see Robert Osgood, *Limited War Revisited* (Boulder, Colo.: Westview Press, 1979). For a discussion of Clausewitz's changing conception of limited war,
see Peter Paret, "The Genesis of *On War*," in Carl von Clausewitz, *On War*, ed. and
trans. Michael Howard and Peter Paret (Princeton: Princeton University Press, 1976),
pp. 21–22.

Chinese troops been used for this purpose). But some sort of compromise if not stalemate is much more likely when both sides have more at stake.

In eras of multipolarity, states often limited their objectives to those that conflicted with only one other major power, thereby attempting to limit the number of adversaries they would have to fight. Thus one reason why Britain found herself in such difficulties in the conflict with France in the 1770s and 1780s was that unlike in the previous encounters, the latter "now resisted the temptation to attack Hanover or to bully the Dutch."[28] To menace several potential participants directly or to convince them that a local victory would give the state sufficient power to turn on them would be to make that victory unlikely. Today, moderation is still often required to keep third parties out of a conflict, a lesson neglected in the Korean War first by North Korea and then by the United States. But the central role of the two superpowers means that much of the limiting processes must involve what each of them is willing to tolerate and forego.

Many of the analyses of limited war concentrate on the reciprocal restraints on weapons and tactics observed by each side. For example, in the Korean War the United States did not attack China, and the Communists refrained from bombing Pusan and other vulnerable targets and, with one exception, did not use mines that could have hindered American naval operations. The processes at work are important and intricate and are not guaranteed to maintain the restraints even if both sides want to do so. But a necessary condition for success is the willingness of both sides to avoid challenging the other's vital interests. The war can inadvertently expand even if both sides are willing to accept its course; it will advertently expand if either side believes that the costs and risks of escalation are justified in order to prevent the other from establishing a settlement that is intolerable or to try to gain sufficient leverage to reach as yet unrealized objectives. Kissinger argued, "We kept [the Korean War] limited, not because we believed in limited war, but because we were reluctant to engage in all-out war over the issues which were at stake."[29] He was not quite correct. The aims, and thus the issues

28. Paul Kennedy, *The Rise and Fall of the Great Powers* (New York: Random House, 1988), pp. 117–18.
29. Henry Kissinger, *Nuclear Weapons and Foreign Policy* (New York: Harper & Row, 1957), p. 48. Kissinger is closer to the mark when he says, "In short, we thought we could not afford to win in Korea . . . because Russia could not afford to lose" (ibid). His attempt to argue that this conceptualization led American statesmen to underestimate their freedom of action is generally unconvincing, however. That General MacArthur never understood the problem of limited war is shown by his claim that "war's very

at stake, were not objective and fixed. We reduced them because we were not willing to fight a wider war.[30]

Wars can be kept limited only if the superpowers do not exert themselves to the fullest, and so attempts to make excessive gains are dangerous because they are likely to lead the other side to expand the level or scope of the violence rather than concede.[31] To succeed too well at one level of violence is to invite the other side to escalate, especially if the state is not willing and able to demonstrate that the political consequences of its victory will remain tolerably limited. For example, America's success in demolishing the North Korean armies tempted it to expand its war aims. But a unified anti-Communist Korea with American troops on the Yalu was seen by China as a threat to its vital interests. Later in the war, if China had been about to push the United States off the peninsula, the United States similarly might have responded by escalating.[32]

The maintenance of limits also requires that each side—or at least the losing side—believe that the other's goals are limited. A state that gains the upper hand in a limited war needs to show that it is willing to accept a reasonable settlement if it is to capitalize on its military prowess. But such demonstrations of restraint are both especially important and especially difficult because states in a conflict tend to impute the most menacing intentions to their adversaries and often believe that the latter seek to cripple if not destroy them. Since decision makers are likely to expect an approximate proportion between the means others use and the ends they seek, a state that employs particularly rough tactics may lead its adversary to doubt that its goals are limited.

---

object is victory, not prolonged indecision" ("Text of General MacArthur's Address to Joint Meeting of Congress," *New York Times*, April 20, 1951.)

30. Many of the issues in the contemporary debate revolved around the question of whether the sort of military measures (e.g., bombing China) that were believed necessary to reach more valued goals (e.g., the reunification of Korea) could be taken without triggering World War III. Given the ambiguities of the information available, the incentives for adversaries to bluff, and the gap between military actions as they are planned and the effects that are produced, the existence of such arguments is not surprising. Indeed, even in retrospect, we cannot be sure what would have happened had General MacArthur's advice been taken. A crucial question facing decision makers in a limited war is what objectives can be pursued that are valuable enough to merit the effort but not so distasteful to the adversary that the latter would rather escalate than concede them. For a discussion of the debate on whether to expand the war or trim American objectives, see Rosemary Foot, *The Wrong War: American Policy and the Dimensions of the Korean Conflict, 1950–1953* (Ithaca: Cornell University Press, 1985), pp. 131–73.

31. Because states are more willing to run high risks to avoid losses than to secure gains, those facing defeat are especially likely to escalate.

32. *FRUS, 1950*, vol. 7, *Korea* (Washington, D.C.: Government Printing Office, 1976), pp. 1348, 1383.

The danger of excessive success is recognized by the "Soviet military writers [who] posit that a NATO decision to use nuclear weapons would most likely be precipitated by a significant loss of NATO territory or a substantial loss of forces."[33] The implication is obvious—to avoid a tactical if not a strategic nuclear war the Soviets would have to limit their gains. Even if major victories do not directly provoke escalation, they may tempt the state to expand its objectives, as the United States did in Korea. It is easy to believe that the other side has little choice but to yield to superior force; it is difficult to stop short of fully exploiting the opportunity that lies before the state, especially if public opinion or elite coalitions are clamoring for what seems to be within the state's reach. Even Bismarck fell victim to these impulses in 1871, although French weakness prevented the ill-effects from being manifested until much later. The Chinese resisted the temptation to raise their objectives when they routed the Indian forces in October 1962, but such cases do not seem common. In a limited Soviet-American war, self-restraint would be both crucial and problematical.

Of course limited wars do not have to end in stalemates, and when carefully linked to realistic poltical goals, military success can produce significant gains. The adversary may find expanding the scope or intensity of the violence too costly to resort to, especially if it does not seem likely either to alter the verdict on the battlefield or to induce the state to concede. Local military resistance can also inflict sufficient cost on the adversary so that it chooses to accept defeat, as the USSR did in Afghanistan. Similarly, the outcome of the conflict in Vietnam could have been different if American military skill had been greater and that of the Viet Cong and North Vietnam less.[34] In Korea, while complete victory was beyond Chinese—and perhaps American—reach, either side could have gained some territory if it had been able to make military progress on the ground. But the goals that could have been reached by better or more skillfully applied force were bounded; to try to push beyond them would have been to incur high costs.

Tensions between means and ends are reflected in attempts to an-

33. Stephen Meyer, "Soviet Nuclear Operations," in Ashton Carter, John Steinbruner, and Charles Zraket, *Managing Nuclear Operations* (Washington, D.C.: Brookings Institution, 1987), p. 514.

34. Here I agree with Stephen Peter Rosen, "Vietnam and the American Theory of Limited War," *International Security*, 7, (Fall 1982), 83–113, without accepting the wider implications of his argument. It must also be remembered that North Vietnam was distinguished by its willingness to accept enormous losses in pursuit of its goal; see John Mueller, "The Search for the Single 'Breaking Point' in Vietnam: The Statistics of a Deadly Quarrel," *International Studies Quarterly*, 24 (December 1980), 497–519.

swer the question of how a limited Soviet-American war might be terminated. Secretary Weinberger gave the official American position: "Should deterrence fail, our strategy is to secure all U.S. and allied interests, and deny the aggressor any of his war aims. We should seek to terminate any war at the earliest practical time and restore peace on terms favorable to the United States that secure all our aims and those of our allies and friends."[35] As far as one can tell from the declassified documents on war termination in the 1940s and 1950s, top secret discussions of this question offer only a little more guidance.[36] Even then, unconditional surrender was seen as too costly to seek. In addition, it was doubted whether such an outcome really was in the American interest. In 1954 the Joint Chiefs of Staff expressed their fear that "full exploitation of our nuclear capability might inflict such chaos and destruction and suffering in the Soviet Union as had not been known in Europe since the end of the Thirty Years' War. Indeed, in the circumstances it was impossible to visualize how the United States could cope with the victory it might achieve over the Soviets, or how it might hope to establish a workable occupational regime."[37] But it is less clear what the United States could realistically hope to achieve.

The attempt to win rather than, in some sense, tie, could easily produce disaster. As I noted earlier, a necessary—although not a sufficient—condition for keeping a war limited is restraint in the objectives that conflict with those of the other side. Current American military strategy puts aside the question of goals, however. Of course it is hard to imagine what issues the war might be fought over, and strategic

35. Caspar Weinberger, *Annual Report to the Congress, FY 1988* (Washington, D.C.: Government Printing Office, 1987), p. 46.

36. See the papers associated with NSC-20/4, "U.S. Objectives with Respect to the USSR to Counter Soviet Threats to U.S. Security," in Department of State, *FRUS, 1948*, vol. 1, *General: The United Nations* (Washington D.C.: Government Printing Office, 1976), pt. 2, pp. 589–669; NSC-79, "United States and Allied War Objectives in the Event of Global War," *FRUS, 1950*, vol. 1, *National Security Affairs; Foreign Economic Policy* (Washington, D.C.: Government Printing Office, 1977), pp. 390–99 (also see the discussion pp. 94–100, 197–200). For the Eisenhower administration's attempt to deal with this problem, see *FRUS, 1952–1954*, vol. 2, *National Security Affairs* (Washington, D.C.: Government Printing Office, 1984), pt. 1, pp. 379–434, 635–44. Also see David Rosenberg, "The Origins of Overkill: Nuclear Weapons and American Strategy, 1945–1960," *International Security*, 8 (Spring 1983), 13–14. It is not surprising that when proponents of current American strategy are interviewed about war termination, their responses are vague or muddled. See Steven Kull, *Minds at War: Nuclear Reality and the Inner Conflict of Defense Policymakers* (New York: Basic Books, 1988), chap. 4.

37. *FRUS, 1952–1954*, vol. 2, pt. 1, p. 637. Eisenhower disagreed (ibid., pp. 640–41), although on other occasions he expressed similar views, see Stephen Ambrose, *Eisenhower the President* (New York: Simon & Schuster, 1984), p. 206.

considerations of politics and bargaining could lead to refusing to discuss war aims in public. But the private deliberations do not seem to
be much better: political objectives are beyond the purview of military
officials, and American political leaders have not been able to come to
grips with the question of war aims. Thus, although American doctrine
relies on the possibility of keeping a war with the Soviet Union limited,
little attention has been paid to one of the crucial determinants of
whether such efforts could succeed.

Similar problems arise when we turn to questions of what either side
can hope to achieve through the threats of limited violence. Even such
a tough-minded statesman as John Foster Dulles recognized the difficulty of prying the Soviet Union out of areas that it believed to be
important.[38] In the defense reviews of the first years of the Eisenhower
administration, the Joint Chiefs of Staff argued that the United States
should make use of its nuclear superiority before the Soviets closed
the "window of opportunity" by acquiring a second-strike capability.
But the president and secretary of state kept pointing out that even
with such a favorable military balance there was little the United States
could do that would simultaneously be of major benefit and limited
risk.[39] The recent proposal that the United States develop a political
and military strategy that could reduce Soviet control over Eastern
Europe merits a similar response. Samuel Huntington argues that a
conventional army that was strong enough to invade Eastern Europe
in response to a Soviet attack on the West also could "provide an
additional deterrent to Soviet military action against a satellite government that is attempting to broaden its independence. It would, con-
sequently, encourage satellite governments to see how far they could
go in loosening Soviet controls."[40] Of course Afghanistan and Vietnam
show that superpowers will retreat in the face of persistent and costly

38. As Dulles put it to the NSC in December 1953: "He could not help but have some
sympathy for the general view of the Joint Chiefs of Staff in favor of greater dynamism
in the American attitude toward the Soviet Union and Communist China. After all,
during the course of the 1952 campaign he had himself called for a more dynamic U.S.
policy vis-à-vis Communism. However, experience indicated that it was not easy to go
very much beyond the point that this Administration had reached in translating a dynamic policy into courses of action" (*FRUS, 1952–1954*, vol. 2, pt. 1, p. 833; also see
p. 837).
39. Ibid., pp. 686–98, 788–97. Marc Trachtenberg believes the Joint Chiefs were actually calling for serious consideration of a preventive war. What else, he asks, could
have put off the day when the Soviets reached parity and so undercut America's ability
to protect its allies? ("A 'Wasting Asset'?"). I think this interpretation reads too much
into the documents and slights the alternative goal of achieving the rollback of Soviet
control of Eastern Europe.
40. Huntington, "The Renewal of Strategy," p. 28.

local resistance, but to try to coerce the adversary into giving up an area it considers vital is more likely to lead to unacceptable levels of violence than to success.[41]

Crisis Management and Bargaining

A second set of implications extends the previous arguments about coercion to the subject of crisis management. A crucial determinant of the outcomes of crises is the extent to which each side's interests are involved.[42] The state's resistance to demands will be roughly proportionate to the degree to which they infringe on its vital interests, as modified by the extent to which it believes that the adversary is strongly motivated to prevail. Although states can gain much of what they seek under propitious circumstances, or, conversely, under adverse conditions can be forced to make costly retreats, such extreme outcomes are not likely when both sides have strong interests and believe they have legitimate claims, which has been the case in many confrontations of the Cold War. Indeed, as one side is forced to retreat in order to decrease the danger of stalemate if not war, it gives up what matters least to it. The remaining values are likely to be closer to its core concerns. Conversely, gaining something is likely to reduce a state's willingness to continue the confrontation since the new status quo is now better for it.[43] The asymmetry of motivation, and therefore the bargaining advantage, will then shift in favor of the state that makes a concession.

Absent a war, conflicts therefore are more likely to end in compromise than in complete victory for one side or the other. Furthermore, as states move to increase the pressure on the adversary to grant crucial demands, they often simultaneously indicate a willingness to make concessions of their own. Thus during the Cuban missile crisis in the same meeting in which Robert Kennedy gave Ambassador Dobrynin

41. For a parallel argument for interactions at a lower level of violence, see George, Hall, and Simons, *Limits of Coercive Diplomacy*.

42. See George, Hall, and Simons, *Limits of Coercive Diplomacy*; Alexander George, "Incentives for U.S.–Soviet Security Cooperation and Mutual Adjustment," in George, Farley, and Dallin, eds., *U.S.–Soviet Cooperation*. Also see Robert Jervis, "Bargaining and Bargaining Tactics," in J. Roland Pennock and John Chapman, eds., *Coercion*, NOMOS, vol. 14 (Chicago: Aldine, Atherton, 1972), pp. 272–89. For a different view, see Richard Betts, *Nuclear Blackmail and Nuclear Balance* (Washington, D.C.: Brookings Institution, 1987), chap. 4.

43. Of course the adversary may attribute the concession to the state's general weakness and expect it to retreat even further if the pressure is maintained. But while states often resist making concessions because they expect others to draw such inferences, perceivers reason in this way only under unusual circumstances. See Jervis, "Domino Beliefs."

something very close to an ultimatum, he also assured him that the United States would withdraw the missiles from Turkey soon after the crisis was resolved. At the height of the Laos crisis of 1961 the United States followed the same pattern, coupling troop movements and a near ultimatum that the Communists cease their offensive with the acceptance of the Communist demand for a fourteen-nation peace conference.[44] Similarly, Rosemary Foot has shown that in the hard bargaining in the spring of 1953 that led to the Korean armistice, the United States made significant concessions at the same time that it was issuing stern threats.[45] The threats received the most attention and some decision makers later remembered only those. But at the time Eisenhower was wiser and realized that agreement would be more likely if the United States was willing not only to increase the pressure but also to relax some of its demands, thereby making the agreement more attractive to China.

In principle, a state could be willing to provoke or stand firm in a crisis either because of the hope of making positive gains or because of the need to avoid losses. In fact, as noted in Chapter 5, the latter pressures are likely to be stronger and more dangerous. Crises are less likely to occur or to lead to war if both sides find present arrangements satisfactory and expect them to remain so in the future. But a state that finds the status quo intolerable can rationally choose to challenge it at the risk of a war, even a war it believes it probably will lose. Of course no magic wand can transform an aggressor into a status-quo power, and concessions to make the other state more satisfied may be excessively costly. They may also lead the other to expect that continued pressure will yield a still more desirable outcome. But deterrence is facilitated when it is accompanied by measures that increase the adversary's stake in the status quo, demonstrate that acceptable solutions can be reached through diplomacy, and reassure the adversary that the state does not seek to undermine its legitimate security requirements.[46] These favorable effects can sometimes be generated by moves

---

44. David Hall, "The Laos Crisis, 1960–61," in George, Hall, and Simons, *Limits of Coercive Diplomacy*, pp. 59–60.

45. Rosemary Foot, "Nuclear Threats and the Ending of the Korean Conflict," *International Security*, 13 (Winter 1988–89), 92–112.

46. For discussions of rewards and inducements as tools of influence, see David Baldwin, "The Power of Positive Sanctions," *World Politics*, 24 (October 1978), 19–38; George and Smoke, *Deterrence in American Foreign Policy*, pp. 604–10; Janice Stein, "Deterrence and Reassurance," in Philip Tetlock et al., eds., *Behavior, Society, and Nuclear War*, vol. 2 (New York: Oxford University Press, forthcoming). But George is wrong to claim that the model of Chicken necessarily "ignores the possibility (and, oftentimes, the necessity) of combining a carrot with the stick" (George, Hall, and Simons, *Limits*

that increase the other side's satisfaction without simultaneously casting doubt on the state's willingness to stand firm if the other infringes on the state's important interests. The American recognition of the People's Republic of China is a good example of such a tactic.

Conversely, attempts to make excessive competitive gains during confrontations, although sometimes worth doing when the incentives are high enough, are likely to have unfortunate consequences. Even if the adversary decides to retreat, its dissatisfaction with the new status quo is likely to increase, thus breeding future conflicts in which the adversary is less likely to retreat. One reason why the members of the Triple Entente felt they had to stand firm in July 1914 was that they had been forced to retreat in previous confrontations. Stephen Meyer sketches a hypothetical situation that illustrates the potential dangers in current world politics. Imagine that

> the following events occurred within two or three months. A coup in Libya installs a pro-Western government; Israel punishes Syrian provocations by marching to Damascus with the apparent green light and logistical support of the United States; Iran breaks diplomatic relations with Moscow. Overlapping with Middle East developments, centrifugal forces in the Soviet empire explode. Rumania withdraws from the Warsaw Pact; the United States reconciles with a revisionist Cuban government that expels Soviet advisers; the Polish government crumbles into catatonia as a reborn Solidarity runs wild.[47]

If the argument here is correct, the Soviets would be especially likely to run high risks in the later stages of such a series.[48]

A corollary is that crises are most likely to be resolved peacefully without creating a dangerous and self-defeating backlash when the bargaining tactics are built on common as well as competitive interests. In contrast, if the tactics increase the cost the other side will pay if it acts reasonably, the prospects for successful crisis management are diminished. More concretely, tactics that are focused on the specific issue at stake can minimize the general threat posed to the adversary.

---

of *Coercive Diplomacy*, p. 29). Although many theorists have made this error, it is not inherent in the formal model.

47. Stephen Meyer, "Soviet Perspectives on the Paths to Nuclear War," in Graham Allison, Albert Carnesale, and Joseph Nye, Jr., eds., *Hawks, Doves, and Owls* (New York: Norton, 1985), pp. 63–64.

48. See Richard Ned Lebow, "The Paranoia of the Powerful: Thucydides on World War III," *PS*, Winter 1984, pp. 10–17; Jervis, Lebow, and Stein, *Psychology and Deterrence*.

There may, then, be a political and bargaining counterpart to the ways in which military postures affect the security dilemma.[49] When defensive military postures are different from and stronger than offensive ones, states can increase their own security without greatly decreasing the security of others. When offense and defense cannot be distinguished and when the former is more powerful than the latter, the security dilemma is greatly heightened.

Bargaining tactics that stress the state's overall military superiority, its right to dictate the settlement of a wide range of disputes, or its general resolve create a strong security dilemma because the other side cannot easily retreat without endangering its ability to protect many other values. Similarly, if the state employs the tactic of "the rationality of irrationality"[50]—for example pretending not to understand how serious the crisis is or feigning a lack of self-control—it may prevail, but the long-run consequences will be unfortunate if the other side concludes that it cannot deal with the state on reasonable terms.

On the other hand, the use of claims, threats, and military forces that are more closely linked to the particular issue and the state's well-established interests in protecting its position can succeed without simultaneously menacing the other's ability to maintain its core interests. Thus commitment, especially when linked to important intrinsic interests, can be used to safeguard one side's concerns without threatening those of the other: each side can be committed to defend the principles and areas of the world that matter most to it when these are less important to the other side. For example, the American commitment to Western Europe does not diminish the Soviet ability to dominate its sphere in Eastern Europe, and vice versa, although the specific political and military tactics that are developed to support this commitment (e.g., offensive military technologies and doctrines) could invoke the security dilemma. Similarly, the United States could reassure the Soviet Union that it had no intention of trying to reduce the latter's control of Eastern Europe—and would do no more than voice moral

49. See Robert Jervis, "From Balance to Concert," *World Politics*, 38 (October 1985), 62–64, and Jervis, "Realism, Game Theory, and Cooperation," *World Politics*, 40 (April 1988), 332–34. Of course if the other can feel secure only if the state is weakened or destroyed—if the other believes with the czars that "that which stops growing begins to rot"—then containing the other side and deeply menacing it are the same (Quotation from Adam Ulam, *Expansion and Coexistence* [New York: Praeger, 1968], p. 5; I have analyzed this problem in *Perception and Misperception in International Politics* (Princeton: Princeton University Press, 1976), pp. 63–64 and "Cooperation under the Security Dilemma," pp. 183–86).

50. See the discussion in Thomas Schelling, *The Strategy of Conflict* (Cambridge: Harvard University Press, 1960), pp. 16–19.

outrage if the Soviets had to crush national uprisings—without undercutting the credibility of its threat to fight if they attacked the West.[51]

SECURITY AND MUTUAL SECURITY

Of major importance are the relationships between power and security and the related questions of whether the goals that either side seeks require it to make the other side highly insecure. Many decision makers believe that the more economic and military power a state has, the greater its security. But since increasing such power often renders others less secure, the links between increased power and increased security are far from certain and invariant. In this light it is important to remember that power is not a goal in itself but is a means to reach other objectives.

In 1953, the Eisenhower administration decided that "the United States must seek to improve the power position of itself and the rest of the free world in relation to the Soviet bloc." The Defense Department went a bit further and argued that the Soviet willingness to settle disputes would increase "if Soviet stability and influence are reduced."[52] These statements seem unexceptionable: weakening the other side will increase the chances of peace because a weak adversary is less likely to think that it can win a war and is therefore less likely to start one. This line of reasoning is flawed, however; an insecure Soviet Union may be more of a threat to the United States than a stronger and less vulnerable one. First, a state that is being weakened will often try to reverse the trend. Some ways of doing this, for example, the USSR's putting missiles in Cuba, will sharply menace the other side. Second, weakness that leads a state to believe that it cannot win a long or defensive war can stimulate it to develop more dangerous plans. In the extreme, it can lead to a preventive or preemptive war. The Israeli decision to attack in 1967 was due in part to the belief that it was not strong enough to cope with protracted pressure. Understanding dynamics of this kind, many defense analysts have argued that American security would be decreased if it were able to disarm the Soviet Union

---

51. Such reassurances, of course, would be a sacrifice of the Western value of encouraging democracy throughout the world. Furthermore, the Soviets may no longer need Eastern Europe for their security, as Zygmunt Nagorski argues in "To Moscow: Let Your Satellites Go," *New York Times*, January 30, 1988.

52. NSC-162/2 in *FRUS 1952–1954*, vol. 2, pt. 1, p. 594; the Defense Department statement is in ibid., p. 512, and relevant NSC discussion is on pp. 529–30.

in a first strike.[53] Third, if the state expects to grow even weaker and thus sees the status quo as likely to deteriorate, it may rationally start a war even if the prospects for victory are slight, especially if it sees the costs of losing as not much greater than those of accepting the unfavorable trends of a peaceful world.[54] The Japanese decision to attack Pearl Harbor may have been an example of this thinking. The alternative to attacking was to be forced out of China, which, the Japanese felt, was almost as bad as being defeated in a war. Fourth, desperation may reduce rationality. When peaceful paths to a strongly desired goal are foreclosed, statesmen may come to see threats and war as more likely to succeed than they are.[55] The psychological discomfort of facing an unpalatable choice can lead statesmen unjustifiably to see a course of action as feasible when the alternatives to it are very grim. Thus the Japanese decision to go to war with the United States was based on the assumption that the United States would be willing to fight a limited war. The Japanese leaders never analyzed this erroneous assumption with any care because they did not want to face the possibility that their real choice was between giving up China and suffering defeat in an enormously destructive war.[56]

This analysis of the undesired effects of an adversary's being excessively weak is consistent with the fact that the three most dangerous incidents of the Cold War were the Berlin blockade, the Korean War, and the Cuban missile crisis. All these incidents occurred when the Soviet Union was vulnerable; the first and the third, furthermore, can be traced quite directly to Soviet fears. In the first case, not only did the Soviets hope to prevent the West from consolidating its sectors of Germany, but they feared that their own position in East Germany and Eastern Europe would be endangered by a strong West Germany tied to a Western bloc. Although not all the Soviet goals and calculations in the spring and summer of 1962 are clear, a major impetus for their move seems to have been their drive to remedy the "missile gap" the United States had opened up.

Nuclear weapons have simultaneously magnified and diminished the dangers that arise from weakness and fears. Most obviously, they have reduced the chance that war will occur through the mechanisms

53. McNamara publically took this position (Stewart Alsop, "McNamara Thinks about the Unthinkable," *Saturday Evening Post*, December 1, 1962, p. 18).

54. See Robert Jervis, "War and Misperception," *Journal of International History*, 18 (Spring 1988) 677–79.

55. Jervis, Lebow, and Stein, *Psychology and Deterrence*; Lebow, *Between Peace and War*.

56. For a contrary argument, see Scott Sagan, "The Origins of the Pacific War," *Journal of Interdisciplinary History*, 18 (Spring 1988), 914–19.

outlined in the previous paragraphs, just as they have reduced the chances of war from other causes. The fact that each side knows that there is nothing it can do to remove the other's ability to destroy it should remove the glimmer of hope that facilitated desperate adventures in the past. (Although note that the Japanese realized that their country would be defeated in an all-out war.) Furthermore, the fact that the worst outcome no longer is defeat but unimaginable devastation means that even a badly deteriorating status quo will look good by comparison. It is far from clear that if nuclear weapons had existed, the Japanese would have developed the distorted perceptions that characterized their decisions in 1941 or that, even if they did, they would have taken the gamble.

On the other hand, attempts to gain security through unilateral advantage are still common in both sides' military policies. The American countervailing strategy with its stress on counterforce targeting sets force requirements that are incompatible with the security of the Soviet Union.[57] Soviet doctrine seems similar. Robust second-strike counterforce capability probably cannot be attained without simultaneously giving the state quite a good first-strike capability.[58] Furthermore, the American belief that its commitment to NATO requires that it be prepared to use strategic nuclear forces in a way that would beat back a Soviet attack or destroy much Soviet strategic nuclear capability produces requirements that heighten the security dilemma.[59] One of the benefits of understanding that limited force cannot be used to gain major objectives without incurring a grave risk of escalation is that force requirements can be moderated because we can see that deterrence by denial is not needed to protect allies. Without this understanding, military policy, whose object is to serve the state's security, is likely to remain a major source of international tension that may make both sides less secure.

Similar effects are produced by the failure of states to assimilate the implications of the well-known fact that deterrence requires promises as well as threats.[60] As Schelling pointed out, threats to punish the

57. See Robert Jervis, *The Illogic of American Nuclear Strategy* (Ithaca: Cornell University Press, 1984), pp. 122–24.

58. For an attempt to deal with this dilemma by measured and slow counterforce, see Scott Sagan, *Moving Targets: Nuclear Strategy and National Security* (Princeton: Princeton University Press, 1989), chap. 2.

59. See Herman Kahn's classic discussion of "not incredible first-strike capability" in *On Thermonuclear War* (Princeton: Princeton University Press, 1960), pp. 126–60.

60. For a good summary of the arguments and evidence on this point, see Stein, "Deterrence and Reassurance."

other side if it takes prohibited actions can be effective only when coupled with the promise not to do so if the other abstains.[61] Thus in a crisis, deterrence cannot succeed if the adversary believes that war will occur no matter what it does. Similarly, negotiations for restraints on arms building or interventions in third areas require credible promises to match the adversary's restraint. This latter need is both great and difficult because states tend simultaneously to underestimate the extent to which their behavior threatens others and to attribute the ill-effects of the other's behavior to its aggressive intentions.[62] Because it is rarely self-evident to an adversary that the state will reciprocate its cooperative behavior, both may miss opportunities for mutually beneficial arrangements. For example, during the Cuban missile crisis American leaders were very slow to put any credence in the Soviet claim to believe that the United States might have been planning to invade the island before the crisis. Therefore they were slow to see that a noninvasion pledge could be an efficacious inducement to be deployed along with their strong threats. Indeed, it took Soviet overtures to make the United States focus on this tool of influence.[63]

While states—or at least the United States—seem preoccupied with the credibility of their threats, they pay much less attention to that of their promises.[64] As a result, attempts to gain security by deterrence may fail or even increase conflict because they are not coupled with measures to reduce the adversary's fear that it cannot cooperate with the state on reasonable terms. At times, American decision makers have realized that Soviet weakness is not all to their advantage. In the late 1940s, State Department officials feared that Soviet political defeats would lead, not to withdrawal and quiescence, but to frantic attempts to reestablish their position, which could even trigger a war.[65] Similarly,

61. Schelling, *Strategy of Conflict*, pp. 43–46, 131–37.

62. For elaboration, see Jervis, *Perception and Misperception in International Politics*, pp. 62–82, 354–55; Jervis, "Realism, Game Theory, and Cooperation," pp. 336–40, and Chapter 2 above. For thorough documentation of these points as applied to recent Soviet-American relations, see Raymond Garthoff, *Détente and Confrontation* (Washington, D.C.: Brookings Institution, 1985).

63. Raymond Garthoff, *Reflections on the Cuban Missile Crisis* (Washington, D.C.: Brookings Institution, 1987), pp. 44, 117; Harold Macmillan, *At the End of the Day* (London: Macmillan, 1973), pp. 209–10. The idea had occurred to Kennedy the day before the Soviets suggested it, but neither he nor his colleagues saw its potential significance.

64. For a further discussion, see Jervis, "Domino Beliefs and Strategic Behavior."

65. U.S. Department of State, *FRUS, 1948*, vol. 3, *Western European Unity and Defense* (Washington, D.C.: Government Printing Office, 1973), pp. 238–39; *FRUS, 1951*, vol. 1, *National Security Affairs; Foreign Economic Policy* (Washington, D.C.: Government Printing Office, 1979), pp. 2–3, 85–87, 126–27, 131, 166–67, 847; *FRUS, 1952–1954*, vol. 2, pt. 1, pp. 150, 265, 551–52, 816.

in 1953, a National Security Council report said, "the Kremlin would probably not be deterred by the risk of general war from taking counter action against an action by the U.S. or its allies which the Kremlin would consider an imminent threat to Soviet security."[66] But these appreciations are unusual and limited to immediate and unlikely circumstances. There is less grasp of the general connections between the level of security two sides enjoy. Thus immediately after noting that one of "the greatest danger[s] of ... a war would come ... from further free world success in the alleged encirclement of the Soviet bloc," Secretary of State Dulles declared that "by all odds the greatest single prevention [*sic*] of global war was a strong and vigorous United States."[67] Both of these statements may be true, but the latter sentiment tends to drown out the former.

THE CONTINUING RELEVANCE OF CLAUSEWITZ

It is a commonplace that military policy should aim at greater force than the other can muster and, if war should come, at gaining a military advantage. But this notion mistakes means for ends. As Clausewitz said, "there can be no question of a purely military evaluation of a great strategic issue, nor of a purely military scheme to solve it."[68] For a country like the United States, the goal is security and the propagation of the democratic values that characterize its society. Although it is of course difficult to tell which policy will best serve these goals, it is important to remember that, as Clausewitz stressed, military policy must be their servant, not their master. States can gain competitive advantage and power at the expense of security and other values. Henry Kissinger understood this well when he analyzed the Congress of Vienna:

Could a power achieve all its wishes, it would strive for absolute security, a world-order free from the consciousness of foreign

66. *FRUS, 1952–1954,* vol. 2, pt. 1, p. 757; also see pp. 529–30 and *FRUS, 1948,* vol. 3, p. 848.
67. Ibid., p. 265.
68. Quoted in Paret, "The Genesis of *On War*," p. 7; also see Clausewitz, *On War,* pp. 78, 90. Bernard Brodie, who stressed the contemporary relevance of Clausewitz (see especially *War and Politics* [New York: Macmillan, 1973]), originally thought nuclear weapons had made these ideas of historical interest only. His thinking on this point started to shift in 1949 and 1950; the change was accelerated as he considered the implications of the planned H-bomb. See Marc Trachtenberg, "Strategic Thought in America: 1952–1966," *Political Science Quarterly* (forthcoming).

danger and where all problems have the manageability of domestic issues. But since absolute security for one power means
absolute insecurity for all others, it is never obtainable as a part
of a "legitimate" settlement, and can be achieved only through
conquest.

For this reason an international settlement which is accepted
and not imposed will always appear *somewhat* unjust to any one
of its components. Paradoxically, the generality of this dissatisfaction is a condition of stability, because were any one power
totally satisfied, all others would have to be *totally* dissatisfied and
a revolutionary situation would ensue.[69]

Even before the development of nuclear weapons, complete victory
was not always a wise political goal. The expected costs often outran
the likely gains. To seek this objective would usually be to place the
state at enormous risk, since a defeat in this kind of struggle could do
irreparable damage. Furthermore, in a multipolar war even a total
victory might not benefit the state: its current allies might be its adversaries in the next war and the state it had smashed might be needed
as an ally in the future.[70]

Because international politics is a dynamic process in which nations
react to each other, short-run advantage and gains do not always produce long-run benefits. As Michael May argues, "It would lessen, not
improve, Soviet security if the Soviet Union were to 'win' in the Carib-
bean, particularly if it won big and began to be a military factor in,
say, Mexico. The extraordinary insecurity created in the U.S. would
greatly overbalance whatever conventional military advantages might
accrue."[71] The state can successfully and safely undermine the adversary's influence and security when the latter is not only too weak to
react effectively but also is willing to recognize this—as Japan was not

69. Henry Kissinger, *A World Restored* (New York: Grosset & Dunlap, 1964), pp. 144–
45, emphasis in the original. Secretary of Defense Weinberger noted that "to paraphrase
Clausewitz, policy cannot make demands on military strategy which strategy cannot
fulfill" (Department of Defense, *Annual Report for FY 1983* [Washington, D.C.: Government Printing Office, 1982], p. I–23). But he does not seem to realize that his accompanying plea for increasing military power overlooks the possibility that his military
policy may endanger rather than support political goals.

70. For a discussion of these principles in the Napoleonic Wars, see Schroeder, "The
Collapse of the Second Coalition," pp. 287–888. Of course the war against Hitler had to
be fought to something close to unconditional surrender. But this case is not a usual
one and the fact that it looms so large in our consciousness should not lead us to see it
as the standard model.

71. Michael May, "The U.S.–Soviet Approach to Nuclear Weapons," *International
Security*, 9 (Spring 1985), 150.

in 1941. This description is not likely to apply in a world of superpowers and mutual vulnerability. It is not surprising, then, that actions that bring military gain can lead to political defeats. Even if using nuclear weapons in Vietnam would have won the war without triggering a wider conflict, the outrage among allies and U.S. citizens probably would have meant that the credibility of future use would have been decreased, not increased. To take a real rather than a hypothetical example, crossing the 38th parallel may have been the best way to destroy the North Korean army, but it was not an adequate means to reach American political objectives. Similarly, current American strategic doctrine is constructed with little attention to why the numerous options in the war plan could be expected to terminate the conflict; the crucial nexus between how the war would be conducted and how it might be stopped has been slighted.

Narrow military effectiveness may have to be sacrificed to achieve political ends. Thus naval officials were surely correct in 1940–41 when they repeatedly told President Roosevelt that it was militarily foolish to keep the fleet at Pearl Harbor. But the reasons the fleet was there were not military but political: to signal resolve to Japan, Britain, and domestic opinion. The military price turned out to be much higher than FDR expected, but his reasoning made a great deal of sense. Israeli Prime Minister Golda Meir faced an even sharper choice in October 1973. Although she received an unambiguous warning that Egypt would attack within several hours, she nevertheless decided against launching a preemptive strike, calculating that the expected military advantage, although significant, was outweighed by the expected loss in world opinion and American political support. Eisenhower reasoned the same way in the offshore islands crisis of 1955 when he opposed nationalist air strikes on the Chinese mainland, saying: "It is oftentimes necessary to take heavy liabilities from a purely military standpoint in order to avoid being . . . an aggressor and the initiator of war. This is a price which often has to be paid and which may have to be paid in this case."[72] During the Cuban missile crisis Kennedy pulled the blockade line back in order to give the Soviets more time to think before their ships reached the American forces even though doing so increased the military danger by bringing the navy within range of Cuban fighters.[73]

72. *FRUS, 1955–1957*, vol. 2, *China* (Washington, D.C.: Government Printing Office, 1986), p. 476; also see p. 494.
73. Graham Allison, *Essence of Decision* (Boston: Little, Brown, 1971), said that the navy failed to obey the president's order. This is not correct; see Daniel Caldwell, "A

In some of the the cases discussed in the previous paragraph, eventual military victory remained an important goal. But such victory is not always necessary to reach political objectives. As Schelling has argued: "One does not have to be able to win a local military engagement to make the threat of it effective. Being able to lose a local war in a dangerous and provocative manner" may produce desired political effects.[74] The Middle East war of 1973 again provides a clear example. Sadat's goal was to regain the Sinai. Militarily retaking the territory was both impossible and, if it could have been done, might have triggered an enormously destructive Israeli response or deprived Israel of the self-confidence that enabled it to respond to Sadat's overture in 1977. But victory was not necessary. Instead, Egypt had to show Israel that its policy of unyielding deterrence could not indefinitely keep the peace at a reasonable price. Egypt also needed to demonstrate to the superpowers that the status quo was too dangerous to be permitted to continue. By fighting the war—and losing it—Egypt created an international crisis and started the peace process.

As Alexander George has stressed, crisis management often requires states to subordinate purely military considerations to the driving concern to keep the crisis under control. "The military options ... must not confront the opponent with an urgent requirement to escalate the conflict himself in order to avoid or compensate for the military or political damage inflicted upon him. A demonstrative use of force may be self-defeating if it punishes the opponent to the extent that it requires an immediate strong military reaction on his part."[75] Time is required for bargaining, and while military threats and maneuvers are crucial for bringing pressure to bear on the adversary, if they dictate when and how measures are to be taken they could produce undesired escalation. Actions that put the state in the best possible position should major war break out may not be those that are best designed to bring about a peaceful outcome. By seeking military advantage, a state can convince allies that it is reckless or lead adversaries to conclude that it believes war is inevitable.

Research Note on the Quarantine of Cuba, October 1962," *International Studies Quarterly*, 22 (December 1978), 625–33.

74. Schelling, *Arms and Influence*, p. 104.

75. George, Hall, and Simons, *Limits of Coercive Diplomacy*, p. 10. As Robert Osgood put it, "In order that military power may serve as a controllable and predictable instrument of national policy, it must be subjected to an exacting political discipline" (*Limited War*, p. 14). Also see Alexander George, "Crisis Management: The Interaction of Political and Military Considerations," *Survival*, September/October 1984, pp. 223–34; Richard Ned Lebow, *Nuclear Crisis Management: A Dangerous Illusion* (Ithaca: Cornell University Press, 1987).

Military decisions taken without proper attention to political objectives can do political harm even—or especially—if they are successful. Thus the British sinking of the Argentine cruiser *General Belgrano* in the South Atlantic war foreclosed a quick termination of the conflict by enraging the Argentinians, undercutting their willingness to accept defeat, and halting the negotiations. Some have argued that the purpose of the attack was to scuttle the peace negotiations, and if this is the case the tactics were appropriate. But if the British wanted to maximize the chances of a peaceful settlement, the military victory did not serve them well. Indeed, it appears that the weapons selected by the submarine commander maximized the chance of sinking rather than simply disabling the Argentine warship and so gained tactical military advantage at the cost of possible political goals. Two torpedos rather than one were fired, and older, reliable but less accurate torpedoes were selected over the modern wire-guided ones that could have been used to try to strike the rudder and propellers of the ship, thereby taking it out of action without sinking it.[76]

Even more dramatically, the Japanese attack on Pearl Harbor was a major military victory that may have been foolish because it destroyed the slight possibility that the United States would be willing to fight a limited war, a possibility upon which Japanese fortunes depended.[77] The alternative—assuming that war was necessary—would have been to attack only British and Dutch territory, or at most to strike the Philippines. Such courses of action would have entailed military risks, but they might have preserved the chance that the United States would be restrained. Similar dynamics can be at work in a guerilla war when the authorities use ruthless military tactics that temporarily limit the guerrillas' military activities at the cost of alienating the populace and thereby increasing potential support for the rebels.

In other cases, gaining a military advantage in a limited war may incur great costs in terms of the chances of escalation. Thus Schelling argues that the first use of nuclear weapons must be guided by concerns for bargaining and war termination and that battlefield advantage must be viewed in this wider context. The result might be to use nuclear weapons sooner or later than if purely military considerations governed or to use them in a different way.[78] In a limited war in Europe, for

76. See George Quester, "The Nuclear Implications of the South Atlantic War," in R. B. Byers, ed., *The Denuclearisation of the Oceans* (London: Croom Helm, 1986), pp. 120–21.

77. See Sagan, "The Origins of the Pacific War."

78. Thomas Schelling, "Nuclear Strategy in Europe," *World Politics*, 14 (April 1962), 421–32. (I am grateful to Marc Trachtenberg for the information that this article is a

example, a focus on the battlefield could call for the use of nuclear weapons, which could easily produce a large, immediate gain. But the next result could be matching escalation by the adversary, if not explosion to total war. Of course the adversary could also make major concessions rather than accept the costs and dangers of continuing the war, but the considerations that should control the decision are not narrowly military ones.

Military advantage could be self-defeating in nuclear exchanges between the superpowers' homelands as well. Gaining a significant advantage over the other side in a strategic counterforce war could lead the adversary to launch a full strike while it still could. Attacking Soviet missile-carrying submarines, for example, might perceptibly reduce Soviet nuclear capability, but at the price of triggering an all-out response if the Soviets believed that restraints were no longer possible. Threatening to attack the adversary's political leadership and C^3 could produce a similar reaction. Actually carrying out such an attack, while greatly reducing the other's ability to fight a militarily effective war, could lead it to strike against cities. None of these consequences is certain, of course, but it is certain that war termination, not military advantage, should be the primary goal. Trying to decisively win a limited nuclear war makes it likely that both sides will lose very badly.

At the start of the nuclear era, one Soviet official explained his country's rejection of the Baruch Plan: "The Soviet Union is not seeking equality, but, rather, freedom to pursue its own policies in complete freedom and without any interference or control from the outside."[79] This drive for autonomy is common and understandable. People and states do not want to leave their fates in the hands of others. Even though the outcome of any interaction must be the resultant of what each actor does and so the idea of complete freedom to pursue one's policies is a chimera, the illusion is a strong one. Thus when evaluating arms-control proposals, states often focus more sharply on the restric-

---

version of a classified paper written for the Berlin task force and passed on to President Kennedy by his national security adviser. The urgent tone of the article strikingly contrasts with that of most of Schelling's publications.) McNamara appears never to have understood the argument; see his comments in Michael Charleton, *From Deterrence to Defense* (Cambridge: Harvard University Press 1987), p. 18. Also see Schelling, "The Role of War Games and Exercises," in Carter, Steinbruner, and Zraket, eds., *Managing Nuclear Operations*, pp. 426–44. Compare Schelling's argument with those of Albert Wohlstetter and Richard Brody, "Continuing Control as a Requirement for Deterring," in Carter, Steinbruner, and Zraket, eds., *Managing Nuclear Operations*, pp. 142–96.

79. *FRUS, 1946*, vol. 1, *General; The United Nations* (Washington, D.C.: Government Printing Office, 1972), p. 957.

tions on them than on those that bind the adversary. The former generally hurt more than the latter reassure in part because of the psychology of loss aversion discussed above. Statesmen often think that by minimizing the explicit restraints they accept and concentrating on the immediate advantages that their policies will bring them, they will maximize their security. The desired results in fact will not follow.

Retaining a focus on Clausewitz's central insight reminds us that unilateral military advantage cannot provide security in an era of mutual vulnerability. Trying to undermine the adversary's security can yield short-run gains but is likely to produce a reaction that endangers both sides. Just as the two sides' fates would be linked together in a nuclear war, their general levels of security are also linked: if one is highly insecure, so will the other be. As President Nixon pointed out: "both sides are threatened . . . when any power seeks tactical advantage from a crisis and risks provoking a strategic response."[80] Gorbachev put it even more sharply when he argued that there can be "no security for the USSR without security for the United States."[81] If both superpowers will act on these principles the world will be safer.

80. Richard Nixon, *U.S. Foreign Policy for the 1970's: A New Strategy for Peace*, a report to the Congress, February 18, 1970, p. 133.
81. Quoted in Robert Legvold, "War, Weapons, and Soviet Foreign Policy," in Seweryn Bialer and Michael Mandelbaum, eds., *Gorbachev's Russia and American Foreign Policy* (Boulder, Colo.: Westview Press, 1988), p. 103.

Index

Library of Congress Cataloging-in-Publication Data

Jervis, Robert, 1940–
    The meaning of nuclear revolution : statecraft and the prospect of
Armageddon / Robert Jervis.
       p.   cm.—(Cornell studies in security affairs)
    Includes index.
    ISBN 0-8014-2304-X (alk. paper).
    1. Nuclear warfare. 2. World politics—1945– I. Title.
II. Series.
U263.J47 1989
355'.0217—dc19   88-43443